D0493164

Long Way Down

Also by Ewan McGregor and Charley Boorman

Long Way Round
Long Way Round: The Illustrated Edition

By Charley Boorman

Race to Dakar

Long Way Round is also available as an audiobook from Hachette Audio.

Long Way Down

EWAN MCGREGOR *and*
CHARLEY BOORMAN

with JEFF GULVIN

sphere

SPHERE

First published in Great Britain in 2007 by Sphere

A CIP catalogue record for this book
is available from the British Library.

HB ISBN 978-1-84744-053-2
C FORMAT ISBN 978-1-84744-052-5

Typeset in Times by M Rules
Printed and bound in Great Britain by
Clays Ltd, St Ives plc

Sphere
An imprint of
Little, Brown Book Group
100 Victoria Embankment
London EC4Y 0DY

www.littlebrown.co.uk

For Olivia, Doone and Kinvara for being there for me. I love you always.

Charley Boorman

For Sheila, who loved the tales of our first trip; for Lou, who I wish I could tell the stories of this one, and for Eve and the girls, who I rode every mile to get home to.

Ewan McGregor

Contents

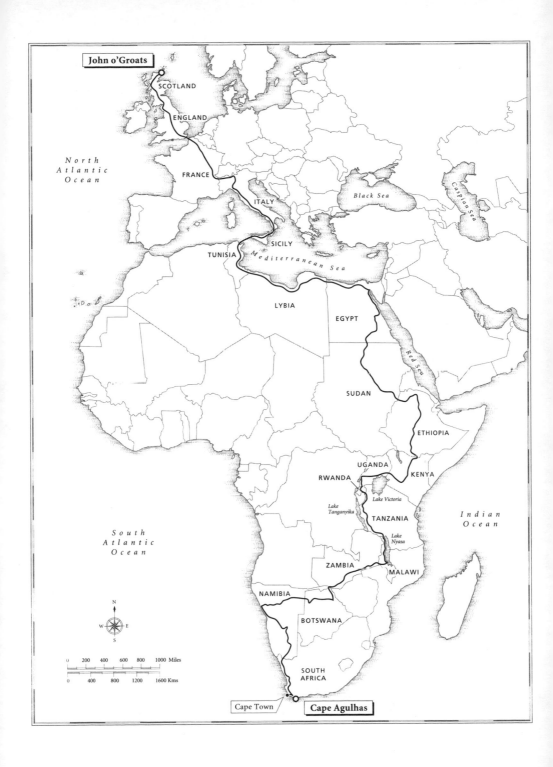

Prologue

EWAN: I said goodbye to Charley and left the workshop around 4.30 p.m. It was a Friday afternoon in the middle of February and we were heading out with our families for a joint skiing trip the next morning. We were both looking forward to the break: things had been so hectic lately with the move to the new premises, and preparations for our Africa trip really beginning in earnest.

I was on my BSA Lightning, the roads choked with rush hour traffic. I've lived in London for years, though, and I'm well used to it. It's only traffic, after all; it isn't sand or deep gravel; it's not 'The Road of Bones'.

Charley and I had crossed Kazakhstan on our motorbikes, we'd negotiated the steppes of Russia and the wilderness of Siberia. Only a couple of weeks ago the GS1150 I'd ridden round the world had been delivered to our workshop. It was now standing next to a dramatic-looking Mongolian Warrior's costume that we'd bid for in an auction at their embassy. An armoured breastplate, the bike's patched and resewn leather seat – they were a reminder of all we'd achieved.

February had been a morbid month in many ways. I'd had surgery to test a mole and more surgery to remove a hint of skin cancer. Then I'd fallen sick while were on a hostile training exercise. But I was chilled out now – the date of departure had finally been set and I was really looking forward to not thinking about work for a while and riding again with Charley. Just a couple of months now and we'd be gone, the two of us riding through Africa, relying on each other the way we did before. The start of another adventure. It made me tingle just to think about it.

The traffic was at a standstill. I was filtering up to the lights thinking about getting home and helping my wife Eve with the packing; it would be great to spend some quality time with the family. I couldn't wait to get on the slopes and watch my three gorgeous daughters learning to ski.

Suddenly without warning a pedestrian stepped between the vehicles right in front of me.

He wasn't looking my way.

And he was close, he was way too close.

My God, I was going to hit him.

Instinct took over and I grabbed everything; front brake, back brake; I grabbed the clutch. Shit, now I had no engine braking.

It was all happening so fast. I knew I wasn't going to stop and could only wait for the impact. Brakes on, I was into a skid and shouting, 'Watch out! Watch out mate!' But he didn't see me.

There was no time and I had no choice but to throw the bike away from him. I was off, chucking the machine to my right, flying through the air. I clattered into him and he was down but at least the bike hadn't hit him. I was still flailing forwards, the road coming up to meet me with sickening speed.

There was nothing I could do. I was going to hit the tarmac way too fast and the bike was still revving above me.

The holiday – Eve and the kids waiting for me at home. Charley and all the team – everything we'd planned together. My body slammed into the road. Was it all over before we'd even begun?

1
Where's Charley?

CHARLEY: I remember the moment it started. It was October 2004, very late one Friday night. We were in the old office in Bulwer Street with boxes all around us, bits of paper, all the office equipment gone. For a few minutes we just stood there reflecting. This is where Long Way Round had all begun, where we'd planned everything, checked and re-checked the maps: it's where we'd first seen the bikes.

It was over, finished: we'd ridden around the world, a mammoth journey; an epic adventure. But it was over now.

The maps were still on the wall and we stood before them once more. Ewan glanced at me.

'What do you reckon, Charley?'

'I don't know.'

'South America, India maybe?'

I looked up at him. 'What about riding through Africa?'

Ewan and I first met on a film set in County Clare more than a dozen years ago, our friendship born out of our passion for motorbikes. We've been best mates ever since. We'd always talked about riding together; France maybe, Spain. But then Ewan walked into a map shop, and over dinner that night we decided to forget France or Spain, we'd go the whole hog and ride around the world. The adventure of a lifetime, the two of us off on a couple of bikes. I wasn't sure we could pull it off; I wasn't sure it would even happen.

But it did. A late-night conversation became a dream, the dream became an adventure and that adventure proved to be a pivotal point in my life.

I grew up in the movie business, but I'm dyslexic . . . and I mean badly: if it hadn't been for my dad taking a year out to teach me to read, life could've been very hard. Even so, reading for acting parts could be difficult sometimes. Historically I'd enjoyed success in movies like *The Emerald Forest*, but after Long Way Round the direction of my life altered completely. I found myself in places like the pit lane of Moto GP circuits with heroes like Kenny Roberts grabbing my arm and telling me how much he'd enjoyed watching our journey.

I was no longer just John Boorman's son – in fact my dad rang me up the other day to tell me he'd introduced himself to someone and they'd said, 'Oh, Charley Boorman's dad'.

My career was now in motorcycling – albeit not in a conventional way – and the success of *Long Way Round* enabled me to live another dream. Ever since I can remember I'd always wanted to race bikes, so together with Russ Malkin, a very good friend and producer/director of *Long Way Round*, I entered the world's most dangerous race: the 2006 Dakar rally – five days in January where I rode ridiculous distances at ridiculous speeds before an innocuous crash tipped me off and I broke both my hands. (I never made it to the sand dunes and I've unfinished business there.) That dream was over for now, but another was just beginning.

Ewan flew in for the end of the Dakar to congratulate us all (my fellow teammate Simon Pavey had made it all the way to the finishing line). He was joined by film maker David Alexanian, the fourth member of the team that created *Long Way Round*. There we were in Dakar – all together again. And there in the scorching sun we confirmed what we had first mapped out over a year before in Bulwer Street. The adventure was on again – John O'Groats to Cape Town: we would ride the Long Way Down.

Once my hands were healed, the first thing Ewan and I did was return to the Royal Geographical Society in London, the place where we'd mapped out the first trip. Our bikes parked outside, I took my helmet off. The old red brick building seemed very familiar.

'So here we are again, Ewan. What do we say to them this time?'

He laughed. 'How about: Hi, remember us? We're back for more.'

Inside I quickly recalled how solemn the place felt; the arched windows, blue carpets and the magnificent ancient maps that decked the walls. One in particular dated from 1920 and at the bottom it was engraved with images of the old continent, names and places going back to colonial days when just about every European country fought for a share of the spoils. Ewan pointed to a picture of a guy in a pith helmet in a pretty compromising position with a tribesman. 'Hey, Charley,' he said. 'Here's how you made friends with the natives back then. See, you grabbed a man by his willy.'

In the journey-planning office we met the same assistant we'd spoken to before and she had yet more large-scale maps spread on a mahogany table.

'Have you decided on a route?' she asked us.

I shook my head. 'Nothing definite yet, but we're going to ride down through Europe, I think, probably cross from Sicily.'

'We'd like to follow the Nile,' Ewan added. 'It's one of those journeys, you know; one of the great trips of the world.'

She nodded. 'Sudan is pretty unstable and so are parts of Ethiopia. You'll need to be up on your paperwork.'

I rolled my eyes. 'Jesus, paperwork. The Ukraine, Ewan. Remember?'

'You mean when we waited nine hours to get in – how could I possibly forget?'

'Ethiopia is absolutely beautiful though,' the assistant went on, 'and despite the problems they're really trying to build up tourism. Sudan is full of open spaces, the Africa of the movies, if you like.' She smiled then, a little warily. 'There are security issues, however.'

I cast a glance at Ewan. She was right, as we knew only too well. We'd only just started investigating the route and already knew we'd need armed guards to get us through places like northern Kenya. We were thinking about going into the Democratic Republic of Congo, and weren't sure whether we'd have to go through Zimbabwe. This was going to be a very different journey from Long Way Round, and I think we were only just beginning to realise how different.

Having reacquainted ourselves with the Royal Geographical Society we headed for the wilds of Devon and a weekend's survival course. The weather was shit, a cold, drizzling rain, and to make things even more miserable, Ewan had his tent up before me. He was crowing about it. I mean, he *never* gets his tent up before me. It was galling. There was some consolation however: he'd put it up at the bottom of a hill and it was raining, which meant there was every chance he'd have a river running through it before long.

After that, we got lost in the 'wild wood' whilst hunting for strategically placed survival rations, and then we had to build shelters from fallen branches and bits of foliage.

Not that we're competitive or anything, but my A-frame and ridge was up, the sides constructed and I was already onto the roof whilst Ewan was still going on about a 'long ridge pole' and the 'bell end' being big enough. After making a wall of branch and fern, the last layer was leaves. Lying inside I could still see daylight and my feet stuck out, though I only discovered that when the instructor kicked them. He proceeded to tell us about a friend of his who went to sleep with his head sticking out of a similar shelter in Africa, only to be woken by a hyena ripping off his face. Our instructor liked telling those kinds of stories: he liked to tell them a lot.

He was complimentary about my shelter, however, testing the structural quality by climbing right over it while I was lying inside. In his own words, it didn't budge an inch.

Ewan was arranging leaves and ferns and other bits and pieces; like a boy scout he was, having a whale of a time. 'Colour coding confuses your enemy,' I heard him mutter.

Finally he was finished, the branches covered with sprays of fern and leaf. He was stretched out inside and the instructor asked him if he felt confident that it was structurally sound.

Ewan replied that he did.

'Good,' the instructor said, 'because I'm going to walk on it.'

He'd barely shifted his weight when the 'bell end' Ewan had been so proud of collapsed, showering our Jedi Knight in broken branches.

For a moment there was silence. Then from the depths we heard him: 'Yeah, well, I think obviously there's room for improvement. But generally . . .' We could see his hands, gesticulating from under the crushed ridge. 'I was quite happy with its . . . you know, I liked the feel of it and it smelled really nice.'

On cue and not without a certain sense of ceremony, the rest of the shelter collapsed; a few moments later Ewan emerged: half a beard, his woollen hat askew.

'Shame,' he said. 'I put a lot of love into that.'

EWAN: What Charley didn't mention was that his A-frame was put together by the instructor. That's why it was so solid. I did mine myself. Not quite the same thing, is it?

The instructor really did like his tales of horror: hyenas eating people; elephants trampling our campsite; not to mention the machete-wielding madmen lurking outside every bar. Having said that, he also told us that despite our laid-back attitude, I was 'wily' and Charley was really 'industrious'.

From Devon, hyenas and elephants, it was Essex and a replica of the border between the Democratic Republic of Congo and Rwanda. Driving down a track in a 4x4 we had the feeling we were about to be ambushed. We were right – just as we were considering potential escape routes a mine exploded in front of the truck.

David Alexanian, who would be joining us on the real trip, was driving. He immediately started backing up. More flash bangs went off, mines, or grenades maybe, exploding behind us.

Now we heard the rattle of gunfire and a man appeared on our right. Heavily built, he approached the vehicle at a crouch, wearing camouflage and carrying an AK-47. We dived for the doors on the passenger side only to find another guy bellowing at us and brandishing not a gun, but a couple of vicious-looking axes.

We piled out of the vehicle. Hands in the air, we tried to talk to the gunmen – a whole gang of them now. We tried to explain about UNICEF, and what we were doing. They weren't listening or didn't understand: they didn't care. Before we knew it we were forced away from the vehicles, our captors demanding money, jackets, our watches.

We'd discussed such a situation with our instructors and they had advised us that in really dangerous areas, convoys of vehicles were put together under armed guard. Our trip was high profile and we knew we were potential targets. On the bikes, Charley and I had decided that if we were attacked we'd just try to get the hell out of there and double back to the last town we'd been through where we could raise the alarm. We would have no idea what lay ahead but we'd know what was in the towns we'd been through – if there were medical centres or police stations.

During the exercise however, with explosions going off and

gunfire ringing out, we had no time to do anything except put our hands above our heads and try to explain what we were doing.

'Watch!' One AK-wielding guy pointed at my wrist. I took off my watch and gave it to him. Not just my watch; he wanted my wedding ring, my wallet, all my money. It was the same with the others: watches, wallets, jewellery. In the briefing we'd been told that if a ring didn't come off the likelihood was the finger would come with it.

Every now and then our captors made their intentions all the clearer by firing warning shots over our heads. I was on my knees with my head down but my gaze was dragged to the dumped body of some other victim they'd already executed. If they had shot him they would just as easily shoot us and we had no option but to cooperate. They fired yet more warning shots – pistols now – rapidly into the air. My captor demanded my jacket and made me take my trousers off.

From the corner of my eye I saw another man wearing a black ski mask marching Charley away. For a split second I imagined how I'd feel if this wasn't Dorset and an exercise, but the real border. I didn't know what was going to happen but Charley's captor pressed him onto his knees some twenty yards from the rest of us. Whether this was just a scare tactic or not I have no idea, but we'd all been told to keep our heads down and avoid eye contact. For a moment the masked man stood over him then came back to the main group leaving Charley on his own.

The others were being stripped of their possessions, the gunmen moving around us and talking rapidly. Every now and then they fired their guns in the air, and looking up again I noticed Charley was gone.

Without thinking I opened my mouth. 'Where's Charley?' I said. He must have made a run for it.

Of course our captors heard me and the next thing I knew the man in the ski mask stalked over to the trees at the edge of the clearing. We couldn't see anything but moments later a single shot rang out.

We were on our knees, hunched forward, elbows on the ground and our hands on our heads.

'Is Charley dead?' someone whispered.

'Yes,' I said. 'Charley's dead.'

The exercise over, Charley appeared alive and well and grinning from ear to ear. I wagged my head at him. 'Charley,' I said. 'You stupid fucking bastard.'

It was only an exercise, but given the times we live in not unrealistic. It was very dramatic, very believable and also very sobering: one of us being marched away and the sound of a single gunshot.

Charley felt a bit guilty, but then he reckoned he'd had the chance and took it. He told us that in a real situation he wouldn't have been caught behind a tree, he'd have kept going until he could raise the alarm. Later we found out that there had been a real kidnap, involving British Embassy staff in Afar, where that's pretty much exactly what happened.

CHARLEY: The hostile training exercises were hugely constructive. In the next one we arrived at a checkpoint to be confronted by a couple of armed men standing beside a massive lorry. I left the engine running and another Kalashnikov-toting guard came up to the vehicle. He wore a machete at his side and I thought about the horror stories.

'ID.' The guard was peering at me out of cold and humourless eyes.

Ewan, David and I were in a twin cab pickup with Russ perched on the flatbed. Ewan passed me the polythene bag containing all our papers and permits.

'We're tourists,' I told the guard. 'We're going to Cape Town.'

He wanted to see our passports and made me switch off the engine. He told us we couldn't film and insisted we get out of the car. Two more guards arrived and with them a white guy in sunglasses wearing a folded Arab keffiyeh around his head. He told us the road was closed, but I assured him we were working with UNICEF helping children, and his government had issued us with the requisite travel permit. He demanded to see it and Ewan dug it out before another guard took him off a few paces and made him kneel down.

He didn't say why, he just made Ewan drop to his knees. Even in an exercise it's hard to keep smiling and the tone of the conversation agreeable, when your mate is on his knees with a pistol pointed at his head.

The man with the headgear kept asking us where we'd come from and where we were going. He was interested in our truck and our gear, which the other guards spilled out on the ground. He was really interested in the fact that neither Ewan nor I could get the back seat on the crew cab folded forward. We told him we'd never used it, but it only made him suspicious. We had the right papers but it was clear he thought we'd stolen the truck. He wanted to know what we were doing with hand-held radios and we tried to explain about filming and staying in contact with our other vehicle. What other vehicle? It hadn't turned up yet and now he was even more suspicious.

I tried to lead the conversation, offering him cigarettes, and all the time he was looking at the camera and asking me what it was worth. Foolishly, I told him about $400, which is roughly what it cost from new. With hindsight I know I'd just set the amount he needed to be bribed otherwise he'd confiscate it.

Ewan was still on his knees and he was trying to explain that we had to have the camera because we were filming in order to help the children in their country. Finally he was allowed to get up and we bribed our way back into the truck, being very polite and friendly, smiling a lot, the nerves all too real even in role play.

They lifted the barrier and we crawled through, travelling all of ten or twelve paces before they stopped us again and insisted we switch off the engine. And all the while these other armed men were watching us from the big truck.

'Fuck this,' Ewan muttered. 'If we ever get going again – just drive, Charley.'

This was only an exercise, but we found ourselves jabbering away, saying all the things we probably would say if it was real. There's nothing quite like being confronted by a bunch of testosterone-fuelled warriors sporting Kalashnikovs.

Finally we were allowed to move on but just a few hundred yards down the track we came across a wrecked car. An old Fiat had flipped on its side and we saw an injured girl – a tourist – lying on the ground. She was bleeding heavily from her thigh, and we could hear her terrified screams even before we stopped. Again it seemed very real; the car, the way she was lying, her cries of pain and fear. Grabbing the medical bag Ewan was at her side in a flash.

'All right, my darling, you're going to be all right.' He set about staunching the wound. 'We're going to help you. You've had quite a turn, but you'll be all right now.'

David helped him while Russ and I took a look at the car. Inside we found another girl unconscious and trapped in her seat. I was instantly reminded of the time my wife Ollie and I spent in Australia before we were married. We were driving in the mountains somewhere and we came across just such an incident. A car had flipped off a bridge and a woman was trapped upside down inside. She was screaming about her children. At the time I could see no sign of any children and I didn't know whether she might have banged her head or something. But fuel was dripping and I knew that if I was going to get her out of there I had to keep her calm. I told her the children were safe, that they were up the road with my girlfriend. She calmed down and I managed to cut her out of the seatbelt.

We discovered that she did have children and they'd been thrown from the car in the crash. They were all right, thank God, and were up the road with another passer-by. It had really shaken us up and even though this was just an exercise, it brought it all flooding back.

Our victim was unconscious: her lips were blue and she was bleeding from a wound in her back. Though the screaming girl had drawn our attention, this woman was much more seriously injured. We decided we had no choice but to lift her into the pickup and turn back for the checkpoint.

When the training was over we returned to London with an even stronger sense of the dangers we would be facing on the trip. There was no doubt this was going to be an adventure of a lifetime, but with every adventure there is always an element of risk, and we would be facing more than we'd ever known before. But little did we know that the first genuine accident would take place not at some remote African border, but on a busy street in west London. And it was an accident that could put the whole trip in jeopardy.

2
Three's A Crowd

EWAN: Just like Charley, I had found that Long Way Round had a very positive effect on my career. These days far more people come up and ask me about the bike trips than they do *Star Wars* or any of my other movies. Since those four months on the bikes I've been very busy: various smaller films but also the third episode of *Star Wars*, as well as *The Island* and a stint on the stage in *Guys and Dolls*. It was whilst rehearsing for the musical that the idea of starting at John O'Groats actually came about. I made a throwaway comment that made it into print, and from then on (whether we liked it or not) we were starting in the north of Scotland.

Our plans were well advanced now, and Charley and I were sitting in the temporary office we were using in Battersea, just the two of us on the couch, talking about the route, the kind of back-up vehicles we'd use, what modifications we might make to the bikes this time round.

'Charley,' I said. 'Eve really wants to come.'

This wasn't the first time I'd mentioned it, but I wanted to discuss it properly. Long Way Round had been about Charley and me – this was different again. His smile was wide, mine awkward.

'What do you think about it, really?' I asked him.

'What do I think about it? Well, I suppose I have the same reservations that you do.' He scratched his neck. 'I suppose, yeah, I'm open to everything.' There was another awkward silence. 'My main concern would be safety. But obviously it changes the dynamic of what we're doing.'

'Yes,' I said, 'it does. Do you think it's a terrible idea?'

'Truthfully?'

'Of course.'

He was laughing. 'It's a terrible idea.'

After we had announced in Dakar that we were definitely doing Long Way Down, we'd followed up with a celebratory meal back at our house in London. Eve had been a little quiet then, and I thought it was just the reality of another long trip, the issues it created at home and the dangers I'd face riding so far once again. But it wasn't that at all, it was the fact that she had decided that she wanted to join us.

She told me a few days later; she'd woken up on Sunday morning just knowing she had to be part of it.

She'd been to Africa before on holiday, but as she pointed out, scuba diving and staying in hotels was hardly the same thing. She'd not seen any of the real Africa and it evoked incredible emotions for her; the landscape, the people, history. She could think of nothing better than camping under star-filled skies or going into villages, meeting people she would never normally meet.

My first reaction was absolute delight. We've been married twelve years, we're a close family and one of the most difficult things about Long Way Round had been the long separation. Also, Eve told me that if she was able to come she really wanted to ride. I couldn't believe it: in all our years together she'd hardly been on the back of my bike, let alone expressed an interest in riding herself.

We didn't decide for certain of course; it was something I had to discuss with Charley, David and Russ, and overnight all sorts of things began to occur to me. The safety issues, first and foremost; how long Eve would come for, our children. I wasn't sure how she'd get on with learning to ride or whether she'd have the time to gain the necessary experience. The next morning I spoke to her about it and I suppose, given my initial enthusiasm, it must have looked as though I'd changed my mind.

I hadn't. It was just that the realities were beginning to dawn. I really did love the idea of having her along, but we'd been talking about her joining us for six or eight weeks and I started to realise what that would actually mean. I've been riding a bike since I was nineteen and on Long Way Round we encountered road conditions that in some areas challenged me to the point of a standstill. Eve hadn't been involved in that trip and it was hard to convey the sort of situations and challenges we might encounter.

She wondered if the real reason behind my apparent change of heart was the fact that she might be treading on hallowed ground. And I had to admit there might have been a grain of truth in that. But we have three children and with both of us riding on difficult terrain, in the end it was fundamentally the safety issues that concerned me.

Anyway, we were on and off the phone all day, pretty abrupt with each other and nothing was resolved, at least not to begin with. Eve told me later that she was thinking: 'I don't need him, I'll plan my own trip; I don't have to go on his trip, I can go on my own.'

I ended up being late for lunch and I'm never late for anything. When I arrived I told the others about her wanting to come.

CHARLEY: I didn't really think it was a terrible idea. I'd had reservations about the dynamic, of course. One of the reasons I enjoyed Long Way Round so much was because it was just Ewan and me. We'd made it round the world without seriously falling out and I know people who have been on much shorter and less challenging bike trips only to fall out badly, sometimes to the point of never speaking again. Friendships can be fragile things when you're travelling and if we were to add a new person into the mix, we had to think it through. Logistically, it was not a problem – we just had to work out where she would join us and for how long – but the safety issues were a concern. I brooded about it, mulling it over, wondering how it would affect us and the rest of our trip.

Of course Ewan and Eve resolved their disagreement. By the end of that Monday they were fine and a couple of weeks later David, Russ and I went round to dinner and the five of us discussed how it might work. David pointed out that even for experienced riders it was a dangerous trip. He suggested that if Eve really wanted to go, we ought to get her a bike so she could clock up some miles. Eve thought it was a good idea, the only sensible way to gain experience, and then she'd know for sure whether or not she could do it.

In the meantime we located premises on Avonmore Road in West London so we could begin to prepare properly. It was massive, big enough for the bikes, trucks and all the gear we were taking. It was an atmospheric place; it had a real workshop feel with a corrugated iron roof, and red girders where we hung the flags of each country we would be riding through. The roof also leaked.

We fixed the leak, and kitted the place out. All we needed now were the bikes: JFK and JLO. It turned out that these were the registration suffixes we'd been assigned by the DVLA. A US president and 'Jenny from the block': strange or what? They were coming from Germany and I was itching to get working on them, but that Friday afternoon when we left the office, all set to go skiing, JFK and JLO were still in transit.

3

Break A Leg

EWAN: 'Watch out, mate. Watch out!'

I clattered into him with my shoulder and flew to the ground, finishing up sprawled on my face. The bike came with me, slamming its full force right into my leg.

For a moment I just lay there, head to the side, looking up at this guy who was looking down at me with his eyes popping out of his head.

'Jesus,' I said. 'Are you all right?'

'Yeah, I'm fine.' Still he stood there, arms at his sides, just gawping at me.

'Can you help me get up?' I asked him.

He didn't seem to know what I was talking about. He was in shock. I was in shock.

Then another guy arrived and picked the bike off my leg. Somehow I staggered to my feet but as I did so I felt something go and a sickening sensation worked through me. I knew I was in trouble and hobbled off the road as quickly as I could. I sat down on the steps leading up to some flats.

The bloke got my bike to the pavement and settled on its centre stand. He asked me where the key was because on the Lightning it's not obvious. I had to get up again and limp over to switch off the engine. Back at the steps I stripped off my gloves and helmet. Then I took off my boot.

My leg was burning, and I could see I'd grazed it quite badly. I could feel a weird sensation just above the ankle: like a sprain maybe, that's what I was thinking, what I was hoping. I'd twisted something and this was only a sprain.

Finally the man I'd hit seemed to come to, and he walked over and asked me if I was all right.

'I don't know,' I told him. 'I think I might've broken something.' The words sort of tumbled out and then the possibility struck me. 'I think I might've broken my ankle.'

'No, you couldn't have.' Another voice, Scottish, a thick accent belonging to the man whose steps I was sitting on. He'd heard the commotion and had come out to help. 'You couldn't have broken it,' he told me. 'You wouldn't be able to walk on it, would you? Not if it was broken.'

For a moment my spirits lifted. 'No,' I said. 'You're right. I probably wouldn't.'

A policewoman arrived on a horse. Or at least I think she did because the whole thing was happening so fast I was sort of detached. It all felt really surreal.

She asked if everyone was OK.

The guy I'd hit was apologising, telling me he'd been looking the other way, that he'd been conscious of oncoming cars.

'Look,' I said, 'so long as you're OK. I'm fine, I might've done something to my ankle but I'm all right.' Sitting there I was just delighted he hadn't been hurt.

The policewoman asked about a van driver that I didn't remember; if he was there I don't think he had anything to do with it. They talked about calling for an ambulance. The guy who owned the flat suggested I come in and have a cup of tea, but all I wanted to do was get home. I didn't want to go to casualty. I didn't want to be in the back of an ambulance. I was in shock, but if I could stand I could ride and pulling on my boot I grabbed my helmet and gloves.

All at once everyone was gone. The policewoman wasn't there, the guy I'd hit was gone; the other man had disappeared back inside his flat. It all seemed so surreal, as if it was happening around me yet there I was hobbling across the pavement with this weird clicking sensation in my leg.

Checking the bike I noticed the right hand foot peg was buckled to the point of being vertical, which kind of made it useless but with hindsight it was actually a blessing. It meant I could get my foot fully under the gear shift so I could change gear without having to flex my ankle.

Somehow I got on and got the bike kick-started. I managed to nudge it into first and then I was in the traffic and completely focused on getting home. Nothing else mattered. Every time I stopped, however, I had to put my foot down. That hurt like hell and I thought: fuck, this is bad.

Eve thought I was joking when I rang the intercom at home and told her I'd had an accident. I couldn't get the bike in the garage and needed her to help me. Later she told me that she thought I was making it up and had some sort of surprise for her. I suppose I did, only the surprise wasn't very pleasant.

When she opened the door I could see the concern in her face. Eyes wide, she stared at me as I hovered there, half-balanced on one foot.

'Ewan, my God! What happened?'

'I hit someone, crashed into him on Holland Road.'

'Are you all right?'

'I've done something to my leg, Eve. I think I need it X-rayed.'

I was still optimistic: in the car I felt my ankle and there didn't seem to be any real swelling. I thought I'd be OK, it was a sprain at worst and I'd still be able to ski. But then I noticed a little lump pressing the skin on the back of my right calf. I pushed it and a wave of panic washed over me. I could feel it move, a hideous sensation. I'd never broken anything before, but I knew what I could feel was the movement of bone over bone.

I could've cried.

My leg was broken and one by one the implications began to hit. There was the skiing trip and a month from now I was due on the set of a film. Fucking hell: Long Way Down, we were leaving on motorbikes for Africa. All the hard work, the massive amount of organisation: D-Day was 12 May and here I was en route to hospital. The sudden silence that swept through me seemed all-consuming; a numbing realisation that I didn't want to acknowledge. It could all be over.

Not long after I was lying in a cubicle in casualty with the heavy blue curtain pulled across and a nurse examining my leg. Still I was telling myself, telling her, that it was all right and my leg wasn't really broken. It was a twist, a sprain, nothing more, and I desperately wanted her to confirm it.

But she didn't.

Instead she flashed the X-rays onto the machine and there was the two-part image of my lower leg. Except that above the ankle it was now in three parts not two: the fibula, the smaller bone at the back, was snapped. I could see it clearly. I didn't want to believe it but there it was in black and white. It wasn't sprained, or cracked even. For a moment I just stared. I was dumbfounded. 'That's broken,' I said.

The nurse took a deep breath. 'Yes,' she said. 'That's a break.'

CHARLEY: Ewan phoned before he left for casualty and told me what had happened. I was gobsmacked. Of course accidents happen and you're vulnerable on a bike, but we'd ridden away from the workshop together and you just don't expect it.

'I can feel a sort of clicking when I move my foot,' he'd said.

'But you rode home.'

'Yeah.'

'Well, if you stood on it and you rode home, I'm sure it's just a sprain.'

But of course it wasn't. He phoned again as soon as he got back from the hospital.

'Fuck it,' he said bitterly.

'Definitely broken?'

'I saw the X-ray. Clear as day, snapped above the ankle.'

All sorts of thoughts began racing through my head; first and foremost concern for my friend, then the ski trip, and of course Long Way Down. Jesus Christ, this could be a show stopper. A wave of concern washed over me.

'Do they think it's a clean break?' I asked him.

'I don't know. I think so.'

'Did the nurse tell you how long it would take to heal?'

'Four to six weeks.'

'Then we're OK. Don't worry about it. It's just one of those things.'

'That's what I thought.' I could hear the relief in Ewan's voice and I knew he was trying to make the best of a bad situation. 'We're not leaving for Africa until May,' he said. 'It's plenty of time. It just means I can't go skiing which is a real pain for Eve and the kids. But we need to talk about it. I want you to phone Russ: phone David. I want you all to come round.'

I could imagine him sitting there with his leg in a cast and Eve packing to go skiing, having to deal with the fact that she was now going without him. She'd just love the prospect of the three of us descending on them as well.

'You know what, Ewan,' I said, 'I don't think that's a good idea. Not tonight.' All at once I was laughing, trying to lighten him up. 'You fucking idiot, you ride round the world with barely a scratch then bin it ten minutes from home.'

I put the phone down, my smile fading. Missing a ski trip was one thing, a family holiday: Ewan would be gutted but I knew he'd make it up to Eve and the kids later. If this wasn't a clean break, however, it could jeopardise the whole trip.

I told myself to chill out and that it would be a simple leg break. There was no point worrying unnecessarily. Then it started sinking in how lucky he'd been, how lucky the other guy had been, stepping out of the traffic and getting in the way of a motorcycle. Hitting a pedestrian – it was scary: like a marker, some kind of warning. It was only a few weeks before we set off and our biggest concern about riding bikes in Africa was hitting someone. When we rode round the world we went through some serious country but often it was remote and the terrain was the challenge. Africa was a whole different ball game altogether. In Africa roads are the lifeblood, the arteries that feed the continent and they're very busy. Hitting someone was our worst nightmare.

It hadn't been Ewan's fault, the guy stepped out, it was an accident; it was just a miracle no one was badly hurt. But it was weird, spooky almost, so close to the beginning of the trip. Vividly I recalled snapping my collarbone not long before we were due at the Dakar. Just like Ewan I'd tried to sell the doctor the idea that it wasn't broken. Of course he'd sat there with his arms folded, peering at the splintered bone trying to force its way through the skin at my shoulder.

I could feel an ache in my hands, the memories of my own injuries returning to haunt me. It wasn't that long ago I'd been in plaster myself with the scaphoid, the most important bone in my wrist, dislocated, not to mention shattered knuckles in my other hand. Just as Ewan had ridden home with a busted foot, I picked the bike up and carried on. I'd had no choice and at that moment no idea how bad my injuries were. In the end I rode another four hundred and fifty kilometres.

EWAN: It was hard seeing them all leave and I was glad Charley and Ollie would be there. The trip had been booked a long time ago and there was no way it could be postponed, but as Charley had predicted I was gutted to have to stay behind. I'd been looking forward to it for ages.

Alone now, I started going over the accident again. Russ and David came round and I showed them the X-rays. Russ was delighted to see me smiling and David suggested that maybe this was a warning that we all just needed to slow down and take stock for a moment: so much had been happening and so fast that none of us had had time to pause for breath. They were concerned that I was on my own so soon after an accident; depression can hit after a shock like that and they wanted to make sure I'd be all right. They told me to take advantage of the time, to rest up and read a couple of books. Which I did for a day or two, but the house seemed very empty and all I could think about was my family skiing without me.

The following Monday I was back at the Princess Grace Hospital to have the full cast put on my leg. I was out of the house and anxious to get the healing process under way. The doctor examined me carefully, then started telling me things I really didn't want to hear – specifically that there were two ways for my leg to have broken. The first (and most likely) was that I'd taken a direct blow which snapped the bone. I thought of the bike crashing down on top of me . . . That was straightforward and the healing time was the four to six weeks I was banking on. The second scenario however, was more worrying. As soon as the new cast was on I phoned Eve and Charley in France.

CHARLEY: When Ewan mentioned the MRI, I wasn't surprised; I'd been through a couple myself.

'The doctor told me there was a chance I might've broken it by twisting it,' Ewan was saying.

'It's a precaution, mate. That's all. When are they doing it?'

'I'm going for it now.'

'OK, well good luck. Let us know when they give you the results.'

Wandering out to the balcony I grabbed a breath of air. The chalet was in a beautiful spot, overlooking a mountain thick with snow. This was a rough road, the first time Ewan had broken a bone. If he did need an operation it could spell disaster.

Ollie knew what was going through my mind and she came out and leant on the rail next to me. 'It puts things in perspective, doesn't it?' she said. 'I feel apprehensive, Charley. I mean, don't get me wrong, the trip is wonderful, it's very exciting. But it's different from you racing the Dakar; different again from Long Way Round.' She gazed across the mountain. 'It's much more dangerous, and not just the politics. The roads are busier and there are people everywhere.' She shook her head. 'It just shows you. I mean London on a Friday, doing no speed at all. It shows how lucky the two of you were when you did Long Way Round. Twenty thousand miles with no major incident.'

EWAN: All I wanted was to have the scan and be told the break was clean and I'd be on the bike come May. But you cannot undergo an MRI if you have any metal in your body, for instance a plate or a clip pinned into a bone. I remembered years back I'd had some iron filings caught in my eye. They'd been removed, of course, but it had to be checked because if there was any residue at all the MRI would force it out of my body, and I mean right through my eye.

That out of the way I lay on my back with my legs in the machine and they gave me a set of headphones to block the weird clicks and noises it makes.

It took about half an hour in all and I waited for the results: nervously. At last the good news came through. I could have jumped for joy if I wasn't in plaster. The MRI was clear; it was a simple break. I rang Charley. By May my leg would be healed, and we'd be riding through Africa.

4
Saddle Bags & Steroids

EWAN: Charley was concerned about Ollie: his wife of fifteen years. He's been in love with her since the moment they met. For the last few weeks she'd had a viral infection she just couldn't shake: Charley hadn't said much but finally he told me he was really worried.

Ollie didn't seem to be getting any better and the date of departure was just days away now. The cast was off my leg and the bikes were prepped. Russ and David were up to their necks trying to finalise everything and emotionally we were all a bit frayed. Ollie's situation was serious and I suppose it accentuated the worries we were all carrying.

David isn't married and doesn't have any children and I guess because of that he doesn't go through quite the same emotions as the rest of us. Russ, on the other hand, has a daughter, Emily, and I knew he was very concerned about leaving her.

On the practical side of things we were ahead of where we were the last time. When we prepared for Long Way Round the support trucks didn't show up until the day before we left. Here we still had a day or so and both Nissan Patrols were ready. We had a team of people coming to the workshop to fit a safe and some bullet cameras. The small, fixed 'bullet' cameras made by Sonic would be fitted in the Nissans and on our helmets and would allow the action to be filmed at all times. The suspension had been upgraded and both trucks fitted with dual batteries; they had long-range fuel tanks, heavy duty bumpers and two spare wheels apiece. The front bumpers had been replaced with ones that carried a winch in case Russ or David had to haul themselves out of a hole somewhere.

Eve had been down to our workshop on Avonmore Road on the 650 she would be riding in Malawi, and we'd talked about the kind of gear she needed to bring with her. It was a difficult period for us – so close to the start now and this time our daughters were much older. Daddy was going away, and although that wasn't unusual because of my work, it was still going to be a wrench. I really felt for Charley. Worrying about leaving the family was bad enough, but with Ollie's condition still so bad, I knew he must be beside himself.

CHARLEY: None of the antibiotics Ollie had been given were working. Deep down I knew something wasn't right and I'd go from worrying about her to excitement about the trip to the heebie-jeebies about ridiculous things. I'd wake in the night and start thinking about the kind of clothes I was taking: shoes, T-shirts, underpants, what kind of razor.

In the meantime, there was nothing to do but keep up the preparation. The bikes had been painted blue and red respectively; one with zebra stripes and the other leopard spots to differentiate them. We'd fitted sump guards and light guards; metal protection plates over the engine casing. We'd also switched the original BMW suspension for what was considered the more robust Ohlins. We changed the weightier exhausts for Akrapovic cans, which were not only much lighter but added around four or five horsepower. They also had the kind of snarling note I wanted when you cracked the throttle. MacTools had provided all the tools necessary to get the Patrols and bikes ready for the road, and Touratech had supplied all the gear we'd need to make an expedition like this work: from tents to camping stoves to mounts for our phones (we were using Nokia's Navigator 6110) that we would use all the way through Africa.

We had also just about nailed our proposed route. We would ride down through Britain and France to the toe of Italy and across Sicily before a boat ride to Tunisia. Once in Africa we would follow the coast to Libya, Egypt and Sudan. We'd always known Libya might be an issue and in particular we were encountering problems getting visas for the two Americans on our team: David Alexanian and cameraman Jimmy Simak. I had my mate Jacob on it: he works for the Libyan government, advising them on their Africa policy, and we hoped he'd be able to exert some influence. Jo, our production manager, was speaking to one of our sponsors, Explore, to see if they could help us out, as they run tours in Libya. The reality, though, was we were just a few days from departure and we'd only just got the requisite paperwork for the Brits and Claudio, the Swiss cameraman who had also ridden with us on Long Way Round.

Visas aside, I couldn't think beyond Ollie. My beautiful wife – she's the rock that holds everything about my life together. She puts up with all the bullshit; she puts up with me; she looks after the kids on her own while I take off and at the same time she runs a business called Share and Care with her sister-in-law Caroline, locating companions for elderly people. She deals with everything, takes it all in her stride and never complains about anything. But it was two days until we left so I took her back to the doctors and they managed to get her in for a scan. It showed up a patch of pneumonia.

Apparently it wasn't uncommon for a virus to cause pneumonia and now they knew Ollie had it they could treat her with steroids. Pneumonia, steroids, Christ I wasn't going to leave for Africa with my wife in this condition. Ollie, of course, told me she would be fine; that once they'd figured out what steroids to give her she'd be better and there was no way she'd let me alter the plans. I wasn't convinced, and I told her I wasn't going to leave until I knew she was all right.

The only way to find out which steroids to prescribe was for the doctors to do a biopsy of the patch of pneumonia and they told us that during the procedure there was a small chance the lung might partially collapse. This was Wednesday afternoon and I was supposed to be leaving on Friday morning. Ollie's parents were in Spain for a few weeks and this coming weekend was our niece's First Holy Communion. Ollie's sister Anastasia had been brilliant, running around and picking up our daughters Doone and Kinvara. But she had forty people coming for lunch on Sunday and if anything went wrong with this biopsy there was no way I was leaving on Friday. Ollie asked the doctor how many times he'd pierced a lung while performing this type of biopsy.

None, he told her.

Of course this was the time he did and the lung collapsed.

To reinflate it they used a local anaesthetic before inserting a massive needle, like a knitting needle, between Ollie's ribs. The pain was excruciating: Ollie all but screaming. She gripped my hand so hard her fingernails drew blood. It wasn't a quick procedure and watching her go through it was heartbreaking. She was determined that the lung would reinflate quickly, though, so she could be home from hospital for my last night. I told her it didn't matter because there was no way I was leaving her like this. She insisted she would be fine, and wanted to be home for Thursday night. So despite the pain she kept the suction on her lung going all Wednesday night.

I was unsure but she was adamant she'd be all right. She argued that she'd find it much easier to recuperate if she knew I was gone – that everything had gone to plan. I still didn't like the idea so I spoke to Ewan about it and he thought we ought to wait as well. But Ollie would have none of it. I know her, and regardless of what she was going through she'd blame herself and that would inhibit her recovery. She was right, reluctant though I was to admit it, so after a lot of soul-searching I agreed. By the time Friday came around Ollie was home and much better and we left for Scotland as planned.

5

Five ... Four ... Three ...

EWAN: 'As planned'? That's not strictly true. We'd been due to fly to Inverness all together, only that's not how it turned out. But as he was the main protagonist, I'll let 'Osama Bin Boorman' enlighten you.

For now let's just say that 'finally' we all made it to the Castle of Mey, the historic seat of the Earls of Caithness, bought by the Queen Mother in 1952. Built in the sixteenth century, the castle is said to be haunted by the Green Lady. A daughter of the fifth earl, she fell in love with a ploughman and was locked away in the attic by her father. She's supposed to have thrown herself to her death from the attic window. Fortunately our hosts waited until the following morning to tell us which rooms she haunted and I had a really good night's sleep. Nothing – living or dead – disturbed me.

My dad and brother Colin were riding part of the way through Scotland with us and I was really pleased about that. I woke early and went for a run. My leg was much better, no twinges whatsoever. But over breakfast I began to feel apprehensive. After all the preparations we were finally leaving and the nerves were beginning to bite.

Like a couple of sentinels our bikes occupied either side of the main door of the castle, and as I made sure everything was in its proper place I was acutely conscious of departure. It wasn't cold, but this is as north as it gets and rain clouds had dominated the sky ever since we arrived. It would be wet on the road today.

Charley had been on the phone to Ollie and she was feeling considerably better. We would never have left if she'd still been really ill. It was great to know she was doing so well now.

The trucks were packed, the bikes ready, and we were all set to go. I pulled up alongside Charley. 'OK, Charley,' I said. 'Good luck, mate. Love you.' Then we were off, Charley leading, his panniers glinting as a brief glimmer from the sun bounced off them.

The sign read 'John O'Groats, a welcome at the end of the road' but for us it was only the beginning. Quite a few people had gathered to see us off. Many of the well-wishers were English, and one couple we spoke to told us that English people came up to escape the rat race while Scots went the other way in search of jobs. I guess I had to count myself among the latter.

Charley was alongside me and I told him I really had to speak to my wife. 'I haven't told her I'm leaving yet,' I said.

He was laughing. 'You mean you've not told her we're doing the trip?'

'No, I just said I was going out to get some milk.'

I spoke to Eve, the whole gathering yelling out 'hello'. And then we were off, five of us in convoy – myself, Charley, my dad, my brother, and Claudio filming. Over the next couple of days the five would become four and the four three – on our way to Cape Town.

I love riding motorcycles. It can be raining, fucking snowing, I don't care. There's no feeling quite like it in the world. I've said it before: the beauty of the trip is the bike, sweeping into bends, banking the thing knowing it's planted, no matter the road conditions. Riding along there's so much time to reflect, which is a rare thing in these days of modern living. I realised that though John O'Groats might have been a throwaway comment initially, it was in fact the perfect place to start. A couple of days in beautiful, barren Scotland – I haven't lived here for years and I don't get to ride these roads very often – was good for the soul. I was relaxed; the Belstaff rally suit was light, comfortable and, most important, waterproof. I was in my element.

Ten miles into the journey, however, I realised I'd forgotten to recalibrate the GPS, which, when you think about it, is a 'page one' thing to do. Stupid – I wanted to know exactly how many miles I'd covered when we rode into Cape Town and here I was with my GPS not reading the distance correctly.

CHARLEY: You may recall that Ewan likes to leave the navigating to me, so I'm not surprised he forgot to reset the GPS. We were heading down the A9 towards Loch Ness before riding through Glencoe and on to Crieff where we would stay the night with his parents. Ewan told me that he'd wondered what it would be like riding into Cape Town on the last day, and if he'd remember that he'd wondered about it way back at the beginning. Cape Town was months away and I had no idea what I'd be thinking when we got there, but I suppose that's the difference between the two of us.

We had a hell of a lot of miles to cover first; there'd been a kidnapping in Ethiopia, plane crashes in the Democratic Republic of Congo, and the situation in Darfur was no better. A couple of weeks previously there'd been a rally in London to protest about the four years of slaughter and we weren't sure what kind of impact that would have on the Sudanese government. I guessed we'd find out.

I was glad to be off at last after all the last-minute stresses and everything that had happened with Ollie. I was pleased we were stopping for a night in London, though, so I could see her again before I left for the long haul. This morning she'd sent me a lovely text, congratulating us on the first day of Long Way Down. That's typical Ollie, always thinking about me. It brought home just how much I was going to miss her and the kids.

I'd needed her yesterday because as Ewan said, it hadn't just been a case of rocking up at the airport and flying north: looking back now it was mad, totally crazy; a really dumb thing to happen.

We'd been in the business lounge waiting for our flight when it kicked off. Before we even got inside a woman, a representative of the airline, was having a go at a passenger who appeared to be in the wrong place. I made some crack and the woman started telling us that this was a business class place and we ought to behave like business people. The reality was there weren't any so-called 'business people' around, just three other guys dressed in jeans like us. It was petty, stupid; but she was really irritated now and with hindsight perhaps she was looking for an excuse to have a go.

Paying customers or not we couldn't do anything right. I had a bag behind my chair and up against the wall; it was no distance from me. I could literally reach over and grab it. She told me to move it.

For Christ's sake, I thought; ridiculous. And then I opened my mouth: 'It's not as if there's a bomb in it,' I said.

Oh God. Charley, Charley; that's not what you say in an airport when you're waiting to board a plane. I knew it as soon as I said it. But it was too late, the words were out and the woman went ballistic.

'Right,' she said. 'That's it; I'm off to get the police.'

I couldn't believe it. I didn't believe it. I just thought she'd gone outside to cool down for a moment.

A couple of minutes later she was back, however, with four police officers and the head of airport security in tow. I was gobsmacked; I mean for Christ's sake all this already and I'd not even left England. They marched me outside and started grilling me.

Rightly so: I'd made a stupid comment, letting my temper get the better of me when only a few weeks earlier on our training course I'd been talking about how daft that was. I know from my own experiences on the last trip that ranting and raving about something gets you precisely nowhere, except into more trouble. Not that I'd been ranting and raving, but I *had* lost the plot and now I was paying the price.

Anyway the four cops and the head of security asked me all sorts of questions and I told them what had happened and that I was sorry, and it had been foolish in the extreme to make such a remark. But I also told them about the woman's attitude, that she'd been in everyone's faces and in my opinion she'd been looking for a reason to get even. While this was going on the flight was called and the three other passengers who witnessed what had happened in the lounge each came out to tell the police that the woman had been totally unreasonable. All I'd really done was make a silly crack.

The thing was, however, no one from the airline was there to hear it so although the police and the head of security accepted my apology, the airline wasn't able to. If they'd sent someone through I might have made that plane. As it was I didn't. They told me there was no way they were letting me on. I wasn't flying and that was the end of it.

Jesus, it was a mess. Immediately Russ said he'd stay behind with me and we'd try and get on another flight. Typical Russ, I can't count the times he's been there to bail me out.

Anyway Russ stayed and the others took off for Inverness as planned. The head of security ushered us out to arrivals. I kept apologising, as did Russ on my behalf, and between us we suggested that she might go and see the airline people for us. She agreed to do that, deposited us in a cafe and told us to wait.

Wait we did and what a nightmare. We spoke to Asia, the *Long Way Down* project manager, at the office and she told us that the airline were going to put the word out to other airlines and make sure no one would fly me anywhere. Not just then, but anytime and anywhere in the world. I was cacking myself.

We sat there and sat there, going over every possible scenario, every outcome; ruing the fact that I'd opened my big mouth. And then the head of security came back. She brought with her the manager of the airline and once again I apologised, grovelled even, and she agreed it had all been a misunderstanding and that we could get on the next flight.

Anyway, we made it; and spent the night in the Castle of Mey with the others. It was all behind me now thankfully. I felt great, relaxed even, if a little emotional. I hoped everything would be all right.

It started well; the roads were sound, the tarmac good and the countryside spectacular. This morning had been weird though; I'd woken up with a black eye. It had been fine when I went to sleep, but now I looked like I'd been in a fight and I began to wonder whose bedroom mine had been historically – the fifth earl maybe; he who'd locked his daughter in the attic?

It was beginning to rain; the clouds that had unloaded the night before had regrouped and were swamping us again. We headed south, a loch on our left and the mountains sombre and grey. Ewan was right, Scotland had been a good idea; the roads were empty, the bike felt like it was on rails and to be riding with my best mate again was fantastic.

I was over the irritations now, all the bullshit at the airport and I'd had last night to fully unwind. As if in warning, however, ahead of me Ewan tried to overtake a car. There was another car coming but the driver he was overtaking wouldn't let Ewan in. He had to back off the throttle and pull behind him again. A boy racer with a big aerial, the twat, he could've killed him.

Beyond the pitch black waters of Loch Ness we headed east through Glencoe. Here the mountains shouldered us on either side and Ewan described the history as 'bleeding off them'.

It had stopped raining but the tarmac was greasy, the road twisty but not technical, shortish sweeping bends, grippy Michelin tyres; the bike pitched into them without missing a beat.

EWAN: The scenery was stunning: mountains banked with heather and massive stands of fir trees, lines of which had been cut back. The way they smelled in the rain was terrific. For the first time in ages I had a little head space. I had no great sense of the journey yet, no overbearing worries about the miles; it felt like a Sunday, I was bimbling along behind my dad just out for a ride on my bike. At breakfast I'd had a sense of scale but right now it was banished. I was travelling in the direction of London though, and that meant towards my family. I knew it would be different when we left again; then I would be going ever further away from them and no doubt the reality of the venture would dawn.

My leg was aching a bit: this morning was the first time I'd been running since I'd broken it. On the set of *Incendiary* I'd had to do a little jog now and then, and during the first week of filming I was definitely still hobbling, but this morning I'd been running and now my leg was complaining about it.

It was getting near lunchtime but we wanted to be south of Inverness before we stopped. It's weird but we'd only been going half a day and already there was the temptation to rush on. Why?

What for? We weren't slaves to any clock and I was determined we weren't going to pressurise ourselves. I wanted to relax and enjoy it, not be cowed by some schedule as we'd sometimes found ourselves on Long Way Round.

I was getting hungry and coming into another town I spied a cafe by the roadside where a couple of rozzers were squatting in their panda car. It was too early to eat. I was thinking about food, though; scampi and chips in particular. What is it about road trips through Scotland that make you think about eating scampi and chips?

Still it rained; the roads slick, puddles opaque as sheep crossed, and a lonely camper van struggled on ahead. Day one and already we'd had as much rain as we'd had during the entire time it took to ride round the world. I remember being in the jungles of Honduras with an archaeologist and he told me about rain. He said you're all right if you can stop it raining in your head. Let it rain inside your head and you're in trouble: you can easily become depressed. So it could rain all it wanted on my helmet, I wasn't going to let it rain in my head. Besides, later we'd be in fifty degrees of heat in places and we'd probably be begging for a downpour.

We spent the night with my mum in Crieff and in the morning we headed for Stirling and then Robin House. Only the second children's hospice to be built in Scotland, it's a place where parents can take their terminally ill youngsters for a certain number of days a year and get a little respite themselves. It's run by the Children's Hospice Association of Scotland, a charity I'm involved with that was founded in 1992 by a small group of committed parents and medical professionals. I'd not been to Robin House since it was completed, but I had been to its sister Rachel House in Kinross. The best way to describe the children is as wonderfully brave little people who aren't going to make it into adulthood. They're feisty, full of life; they're very much alive. How do you deal with it though . . . if you're a parent, I mean? I think unless you're actually in it, it's unimaginable.

Robin House had been finished a couple of years ago and is set within the boundaries of Loch Lomond National Park. We pulled up and were met by the staff: inside one of the kids was hovering. I gave him a big hug. 'Hi, wee man,' I said. 'How are you?'

CHARLEY: For years Ewan had been telling me about CHAS and what fantastic work they did, how incredible the families involved were. But until today I'd never seen for myself. I have to admit I was feeling quite emotional. I spoke to Ewan in the spacious reception area. I said that as well as it being so hard on the children and parents, it must be really tough for the staff.

Ewan nodded. 'What you find being here though . . . it's a really positive experience because it's a place full of colour and life. I've always found it at Rachel House. That's what it's for, for these kids to have a really good time. And so you come away feeling really good. It's only a day or so later maybe, when you've had time to reflect, that it hits you.'

It was an incredible building, wood-panelled with a sloping roof, a tiled courtyard and windows everywhere. The views were magnificent, across the gardens to low and distant hills. The children's bedrooms had little portholes, circular windows at bed level so they could be lying down and still gaze across the gardens. The staff took us into the sitting room where families were gathered and they'd put a big sign on the wall welcoming us. There was the usual hubbub, music in the background, loud and crashy, not sombre or even vaguely melancholy. We met a great lad called William who'd come all the way from Rachel House especially because his greatest ambition had been to meet Ewan. There was a lad called Sean from Stirling, a young lady called Ashleigh, there was Cameron, Keiron, Lee; and a little girl called Rebecca who was running around taking everyone's picture. Outside a wheelchair-bound boy named Paul was flying a kite with one of the carers, while someone's younger brother dressed as Superman dived about all over the place.

The parents had bedrooms downstairs – a sort of escape zone so they could get away from it all for a while. I spoke to a couple who explained that having cared for their little one 24/7 all his life, it was actually quite hard the first time they went to the hospice. It took a while to get used to other people being around to look after him. The families, brothers and sisters particularly, take advantage of the hydro-pool because with one child needing constant care they rarely go to a normal swimming pool. The kids have a main play area complete with a soft play room, where those who can't stand up are able to roll around without getting hurt. They have a fantastic art room where the music is normally so loud you can barely hear yourselves speak.

A lot of the kids they deal with are teenagers – many teenage lads in fact – whose minds are sound but their bodies let them down. They have their own den, where no adult or young child can go; a chill-out zone like every teenager needs. There they can surf the net, watch DVDs or play the drums if they want to. The hospice has what they call the snoozlin: a multi-sensory area with coloured bubble lights, a water bed, a carpet that changes colour and a ceiling made of stars. Children who can't communicate can lie there and perhaps some image or colour will bring a light to their eyes or even the hint of a smile.

Most of the time I was fighting back tears. We met a girl called Jenna whose dad was a biker, another girl called Jenny, there was Leona and John; I'd never come across such brave children or such incredible parents. The whole thing was humbling and left Ewan and me feeling very emotional, particularly after they showed us the rainbow room. The hospice is there to create memories for families who are losing their children. That's what they told us, and it was a terribly sad and yet kind of hopeful way of putting it. For me it was personified in the rainbow room: it looked like any other bedroom but this was where a child was laid out after he or she had died. It was private and separate and could be made very cool very quickly so a grieving family could have as long as they wanted with their loved one. They could play music or read a story, or they could just sit with them until they could face moving on. If they woke in the night in floods of tears they could go to the rainbow room and just be with them.

The carers told us that ironically the room comes to life when a child is lying there; they have hidden projectors and can play images across the walls, photos would be spread, memories. If the child was just a baby, perhaps only a few days old, ceramic imprints of their hands and feet can be made. They told us about a teenage weekend they had, when one of the kids died and all the others went to the rainbow room to say goodbye. Talk about tough, talk about brave; they knew this was what faced every one of them.

It made me think about my sister Telsche, who I lost to cancer some years ago. I missed her. I loved her. I could feel her with me on the bike, almost as if when I slung my leg over the seat she climbed right on the back. She was there on Long Way Round; she was there on the Dakar. I knew she'd be with me all the way to Cape Town.

EWAN: Robin House was very emotional. I've visited Rachel House many times and it puts everything into the sharpest focus. It's a strange truth, but as parents go to a hospital when it's time for their child to be born, so some parents take their children to Robin House when it's time for them to die. I was really touched by Cameron's parents. They were a young couple with two kids who were well and one who wasn't – Cameron – who was such a sweetheart. I was full of respect for his father, a young guy who worked on farms and had such a lot on his plate looking after his family. He seemed a really a decent man, but then all the families are like that. You just have to thank God that places like Robin House are there, because for the families that use them they're an absolute necessity, and the carers, the people that work there, can't be praised enough.

We stayed for lunch then reluctantly said our goodbyes and

rode on to Erskine Hospital, an establishment for ex-service people that my brother is involved with. We spoke to some ex-soldiers – one old boy in particular had been part of the actual Great Escape. He told us that he'd been a private, though, and it was the officers who got to escape; he and his mates had to stay behind and cover for them. The youngest resident was twenty-two and suffering from chronic arthritis; the oldest was a hundred. Charley spoke to a bloke who'd served with Robert Lawrence, a friend of Charley's who had been horrifically wounded in the Falklands. He wrote about his experiences in the controversial book *Tumbledown*.

It had been an incredible, inspiring day. In their different ways both places had taught us something about the nature of true courage and it was a real privilege to have been invited.

My dad left us now. He was a little emotional saying goodbye; he'd loved riding with us and I'd loved having him there. But he was heading home now and we were going to Cape Town and I imagine there was a part of him that wanted to go with us and another part that was nervous for us. We shed a couple of tears and parted company and then there were four bikes on the road. We cut across country to the south-eastern part of Scotland – an area I'd never visited – and from there to the desolate location of Holy Isle. It's built on a promontory beyond a causeway which floods at high tide, and the wind howls in an almost permanent gale. I could only imagine how cold it must be to live there but there was a barren beauty to it even so. A little further on a couple of people came rushing out of their house, waving their arms. I pulled up. They told me that they'd been following our departure on some website. Dave and Claire, both BMW riders: I told them to get the kettle on. They were the first of many along the route who would show us great hospitality – and this was half the fun of the trip for me.

My brother was going to peel off and head back to Edinburgh but I really wanted him to stay and we persuaded him to spend the night. The weather was filthy and he was wet and cold and we could eat together, have a drink and he could take off in the morning. And then the four would become three and that's how it would remain all the way to Cape Town.

Just before we hit the border with England we had our second moment on the bikes – if you can call my brush with 'boy-racer' a moment. Claudio banked into a sharp right and ran wide on the grass. When we pulled up for a breather the Swiss, in his own inimitable fashion, told us he was missing the off-road experience and decided on a little practice before we got to Africa.

We chilled out for a while, drinking water and lucozade. Charley was a little windy (he's known for it) but he claimed it was the altitude expanding the air in his arse.

We rode south and on the third night camped at Silverstone. Right on the race track, the sweeping bend before the start and finish straight; a triangle of grass, between that bend and the chicane that was used for superbike races. Apparently we were the first people in the sixty year history of the place to actually camp on the track itself.

It was the ideal opportunity to test the gear before we hit the continent. If anything was awry we'd have time to rectify it. My tent was great; dry and cosy and plenty big enough for me and all my gear. It rained in the night and again first thing, but when I packed up everything was bone dry.

Before we left Charley and I followed a pace car for two laps of the track with the Nissan Patrols following. It was foul weather, pouring with rain, but still Charley managed a second gear wheelie. From Silverstone it was London. We fuelled the bikes at the same petrol station where we'd filled up on the first day of Long Way Round. From there it was Avonmore Road, the workshop, the gang, and home for one last night with our families.

6

Here We Go, Charley

EWAN: The following morning everyone was gathered at Avonmore Road: our families and friends, and many of the people who'd been there to see us off the first time. It gave us a real sense of support. We said our final goodbyes. Clara, my eldest daughter, was there with my wife, but Esther and Jamyan, my younger two, were both at school.

The bikes packed, the trucks ready, we rolled out of the workshop for the last time and everyone was gathered on the pavement. Flags were waved, we had a line painted on the tarmac just as we had before we set off round the world, and we cut a cake made in the shape of a crash helmet.

Shaking hands with Charley, I looked round for my wife. There she was: a smile, a final wave and that was it. Pulling my best ever wheelie I led us off down the road.

All sorts of emotions rushed through me; my heart was pounding, adrenalin pumping and I was sweating buckets I was so hot. I'd not see my daughters again until Cape Town. I couldn't believe it. I just couldn't believe it. I was suddenly confused about the whole thing. Was I just being fucking selfish, taking off for so long and leaving my family behind? I didn't know. I couldn't get my head round any of it.

I concentrated. I had to: my pulse was racing so much I was in danger of crashing and I'd hit enough pedestrians for one year already. All I could think about was what one wise man was supposed to have said: 'Get me the fuck out of London!'

CHARLEY: Ewan popped the wheelie and I followed him. We were skipping through the traffic when all at once a pickup truck stopped right in front of me. I didn't even see his brake lights. With so much buzzing through my head I wasn't concentrating.

On the line I'd shaken hands with Ewan and wished him luck. Ollie was standing on the pavement and I yelled out that I loved her and then we were gone. Ten minutes down the road and I'd almost smacked a Mitsubishi up the backside. I had to brake suddenly, the suspension working overtime. Ewan came flashing by on my right.

For a couple of seconds I just sat there, telling myself to chill out. It's what my wife had been telling me ever since I'd got home the night before. I'd been all of a twitter and she'd kept telling me to calm down and enjoy it. Ollie always has the right thing to say to me: no matter what's going on in her life. When I'm away she has to cope, and when I'm not away I'm jittery about when I will be. Never mind what angst she might be going through, all she thinks about is how *I'm* feeling. She's my hero, she really is.

It was heart-wrenching to leave, even though we'd said our proper goodbyes at home earlier that morning. Ollie was so much better and I was very relieved as I'd never have been able to go if she hadn't been. At least my walkie-talkie was working now and I could talk to Ewan. Over the past couple of days it had been out, but now we could chat away as much as we wanted. I told Ewan what Ollie had been saying and he told me he'd had similar pangs to mine. Of course he had, he was bound to, and Eve had been just as supportive.

Gradually I relaxed; the traffic eased, we were on the motorway and heading for Folkestone with the Eurostar thundering by on our left. I could think about nothing but Ollie and how she was coping with her lung and all that she had to do; how much I was going to miss her, how much I'd miss the kids.

Two hours later we were waiting to board the train and now I had a real twinge of emotion. This was it; we were leaving the island, leaving Britain. Ahead lay France, Italy, Africa. Ewan pulled up alongside me, killed his engine and complained of a headache, probably due to all the emotion and the stress of finally leaving. For some reason I wondered what his mum was thinking. I knew she'd prefer him not to go; she'd prefer us all not to go. She had admitted that she'd had no real idea what had been going on the last time even though Ewan had phoned from Siberia and told her how knackered he was, how the potholes were unbelievable and we were doing no miles an hour. Until she watched the DVD she had no inkling of how dangerous it was.

She said she'd been delighted when Ewan's brother left the RAF, because it meant he wouldn't have to go back to Iraq: one son safe, now the other off on a bike again; another fourteen thousand miles, this time to Cape Town. She said she'd spent her life worrying about her family and now she was thinking about taking up bungee jumping or something so her family could worry about her for a change. Mind you she was also kind enough to point out that without Long Way Round the fact that in some parts of the world kids lived in sewers might never have been highlighted. She's a remedial teacher and told us that loads of classrooms around the country had followed our journey via maps on the wall. She said that both the DVD and the book were being used as teaching aids for subjects such as geography and modern studies. As someone who had often struggled at school, it was strange to think that something I'd done could help broaden kids' knowledge of the world.

Ewan's mum confessed that she'd finally got her head round

the fact that her son was nuts about motorbikes. She even went with Ewan when he bought his Guzzi and was amazed at his knowledge; the fact that he not only buys and rides bikes, he rebuilds old ones himself. I think she and her husband Jim are very proud of him, of all of us, of how we put Long Way Round together and the impact it's had. It was brought home to Jim when we stopped at Castle Urquhart on the shores of Loch Ness and a couple pulled in, having no idea we were there. Believe it or not they had a copy of the *Long Way Round* DVD in the car and Ewan and I signed it. Jim was very proud, they both were, but it didn't stop them worrying.

EWAN: This was it. We were really leaving now and a rush of adrenalin washed through me. With the train waiting we headed on to the ramp, side by side. I looked over at my mate with a smile on my face and my headache fading.

'Here wc go, Charley,' I yelled. I remembered the last time we'd left Britain, hitting France and swinging east towards Brussels. East, cast, forever it had been east. This time, apart from a little bit of south-west maybe, we were heading south all the way.

Charley looked across with a grin under his helmet. 'Hey, we could always just go back up the ramp.'

Within half an hour we were in the saddle again and pulling out of the train on the French side of the channel. Like a flag over conquered land, Charley hoisted the front wheel and I was laughing now, excited. The first thing Eve had said to me when I phoned from the tunnel was: 'You did a really big wheelie!'

France, and the first leg proper: God it was brilliant. It was overcast but not raining, the skies a feathered grey and the road dead straight: farmers' fields unrolled left and right, very flat, just the odd tree here and there to interrupt the horizon. We drifted south through one-street towns heading for Reims, which was about four hours from the tunnel. I'd always thought it was pronounced 'Reems'. Then I thought it might be 'Rems'. You'd think I'd know, wouldn't you, being married to a French woman for a dozen years. I finally learned it's pronounced 'Rance'.

By six p.m. French time we were an hour from the hotel where we'd booked to stay the night. I didn't recall making any decision about a hotel, in fact I wanted to camp. It was dull but not wet and I'd really enjoyed the night we'd had at Silverstone. It seems to me these decisions have a habit of just being made, sort of remote control, and I always find out afterwards.

I was into the riding, though, and right now that was all that mattered. I'd waited for this for so long that just to be on the road again was fantastic. Some of the driving left a little to be desired, mind you: cars kept overtaking then slamming on their brakes, pulling across in front of me and diving off at the exit. It happened about three times and really began to piss me off.

I ignored them the best I could: when you ride a bike you get used to the antics of car drivers who aren't always as considerate as they might be.

I was conscious of the distance now, the size of the trip, in a way that I hadn't been in Scotland but I settled back, determined not to rush. I knew there was a magnificent Cathedral in Reims and thought we might want to take a look at it, but it seemed there was an urgency to press on. I could feel it, racing the clock – exactly what I'd wanted to try and avoid.

I suppose there was a need to just get to Africa; the trip was about Africa and wouldn't truly begin until we got there. I picked up the same feeling from Ted Simon's book *Jupiter's Travels* – a book that had always inspired me – when he describes the urge to rush through Europe to get to the beginning of the journey.

Oh my God, we're going to Cape Town! Sitting there on the French motorway I could feel the grin stretching my face and I began to wonder what it would be like when we did get there. I tried to imagine arriving in Tunisia; the noise, the colour, the smells of the port town; the coast road in Libya; Alexandria. What was it going to be like in Sudan; in Kenya; Namibia? Sand dunes and God knows what kind of road conditions; that would really test my riding skills.

CHARLEY: Out of the train I pulled a wheelie as I planned to at every border. I was still feeling emotional, though better now I'd had some food in Folkestone. I'd been on the phone to Ollie and that made me a little sad but now we were on the continent and heading south and I was totally into the bike. We had another four hours before we stopped for the night – not a bad day in the saddle and at least it wasn't raining.

Ewan had been up for camping tonight, and we'd been talking about camping in Europe being so different to camping in Africa. There I imagined it would be the cuds, unknown territory, as it had on Long Way Round; in Europe we'd probably have to go to proper sites. We both preferred the cuds, but thought it might be a laugh on a campsite and it was a chance to meet people. We'd just roll up on the bikes, pitch the tents and see who came along.

Not tonight, though. We'd agreed on a hotel and arrived about seven I guess; a nice, modern place just outside Reims. We pulled off the road onto a gravel drive backed by sweeping lawns.

Ewan took his helmet off. 'We should've camped,' he said. 'Pulling up at a hotel like this with all the adventure gear, I feel like a bit of a dick.'

He spends a large part of his life in hotels and he had a point. But though he seemed to have missed it, there had been a consensus about this first night. The weather looked iffy and we had to get through the Mont Blanc tunnel the following aftenoon if we were to make it to the Moto Guzzi factory as planned.

We got settled in our rooms and met up for dinner. Sitting round the table we had what I'd call a substantial discussion about what we were going to do; what the route would be and how it would pan out. It got a little heated with Ewan stating that he wanted to see more of Europe. There was a lot of humming and hawing and Ewan got genuinely upset, partly about the planning and partly because he'd set his mind on camping.

EWAN: I slept well and in the morning when I looked out the window, I was in fact quite glad we'd decided on a hotel. Charley would probably be thinking 'I told you so' because it rained in the night and it was raining now; not heavy but ominous-looking and slanting from an ashen sky. There was no sign of it lifting.

Today was a big push. We were hooning down French motorways to the Mont Blanc tunnel. We'd be in Italy tonight and had some three hundred and seventy miles to cover. We'd see nothing of France which was a shame, because the area around Dijon is particularly beautiful; I've got some great memories from back in the early nineties when I made *The Scarlet and the Black* for the BBC. But then I knew I could always come back another time with my family.

I was really enjoying myself now; I just love riding. These trips aren't about me trying to get away from acting or the movie business. They're more about melding my two worlds, professional and personal if you like. I love the fact that there aren't a hundred and one people ushering me around like there is when I'm working. Fantastic that no one tells me to get off the motorbike because it's too dangerous and we have to get a stuntman in for those bits: if I want to zoom along at a hundred and fifteen in a tunnel I can; if I want to stop at a transport cafe and throw a map on the table I do. It's partly riding with Charley, of course, partly adventure, and partly just the camaraderie of motorcycling. Everything I need is on that bike: that's why when the opportunity is there to just pull over and put a tent up I want to take it.

The rain was light at first and I was pretty relaxed; muscle memory or mind memory had kicked in. This was day six of about ninety and I was looking forward to the rest of the trip. East of Dijon is Besançon where we also did some filming and where

Eve's parents have a house. It's a stunning part of the world, sumptuous countryside, all gorges and rivers, chateaux dotted here and there. It's where George Millar was based during World War II. One of many British SOE agents fighting with the French Resistance, he led a band of *Maquis* that attacked German rail traffic. There's also a nice little love story there – Marie, a French girl I knew long before I met Eve. She was . . . well actually, no, that's another story . . .

The day wore on and the rain grew heavier the further south we went. My boots gradually filled with water. The roads were slick and there was so much spray. We were beetling along at around 80 mph, the bikes perfectly stable, perfectly smooth; the only real bends were the perfect radius slip roads where, in the dry, you can really get the bike cranked over. Not today though, today was as wet as I can remember and forget the three days I told you about from John O'Groats – we'd had more rain this second morning alone than during the whole of Long Way Round. Four hours in the sodding rain. I could feel water moving around my toes, passing back under the arch of my foot and gathering at the heel. My foot was in a spa only the water wasn't hot. *Would somebody get me out of this fucking rain*?

The countryside was dim and grizzled-looking. We were into mountains and lakes that on any other day would've been beautiful, but the clouds hung so low they draped like damp shrouds and all we could see was the swirl of grey and the viciously slanting rain.

We stopped for fuel at a Total garage and I nosed my bike alongside Charley's. 'So, Charley,' I said. 'How do we feel?'

He made a face. 'A bit low actually. Too much sun, a little heatstroke, I think. It's like being on the Dakar.' He glanced at the petrol pump. 'Total sponsored me, actually.'

'Really, Charley?'

'Yeah . . . Hey, did I ever mention I did the Dakar, Ewan?'

'Yeah, I think you mentioned that. Anyway, it's the dryness of the heat that's the killer.'

'You know somewhere in Africa we'll look back and dream of this day.'

'Somewhere.' With a squelch I shifted position. I could feel water running down my sleeves and into my gloves; they were soaked through and my hands, my feet would be shrivelled up like prunes. Charley was the same.

'You know what's keeping me going?' I said with a grin.

'What's that?'

I looked up at leaden skies, the rain rattling off our helmets. 'The thought of finding a really nice campsite and getting the tent up. You know, even if it's still raining, carrying all the kit in and getting it dry.'

'Right,' Charley said, 'right. It's a good job we carry those dehumidifiers for the tents, isn't it.'

Rain ran in a stream, hideously chill, down my neck. 'Maybe we'll hotel it tonight,' I said.

CHARLEY: Yeah, maybe we would. I had a leak in my left boot, my wrists were damp, I was chilled to the bone and all my old bike injuries were hurting me. At the fuel stop, however, I'd spoken to a bunch of people heading for the Moto GP and they cheered me up; horns hooting, people hanging out of windows, giving us thumbs up . . . everywhere I looked there were smiley faces.

We rode south through the rain, the water lying so deep that now and again we'd lose traction for a moment and aquaplane; ever south and no warmer, never any drier. Up ahead, Ewan had gone into iPod mode: he'd been complaining of lute music coming over the headphones that he'd no recollection of ever downloading. I watched the back of his bike, steady as a rock as he kicked up spray. Riding in the wet is fine, it's a matter of keeping your concentration, keeping the pace up but slowing things down in your mind and making sure everything you do is smooth. The bends were big and sweeping, not tight or technical.

The GPS seemed to have taken on a mind of its own for a moment, telling me it was this way, then that way. I told Ewan and his response was to give me some *Star Wars*-style advice across the radio: 'Trust in the machine, Charley,' he whispered. 'Trust in the machine.'

Wet, I kept thinking. This is fucking wet. My body was dry, my trunk I mean, but my feet were soaking, especially the left one. I was taking shallow breaths to stop my visor steaming up and I'm sure that's not a good thing. The mountains were all but invisible though we were climbing hard now, closing on a thousand metres above sea level.

Apart from the weather it felt great to be just the two of us. We were in and out of tunnels and I was concentrating too hard to feel any anxiety. Last night in my room I'd been worrying about the route, the lack of consensus, making decisions that might offend people. This morning though, I realised that all I had to do was make sure I enjoyed the trip. And I was enjoying it. After all the prep it was fantastic to see Ewan loaded with panniers and bags. He was out of iPod mode again and jabbering in my ear, keeping my spirits up. 'Rain's nothing,' he said. 'You and me, Charley, we can ride for days in the rain. We're hardcore bikers and we could ride through anything.' He paused for a moment. 'The tunnels are great though, aren't they; like riding down someone's throat.'

He was right, they were great, they gave us some respite. With Ewan a few yards in front I watched the lights envelop his helmet so it glowed almost blue and he looked like something beaming down in *Star Trek*. I decided I liked the tunnels; no, I loved them: this one was long and warm and dry. It was a bloody nice tunnel.

I could see the end approaching and thought, maybe it won't be raining up there. But of course it was. In fact it was worse, hammering down, rattling off the tarmac, spray lifting in icy sheets from the wheels of passing vehicles. We were really high now and the scenery would have been spectacular and I'd love to tell you about it. But I couldn't see it, could I?!

That's how it was now, mile after mile, hour after hour. If we weren't in dry tunnels, we were crossing saturated bridges that spanned massive valleys, gorges falling to nothing beneath the wheels. Ewan was alongside me and we were climbing. Through a gap in the cloud ahead I could see snow on the Alps.

It's when you stop on a bike that you realise just how cold you are; you start to shiver and shake, especially if you're soaked through, and we were fluctuating from about fifteen degrees in the tunnels to seven or eight in the rain. Ewan was in *Star Wars* mode again. 'Charley,' he told me, 'be mindful of your thoughts for they betray you.'

I had no thoughts except getting through the Mont Blanc tunnel, finding the nearest hotel and getting my sodden gear into some kind of drying room.

EWAN: That was the plan, through the tunnel, first hotel and out of the fucking rain. But where was the Mont Blanc tunnel? Tunnel after tunnel I was thinking: is this it? Is this Mont Blanc, this has to be Mont Blanc. But none of them were and on we ploughed higher and higher on wetter and wetter roads. I realised now that there was a kind of sick pleasure in all this water – the challenge of it, staying upright, getting through: it wasn't without its positive angle. Three hundred and seventy miles and pissing down every inch of the way.

Finally we made it. Through the toll and out of the rain, I looked up at the height of the roof at exactly the wrong moment; visor up, a drop of water smacked me right in the eye.

Now we were under cover the temperature was climbing, but now I had an itchy bum; you know like when you get a wet bum playing out in the rain at school. Then later you're sitting in the maths class and you get an itch in your arse; horrible.

We were through the tunnel and into Italy and still it was raining: our plan had been to find the first hotel but somehow we couldn't get off the road. I don't know why, I imagine Charley will blame me and my so-called lack of navigation skills, but where we wanted to leave there didn't seem to be a junction. There had been one, I'd seen the signs, but the junction just seemed to die. I don't know, maybe it was never there or I'd missed it because of all the fucking water.

Anyway, we went on and on through yet more tunnels and eventually pulled off at a little hotel where they had warm, dry rooms and secure parking. God it was a relief to be inside. Charley took a look at his clutch which had been going a bit soft all day; he thought there might be some air in the hydraulics and he tried to bleed it. If it didn't clear we'd need to find a BMW dealer to take a look at it. Everything was dripping, and within the hour the two of us had clothes draped all over our rooms and were using every means possible to try and get them ready for the next morning. We used tepid radiators, hair dryers; whatever we could lay our hands on. Charley even tried drying the inside of his boot with the heat of the bulb from a table lamp. How was it that the survival instructor described him? Industrious. I couldn't argue with that.

CHARLEY: It had been a tough day, but it was over now and I sat for maybe half an hour in the shower: ironic, I know, but at least this water was warm. There had been so much spray on the roads it was horrendous. Having said that, the bikes had been just wonderful, apart from my clutch anyway. I'd noticed it was soft early on and I'd tried to knock the air out when we got settled. I'd top it up with fluid in the morning. My hands were like shrivelled apples, the last two hours had been a nightmare and now I was cursing the pressure we'd placed ourselves under. Towards the end I was so cold I'd begun to lose a little concentration and there'd been a couple of crazy cars trying to kill me. I'd begun to get anxious again and started worrying about getting into Africa. It was only tiredness and the stress of riding for so long in the rain, but as Ewan said there was something about overcoming the challenge. I had some food, spoke to Ollie and crashed out.

The following morning dawned clear and still and beautiful.

Now we could see the mountains, the valleys, the great overhanging crags of rock. Most of our gear was dry and what wasn't soon became so as the wind rushed through it.

We were heading across northern Italy towards Lake Como and the sun was high, the day almost hazy. I was following Ewan as we figured out which way to go. I was mellow and the morning was so warm that people were sunbathing in the fields. One couple had me up out of the seat. No, I wasn't mistaken, that girl was definitely topless.

Once we'd got off the Milano Road, which was ugly and industrialised and chock-a-block with traffic, it was all green fields and little churches, bits and pieces of ruins dotted here and there. People were working farms and smallholdings; I could smell the wonderful scent of freshly mown grass and began to think how I might like that kind of life, working the land: a farm, a vineyard maybe. This was so different from yesterday, brilliant sunshine, the kind of riding I'd hoped for. I was following Claudio on the camera bike and he was following Ewan and the only thing bothering me was my helmet camera. It kept slipping and if I wanted to film anything that looked like anything, I had to tilt my head. A Ferrari blatted by, very Italian, very chic. I decided I'd probably be bored working the land.

Up ahead Ewan overtook a lorry, a sweet move, and then we were into small towns and heading the right way. The road was great with old buildings pressed up to the kerbs, sand coloured and ochre coloured, and beyond them the mountains shone in the sun.

An hour or so later our longed-for destination appeared right in front of us: the Moto Guzzi factory, a series of 1920s buildings carrying the bend in the main street. Painted a sort of amber it looked more like an old hotel than a bike factory.

EWAN: I was in seventh heaven. It's me that's the Moto Guzzi fan – my first big bike was a Guzzi. I thought it was a 1978 Le

Mans when I bought it but it was only pretending. It was some kind of Guzzi, though only the seat and tank had come from a Le Mans. It didn't matter. I loved it and I've been a Guzzi fan ever since.

We were lucky enough to be shown round the factory, which really comprised one major assembly line where all the component parts are set up and an hour and twenty minutes later the complete bike rolls off the other end; a total of ten thousand manufactured every year. From there the bikes go into an engine testing room and then on to the dyno (rolling road) where the engines are put through their paces at lots of different revs. They had plenty of bikes on display; one in particular we just *had* to sit on, an eight cylinder classic that years ago had won the Isle of Man TT.

Outside they have this amazing test track, old and a little moth-eaten. It's pretty tight, with the factory squashed in the middle and ivy covered walls climbing the perimeter. It's four hundred and sixty metres around and the corners are banked. The tester told us he could get up to eighty on it. He had two bikes sitting there and Charley and I jumped on them and did a couple of circuits. No helmets, with people looking on from the offices and the tester shaking his head and telling everyone how he really enjoyed his job and would be sad to lose it if one of us happened to peel off.

Russ, David and the trucks had left for Florence but Charley and I just wanted to chill out. It was still a beautiful day and, determined to camp, we told the others we'd catch up with them the next day. We were north of Parma and neither of us wanted to ride too far now so we set about trying to find a place to spend the night. A few miles from the Guzzi factory we stopped at a garage and this gentle giant of an Italian used his GPS to find us a campsite. He loaded the coordinates into ours then called the site and booked the three of us in. By seven p.m. we were asking final directions from a sweet old lady who pointed us on our way. Then we were at the gate and being checked in by a smiling, grey-haired Italian with a goatee beard.

We rode beyond an area where camper vans were parked, down to a smaller field that we all but had to ourselves. In no time the tents were up and we were larking about like kids. We'd not been able to buy any food, but we had bread and cheese and stuff we'd got for lunch and not eaten. I kind of wanted something hot, mind you, and as I was thinking about it along came Francine with a pot of pasta.

We'd never seen her before in our lives: but here was this redhead walking towards us with a guy called Walther, and a pot in her hands.

She told us they were bikers and they'd been in their van watching us arrive having just finished eating. They were planning to put the rest of the pasta in the fridge, but thought we looked hungry. The next thing I knew we were squatting on the ground, Francine had opened the pot and indicated the forks she'd brought along with her.

It was wonderful, great food just when we needed it and provided by a couple of people from Zurich we'd never seen in our lives before. It really was moments like these that made the trip so special. We talked about riding motorbikes and explained our route and what we hoped to do. They spoke great English and told us that they had ridden some of the same journey themselves. A few years back they'd biked their way from Cape Town to Dar Es Salaam and were able to give us some insight into what we were undertaking.

They left us to the food and after we'd eaten and Charley had lit a couple of farts, we ended up over at their camper sharing GPS coordinates for campsites in Africa. Eve was coming to Malawi and Francine told us there was great camping on the lake itself. They gave us the coordinates and suggested that the best fish to eat was something called kampango. Charley wanted to know if you could swim in the lake or if there were hippos or crocs to think about. I was much more concerned about the tiny worms that swim right up your willy. Still, I asked Francine again for the coordinates.

'South, 11,53.643,' she said. 'East 03410.013. It's six thousand, seven hundred and thirty five kilometres from this van,' she added.

'That's over four thousand miles.' Charley glanced at me, a sharp lift to his eyebrows.

'Is that all,' I muttered, 'four thousand miles?' I nodded. I smiled. I could feel the hardness of the bike seat already numbing my bum.

7
Cobblestones, Cars & Kissing

CHARLEY: The next morning Ewan told me that he might try and find some kind of sheepskin pad for his seat. It really was bothering him and with ten hours at a time on the bike we had to do something about it.

Last night had been great, meeting Francine and Walther and sharing the GPS coordinates. It was like a new kind of culture, a GPS culture; travellers meeting up and sharing the coordinates of places they'd been, places that other people could go. All you had to do was punch in the details and you'd get there. Not like a map where you faff around and miss the turning or maybe take the wrong directions down. How many times has someone told you about a place you must see and you never get there because you don't write it down properly or can't find it on the map?

I love it, it's great. I'm a gadget guy anyway, but this is about sharing experiences; the beauty of the world witnessed through GPS.

It was another stunning morning in Italy. I liked Italy: it didn't seem to rain in Italy. We said goodbye to our Swiss friends and grabbed a coffee. Earlier Ewan had pointed out the walk of shame: people heading for the toilet blocks clutching their loo rolls. He commented that the real shame was the way back if you returned with just the cardboard inner . . .

I'd slept well, though I'd like to have spoken to my kids. Kinvara was off to Wales on a camp – the first time she'd done that and I'd wanted to wish her luck.

Francine and Walther had told us about some hot tubs or hot springs down by Siena; we were heading there for lunch and thought we might try and find them. Tonight we'd be in Rome, though, which was three hundred and fifty miles so we couldn't hang about too much; another really good day in the saddle and Ewan would be seriously numb by the time we got there.

We headed off with fields on each side. Olive trees growing in symmetrical lines. I saw an old fellow outside his house, his scooter on its stand and his wife wiping the seat and screen. The old guy fitted a cap on his head, kissed his wife and off he went as he'd probably done every day of his life. She stood there waving. God, it was lovely, she obviously adored him. He must have been well past seventy, off to work somewhere: a field, a vineyard, a workshop maybe. I hoped that would be me and Ollie when I was that age.

He wasn't the only one on a scooter, far from it. There were scooters everywhere, not just the towns but out here in the sticks; old or young, everyone seemed to ride them. It reminded me that one had nearly hit me once, in Rome, in fact, where we were now heading. I'd been visiting my old mate Jason Connery who was making a film there, and was on my way back to my hotel late at night. A car hit a scooter, sent the rider spinning and the scooter hurtling towards me. It all happened so fast: I heard the crunch, looked up and there's this Vespa flying towards me. It missed my feet by a matter of inches.

We got to Siena before lunch and Ewan pulled up alongside. 'Fantastic, Charley, I love it. You know I think there's some kind of vintage car rally going on. I've seen old Alfas, an Aston and a beautiful VW.'

EWAN: I'd seen quite a few cars on the motorway; one classic Alfa in particular and a really memorable VW Karman Ghia. I'd left the campsite with Madame Butterfly playing on the iPod and I was really feeling like riding. It was a happy Saturday, the sun shining, the roads good, and it felt fantastic to be part of the brotherhood that is motorcycling. There were so many bikes on the road and everyone acknowledged everyone else and you just knew if you broke down someone would stop. The ride to Siena was brilliant: great tarmac, enough traffic to keep you interested, I was in terrific spirits.

We got there around lunchtime; a wonderful city with the sun falling on wide streets and ancient buildings. Everywhere I looked there were classic cars. We started chatting to two English guys who had a 1932 Alfa painted in the traditional French blue parked up near the square. Historically every country has its racing colour: French blue, yellow in Belgium and of course British racing green. It turned out the guys were doing the Mille Miglia, a classic road race in pre-1950s cars that went from Brescia to Rome and back to Brescia again; a thousand miles. Or kilometres. I think. Don't quote me.

We made our way through the narrow streets where rozzers and ambulances tore around with sirens blaring while thousands of pedestrians wandered among the shops. The streets converged on the Piazza Del Campo in the centre of the old town. The buildings surround the piazza in a circular arena, and in July and August they stage the Palio Di Siena: horse races where the competitors gallop round watched by massive crowds cheering them on from the windows. Siena is a great city – ancient yet vibrant, full of life and colour and the architecture is absolutely stunning. We had lunch, chatted to a few people and wandered the town. We never made it to the hot spa but it didn't matter. It was back to the bikes and the next leg, a big stint down to Rome.

We got there later that afternoon and as we entered the city Charley spotted a white Rolls Royce just like the one his dad had owned when he was a kid, and he told me how one summer his mum, dad, he and his sisters trundled round Europe in it.

We stayed the night at a really beautiful old hotel, the St Regis Grand, in the middle of the city. We were able to park the bikes off the road in a kind of enclosed courtyard in the hotel itself – they were up on centre stands and on either side of carpeted stone steps that led to the revolving door. Road-weary and unshaven, wearing bike gear and weathered T-shirts, we unloaded the bikes while the bellboy, a nervous-looking bloke, hopped about as if he thought he'd get fired any moment.

We were a bit knackered now, and the Italian driving getting worse the further south we ventured, we'd still to get round Naples and that was nightmare alley apparently. Another big day tomorrow. We'd make our way round the Amalfi coast, camp again then head for the Sicily ferry. Only a couple of days to go and we'd be on the boat for Africa.

CHARLEY: Siena was great and Rome too, but I got up on Sunday morning feeling a little bit blah. I think the hotel did it for me: a bit of luxury before we hit the cuds, and with the luxury comes the wine and I'd probably had too much. You know how it is.

We waited while Russ and David sorted the Nissan vehicles. There was stuff they had to tie down and cameraman Jimmy Simak was already perched on the back of David's truck (which they had named Fiona), with his legs wrapped round one of the spare wheels so he could film Ewan and me on the road for a while.

Ewan was wiping his screen clear of insect guts when some guy came over and spoke to him. Ewan gave him an odd look and the man walked away. 'Hey, Charley,' Ewan called, 'that American guy said: "You're not doing it again, are you? Like a dog to its own vomit!"' He shook his head in bemusement. 'What the fuck does that mean?'

We set off, winding our way through one of the most historic cities in the world. It was hot and slow going and given how I was feeling, not the best riding. I could hear Ewan whistling though, singing Italian songs, anthems, ice cream adverts. Jimmy was still in position and I noticed that whenever David braked hard or suddenly, his features would become a little contorted. Over the radio, David asked how he was doing: Jimmy was just fine apart from the chafing.

We passed a pyramid. No, I'm serious; a full blown Egyptian pyramid. It reared up out of the trees and I heard Ewan wondering if it had been removed stone by stone from Egypt, maybe. In fact it turned out that this was the Pyramid of Cestius, a Roman who decided to be buried Pharoah-style after Rome had conquered Egypt. A fashion thing, you know.

We rode for a while on the Via Appia, or Appian Way. This was the most important road in ancient Rome, stretching from the edge of the city to Brindisi down in the south-east. It had been the main thoroughfare for trade and the movement of soldiers. Romans used to build their roads by setting down a layer of dirt then a layer of mortar and small stones. After that the cobbles would be interlocked over the top of it. It was a very effective way of building because the road was still there, though many of the stones were missing now of course. But that didn't hinder us: up on the foot pegs, Ewan and I rode our bikes along the same stretch of highway that the Roman Army marched thousands of years before.

Out of the city we were on open roads and it was thankfully not so hot. We had two and a half hours to Naples and then we would be on the Amalfi coast. It's a rugged peninsula with Sorrento as the main town and the island of Capri a couple of miles offshore. We were camping tonight and I'd be grateful to get there. I was hanging today, not myself; still feeling pretty blah; but once we'd got round Naples I was better. The coast road was stunning: really twisty, the sea on one side, sometimes close by, sometimes hundreds of feet below, with rocks and trees and buildings banked up on the other. In Sorrento I was still admiring it all when a car popped out of a junction right in front of me. Fortunately I was doing just a few miles an hour. The driver looked at me, lifted a hand and went on his merry way. I took a moment to gather myself and noticed that people were hanging out at ice cream parlours in the sun. It struck me as wonderfully old-fashioned. In Britain we hang out in pubs and get shit-faced. The place was humming, streets heaving with cars, scooters and bikes. I saw a horse appear as if from nowhere. It just came out from between the cars, ridden by a guy with an American saddle, nonchalant as you like.

EWAN: The road was fantastic, a biker's paradise, though some of those bends were horrific; one mistake on a corner and it would be the last corner you got wrong: little low walls that your bike would clatter into and you'd be flying hundreds of feet through the air before you got mashed on the rocks below. Great riding though – after hours and hours on dead straight motorways I was just loving it. The road seemed to be bolted onto the cliff, rock walls chiselled in great slabs and the houses built in clutches, clinging there like limpets.

When we left Rome I realised that we'd covered more than 2500 miles now. Fantastic: I'd lost count of the days; in fact I barely knew what day it was any more – morning, afternoon, who the fuck cares? I loved this. Palm trees everywhere and little cobbled streets, orange and yellow buildings with terracotta roof tiles faded by a constant sun. The road was twisted around the coast, hugging like the coils of a snake; sometimes we'd pass through a crude tunnel where the stone had been hacked away leaving it ragged and kind of brutal above our heads.

And the people: everyone seemed to be kissing. Everywhere I looked, every lay-by, couples were snogging. There seemed to be a great deal of love and affection going on in Italy. Sometimes Britain feels so bogged down in rules and regulations; here people were snogging, they were buzzing about on Vespas with no helmets; it all felt so vibrant and alive. Maybe it's the sunshine. The scenery was stunning, a beautiful haze where the sky met the sea. I could smell the salt, and down by the shore fishing boats were up out of the water being repaired or rebuilt.

Leaving the peninsula we continued south towards Reggio di Calabria where we'd make the crossing to Sicily. It was getting dark and we were tired now. 'Charley and Ewan,' I muttered into the video or the radio or maybe just to myself, 'intrepid travellers, too tired to think, too scared to stretch out on the road.'

We made the campsite and got the tents up, no longer any competition between us; too weary for that, though Charley still seemed to be ahead of me. It was dark and I had my head torch on, clipping the inner tent to the web of poles then unpacking the bike and sliding bags into the bell ends.

There was a really nice taverna/café on the site and we sat down to dinner. Russ appeared with a sardonic grin as me and Charley set about stuffing ourselves on fresh melon and antipasto; salads of every kind.

'Well,' he said, 'we might as well take it easy in Europe. You know it's going to get tougher.'

The next morning we set off for Palermo. It was another ten hours of driving, but it meant we had the following day to prepare for our crossing into Africa, do our laundry and get the bikes to a BMW dealer to change the tyres to knobblies. So we rode south, back on the big roads now with the sea on our right as we climbed high, crossing massive bridges with drops that set your hair curling. From the bridges we'd be in tunnels where the engine note was magnified and lights shone in your face: it was like a massive, crazy video game.

Charley abreast of me, I waved him on with a smile. I could see the white rag I'd attached to his bike, flapping now in the wind. A bit of old T-shirt with Long Way Down on it. The trick was to get it onto his bike unnoticed and see how long it would stay there. It had started on Charley's bike, had been on mine and now it was back with him. Silly games, but fun; it's something we'd done when we rode round the world.

CHARLEY: I knew where it was, I'd get him back, bury it somewhere so I could see it and he couldn't. I felt better today, a breeze in the air, riding the coast with spectacular scenery to look at, a rugged coastline with a fort in the distance and the island of Sicily beyond. We were getting closer and I wondered again about Africa. My smile faded. What would go wrong? Something was bound to go wrong.

Descending to sea level we made it to the boat and our crossing to Sicily. There seemed barely time to go up on deck before we were docking again. A half hour trip across the water and we were back in the saddle and gliding down the ramp into the port of Messina. Right in front of us was a massive, half-finished apartment block with the sun going down behind it. We burbled through town, stopping and starting; road works, the scene of a recent accident, a reminder of the dangers. I thought of the monster chopper I'd passed earlier; Captain America riding hard with ape hanger bars, the lack of aerodynamics creating a massive weave on the road.

My helmet cam was now at right angles to my head so whatever I was filming was all but upside down. I didn't care though – we were in Sicily, avoiding road works, and the day after tomorrow we were crossing to Africa.

We could smell wood burning and, as Ewan suggested, school dinners. It was more barren here, less green; most of the way south it had remained pretty green. This was more deserty; dare I say more African.

The next morning I was feeling nervous. I kept thinking about Africa and what could go wrong. Ewan came down and we got the bikes and as we pulled out from the underground car park this guy and his girlfriend stopped us. I don't know if he was an American Italian living in Sicily or an Italian who'd spent time in

America maybe, but he spoke English with an American accent and showed us the way to the BMW dealer.

EWAN: We sat down and had a coffee and he explained that he was a BMW rider and at four thirty that morning he'd been trawling one of the BMW owners' websites. As you do. He'd been told that Charley and I were in Sicily and he decided he wanted to meet us. So off he went down to the docks and asked about ships to Africa. Had any gone? Were any going? One had already gone but they assured him there had been no motorbikes on board, which meant we were still here. So back he went to his computer and after some more investigative work he came up with someone who'd seen us arrive at our hotel. They hooked up, two guys who didn't know each other but had BMW trail bikes in common. A few hours later we were all having a coffee. It was brilliant; we'd met Dave and Clare in Britain when they came rushing out of their house waving their arms, we'd had Francine and Walther arriving with pasta, and now these two Italians who'd moved heaven and earth to hook up with us here in Palermo.

There were a number of old bikes on display in the BMW shop. One in particular, this old black beast from the seventies, was similar to the ones the French police used to use. Again I was reminded of Marie. OK, I'll tell you, some of it anyway. I had a romance with a girl called Marie and we spent three glorious weeks riding a bike just like this one. It was my first real experience of motorcycle touring and maybe that was when I got the bug. But I'd first been reminded in Dijon and now here again in Palermo. I'll never forget riding pillion through the Riviera with Marie hunched at the bars in front of me. That relationship ran its course, but my love affair with the motorcycle had only just begun.

CHARLEY: It was fantastic, the first time in ten days of riding that we'd actually arrived anywhere before about nine at night: it was the one thing that was bugging me about the trip. I liked to get to a place a little earlier, preferably when it was still light, so you could get your bearings and maybe see something of the place before you crashed for the night.

We sorted our rooms, left the bikes and chilled out for a while, taking a moment to soak up some sun. We'd had no days off; Ewan said he didn't think we had another till we were on a boat somewhere on Lake Nasser. We'd been riding hard, ten days from dawn to dusk yet even now all we talked about was bikes. We lay there discussing an idea of going to New York, building a couple of choppers and riding them to LA via Mexico City. It summed up our friendship: it began with motorbikes, it is motorbikes, it will always be motorbikes.

A couple of hours later I was sitting on the shore in the sunshine, the wind in my hair and my back to a rocky outcrop, considering how crystal clear the Med was and talking to Russ about all that had happened since we left London. Bombs and planes and black eyes; John O'Groats, Robin House, camping on a race track. After that it had been France and the rain; the Guzzi factory and riding down here. Russ asked me if I had any fears about Africa and I wondered what fears I didn't have: crashing, bandits, kidnapping; stuff getting nicked off the bikes in busy, built-up areas.

I found it therapeutic talking through my hopes, fears and all the emotions. By the time I went to bed I was thinking about my wife, my children, the tremendous effort put in by everyone back in London, and instead of being nervous about the following day, I was calm, relaxed and contented. The night before Africa, the night I could have been the most nervous, I went to sleep a very happy man.

8
Sea Legs & Security

EWAN: Much as I was excited about getting to Africa there was a part of me that was sorry to be saying goodbye to Italy. It was vibrant and vital and the further south we got, the more I'd fallen in love with it. We'd arrived at the hotel in Sicily in plenty of time to chill out, and Charley and I had taken some time out by the pool discussing yet another bike trip. Later David hired a boat to take us across the bay so I could buy some underpants that didn't pinch my bum when I was riding.

I was drinking coffee as thick as treacle, and when I mentioned as much it sparked a discussion about the relative merits of treacle and golden syrup; neither of which Jimmy Simak had ever come across. Charley and I took a dip in the Med which was much colder than it looked: the only thing that kept my heart going was the amount of really thick coffee I'd been drinking.

It turned out to be a great last day in Europe and in the morning we rode the bikes down to the port at Trapani.

The ship was tied off alongside the dock and we were able to ride right up to it. The roll-on roll-off doors were open, inviting almost, but there didn't seem to be anyone about.

We were first in the queue; not that many people appeared to be taking this particular boat today. Everything felt very quiet. I don't know what I'd been expecting but it hadn't been this. It was calm and tranquil and I suppose we had arrived pretty early but everyone seemed chilled and when the immigration and customs officials showed up Russ had all the relevant paperwork ready. It was the first time we'd needed to produce *carnets* for the vehicles and the lists of equipment we were carrying. A little while later our tickets were torn and we were riding up the ramp. Suddenly my heart beat faster. Africa was just a boat ride away.

I parked my bike alongside a couple of scooters and the loading guy made me put it on the centre stand even though Charley had his on the side stand and was able to keep it in gear. The bike was far more secure like that, but I didn't argue: there's no point getting into it with officialdom. I was concerned, though, any serious movement of the boat could result in the bike toppling over and that was the last thing I needed. Vividly, I recalled waiting for my previous GS to come off the plane at Anchorage when we flew over from Magadan. I watched in horror from a window as it came down the conveyor belt from the hold, on its side and rocking on one of the cylinders.

Locating a hunk of cardboard I folded it over and stuffed it under the front wheel. That kind of wedged it at least, gave it a little more stability.

On deck the sea was calm, the crossing ten hours or so and barely a white top to be seen; the sun was shining, it was a beautiful day and we were all together. I could scent a little tension in the air, we were all tired and none of us knew quite what to expect. As Jim Foster had told us, when things kick off in Africa they really kick off, go down hill very quickly and generally there's no warning. Normally when a situation goes bad you get a sense of it before it happens: a change in the mood, the atmosphere; but not in Africa. Jim was one of our cameramen who'd worked in places like Beirut, Iraq and Afghanistan: he was with us not just to film but to offer a little security should we need it. Forty-five years old, he'd been born in Africa and there wasn't much he couldn't tell us about the politics. He also reminded us that life is cheap and what westerners considered brutality wasn't the same in Africa, particularly Central Africa. It was sobering. We all had our fears and you could sense it now in the atmosphere. There was nothing overt, just a kind of easy unease: a jovial sort of nervousness I suppose you'd call it.

I spoke to Eve on the phone, told her I loved her and we were truly on our way at last. She was going out for a ride and I imagined her on her bike on the busy streets of London. Wow, what a contrast. I took a last look across the empty dockside to the town beyond and the beautiful, renaissance-style buildings that were all pillars and arches. Then we were slipping away from the dock and heading out to sea; finally on our way to Africa.

Russ told us that he'd spoken to the office and it looked as though David and Jimmy weren't going to be able to get into Libya. It was a real disappointment but not unexpected. It appeared that our last hope, Charley's mate Jacob, hadn't, in the end, been able to exert any influence and visas for the two

Americans would not be forthcoming. Jimmy was upset, David even more so – he had been absolutely determined to drive his truck every step of the way. He was certainly going to drive to the border: if they didn't get in, then they didn't get in and they'd have to go all the way back again.

It had been an issue for months and sorry as I was for David and Jimmy, the way I looked at it was that this was all part of the inevitable adventure. The obstacles along the way were just part of the journey, frustrating as they might seem.

Jim Foster had a few ideas for smuggling the two of them in and Charley suggested that Obi-Wan Kenobi use the 'Force'. The reality was, however, that Friday and Saturday mark the weekend in Arab countries and the embassies would be closed. There was nothing more we could do.

CHARLEY: The ferry was making its way along the northern shores of Africa: I could see it now, the Tunisian coast forming part of the peninsula. It was wonderful, Africa finally, almost.

I was nervous, I had the collywobbles; the calm of yesterday was gone and in its place were nerves. Ewan pointed out what looked like a bunch of windmills, some kind of wind farm along the coast; the cliffs were a sandy white and the sea that stunning blue. Beautiful, all of it, but it didn't make any difference to how I was feeling.

As far as the Libyan situation was concerned Russ was a little worried about the carnet and getting everything from Tunisia to Libya. The documentation listed all our names and two of us wouldn't be there. He wasn't concerned about getting out of Tunisia, our fixer's dad apparently knew the people who ran the country so that wouldn't be a problem. No, it was more how the Libyans would react to us coming in when two of the proposed party weren't there. It was a bridge we would have to cross when we came to it.

We were all a little tense now; we'd just had a safety and

security briefing: Jim and Dai talked us through the basics of what we had to consider. Dai was our medic; having trained with the army and also attached to the SAS, he now worked as a remote access paramedic and, like Jim, he'd served in some pretty serious war zones. Jim made it clear that unless it was absolutely unavoidable we wouldn't be travelling during the hours of darkness; there were too many hazards, trucks without lights, pedestrians walking the roads, Bosnian motorbikes, as he called the one-eyed monster that's a car with one headlamp out. We all agreed we'd get to a camp spot and recce at least an hour before darkness, make sure we had plenty of time to set up.

Before we entered each country we'd have an up-to-date briefing on the situation from London; Jim was very conscious of the changing political landscapes. Again he reiterated how swiftly everything can go pear-shaped; we couldn't leap out of the truck like drama queens (as he put it), cameras pointed, and hope to get away with it. We had to be calm and considered; he and Russ would deal with checkpoints and borders. The more people involved the more complicated things would get. That was fine by me, I'd like to avoid vehicle permits altogether after the mess Ewan and I got into the last time.

Jim reiterated that Arab Africa was very different from Central Africa and we'd have to judge every situation on its own merits. We needed to work as a team and consider in advance where we would film and how spontaneous that filming could be. A lot of the areas in Sudan and Ethiopia were mined, and Jim cited a situation with the BBC where the crew jumped out of a truck to film something and found themselves smack in the middle of an unmarked minefield. Explosions started going off, the crew thought they were being mortared and dived into a bunker only to discover they were in a bigger minefield. It had been a disaster and the poor producer ended up losing a leg.

Serious stuff: we talked through safety, what we'd do in given situations, like if we got separated or robbed or attacked. Russ suggested that if any of us were in trouble at any time, the word to use over the radio was 'Magadan'. No one trying to con the rest of us would ever think to use it: it was our agreed Mayday signal. We talked through what we'd do if anyone went missing. Jim reminded us that since the British and American governments embarked on GWOT (their global war on terror), we were always going to be potential targets. Opportunity targets, he called it: we had to be prepared for people just taking offence regardless of any behaviour on our part.

It got a little tense, even more so when the general safety issues were discussed. Dai was almost finished when he looked across at me, arms folded, a serious smile on his face.

'Charley,' he said, 'you're a big boy but I have to tell you you're in real danger of having an RTA (road traffic accident) pulling wheelies all the time.'

I sat there for a moment then glanced at David. I looked round at Russ, at Ewan; all eyes were on me.

'What about blackberrying then?' I said, turning again to David.

'Me?' he lifted his hands, hunched back in the seat.

'If I'm pulling wheelies, you're blackberrying, on the phone all the time using your knee to steer.'

'But he hasn't done it in traffic, Charley, or while driving at speed,' Dai pointed out.

'No, that's right. I haven't.' David sat back, palms spread before him. 'Not at speed and not in traffic. Hey, you know what, you can wheelie all you like. I don't care.'

'OK,' I said. 'How about this: you don't use the BlackBerry and I don't pull wheelies.'

Russ sat forward now. 'It's a serious point, Charley. It's all very well coming off the bike because someone bashes into you, you can't do anything about that. But for fun, when you've got your wife and kids at home? I'm telling you, it ain't worth it.'

David cut in again. 'I'm saying that you're pulling wheelies and you're talking about me on the telephone . . .'

'Booking hotels for us,' Ewan spoke for the first time. 'So should we not . . .'

'Not for you,' David came back at him. 'I didn't say for you.' He turned again to me. 'You were having a go at me . . .'

'I wasn't.' I was shaking my head; this was really kicking off now. 'Dave, I absolutely wasn't having a go at you. The point is I'm doing something that's dangerous. Because everyone's comments are directed at me I'm thinking, so what's everyone else doing? That's why I said what I said: don't take it personally.'

'Yeah, but Charley: wheelies and BlackBerry, it's a separate point.'

'No, it's not. Because we're talking about safety on the road. People are saying stop pulling wheelies and I'm saying, what about everyone else? Don't take it personally.'

He didn't and I took on board what everyone was saying about wheelies. Not that I thought it would stop me necessarily; especially not when it came to border crossings. I recall popping a monster at the Russian border and the exhilaration of the moment will be with me forever. There was no real issue; I mean no deep seated grudges or irritations, we were probably just letting off steam. It hadn't been helped by Libya and the fact that David and Jimmy looked likely to miss out. What I'd thought of as that kind of 'smiling tension' had bubbled over, that was all.

EWAN: I understood the others' concerns, but I wasn't going to add my voice to the fray. There was enough tension around and though we'd been on the road ten days or so, it was still early in the trip. We were finding our feet as a team and everything that had been voiced was a legitimate safety concern. My biggest fear was knocking someone down – it twisted my gut just thinking about it. Having said that, it's true you're not in control of your bike pulling a huge wheelie. Charley does pull these big wheelies and very often the bike comes down sideways, scoots round and all but gets away from him. He feels he's in control, I'm sure he does, but it looks very scary.

The spat at the briefing notwithstanding, I really thought we were gelling; six of us had done this before, Dai and Jim were newcomers, but they were becoming an integral part of the whole. They were also specialists, which helped; both ex-military and I loved the military banter that passed between them. They bore no grudges, none of us did; and when there was a difference of opinion it was important to get it out in the open. Funnily enough I wasn't really nervous. I just wanted to get going; but the security briefing reminded me that this wasn't something to be taken lightly.

Most of all I was excited about the prospect of riding through Africa and as the sun went down we steamed into Tunis. I don't know what I expected, more of a hubbub maybe, noise and bustle, a market scene from a James Bond film or Indiana Jones, all baskets and snakes and swords. It was nothing like that of course, it was a port like any other; quiet really, but it was certainly a border crossing. We docked at around half past eight at night but weren't on the road into town until eleven thirty. That was after we'd furnished the customs man with four, yes four, bottles of vodka which he ferreted away in the boot of his car. Oh, how it was all coming back to me.

It was good to witness the reactions of the rest of the team. Jimmy for example, had never been to Africa before and he was quite emotional. It struck me that I'd ridden all the way from John O'Groats to Africa. There was Charley Boorman in front of me. 'How're you feeling, Charley?' I asked across the radio.

Charley's voice came back: 'Pretty good,' he said, 'I'm actually pretty relaxed. I had the collywobbles on the boat, but we're here now and I'm feeling pretty good.'

I was excited but relaxed. It was brilliant; the trucks behind, the road clear, tarmac good and lights lying low in the distance. There was a very distinctive smell to the place: what was it, eucalyptus maybe? Not quite, it was spicy, a dusty sort of smell. As we headed for the hotel I saw a billboard on the roadside; a girl in a bikini lying on a beach with a massive shark's fin coming up behind her. A soft drink for men also enjoyed by women: 'Shark Attack', they called it. Yeah, right: Africa.

9

Under African Skies

CHARLEY: Three days later I was in a hotel room in Tripoli squeezing the moisture out of my pillow. It was dark outside and from the balcony I could see a group of kids playing football. They weren't the only ones out there, there were people everywhere. It was so hot in the daytime, this seemed to be the best time for everyone to congregate in the fresher air.

Downstairs we had our Libyan fixer Nuri, his driver, someone from the ministry of tourism and a guy from the secret police. On top of that some other guy had turned up and we'd no clue who he was. Talk about entourage; I couldn't see us being on our own again before we hit the Egyptian border. The bureaucracy felt sort of old school – I couldn't remember how long Libya had been open but I did know they only had about thirty-five thousand visitors a year. It reminded me of being in Russia, or Kazakhstan maybe, back on Long Way Round.

My boots stank: thank heaven this wasn't a scratch and sniff movie or the viewers would be switching channels in droves. I was in danger of dying from the smell myself so I shuffled them out to the balcony. Every morning when I woke my foldaway pillow was soaked: the tent would sweat and the pillow seemed to absorb all the moisture. I was tired but happy; three days of good riding, a couple of nights camping, we'd had such a laugh and my wife sent me a really lovely text: *I love you and miss you,* she said: *Try not to worry too much about the unknown. Remember, lots of people have walked, cycled and driven your journey before you, successfully. It's a wonderful, exciting journey you're on. We pray for you every night.*

That first night we'd got off the boat around 8.30 still not a hundred per cent certain that Jimmy and David wouldn't get into Libya. But it didn't seem likely. I was waved over by a policeman and so began the laborious task of getting through customs. By 11.30, though, we were on our way into town but glancing in my mirrors I saw Ewan pulling over, a cop with his hand out stepping into the road. Bloody hell, I thought, we'd only been here a few minutes and already one of us had been stopped. But a couple of minutes later Ewan was on the move again and he came up alongside.

'What was that all about?' I asked him.

'Nothing: the bike, you and me. He was just wishing us luck.'

We rode on and a short while later pulled into the grounds of a lovely hotel. I shook my head sadly. 'Ewan,' I said over the radio, 'here we are in the slums again.'

I took a shower. I was feeling good, and after the altercation on the boat everyone seemed pretty relaxed, almost as if the bubble of tension had needed bursting and now we were all up for it. I'd been edgy throughout the day but coming into port the nerves gave way to excitement and I looked on happily. Jim dealt with the customs men. He had been born here, brought up both in Tunisia and Libya and we were content to let him take care of this kind of bureaucracy. There was a discussion about the walkie-talkies listed on the carnet and we thought they might be confiscated. Some countries are nervous about why you have short wave radios: ours are primarily for filming purposes and we really do need them. Jim managed to convince customs that the walkie-talkies listed were actually the radios in our crash helmets so in the end it was only three of the satellite phones that were confiscated. The satellite phones were vital to our trip and our only lifeline when we were in the middle of the desert. A company called AST loaned all the satellite phones to us, so really they belonged to them: I hoped we'd get them back.

EWAN: The following morning I woke up tired. I had bags under my eyes and no matter how much water I splashed on my face I still thought I looked bleary. It had been a strange boat trip; weird, really, the way it all kicked off. Subliminal nerves I think, the tension of what lay ahead getting to all of us. But that was over now and I was thrilled about being in Africa, even though the port and everything hadn't been quite what I expected.

It was very hot on the road; the tarmac good, really smooth and flat. As we left Tunis the buildings, white and clean and well spaced, fell away and the highway opened up. I was determined to soak up the sights, the sounds, the atmosphere. Palm trees sprang from the pavements and between the lanes the central reservation was sand, the verges the same; the fundamental difference, I suppose, to anything we'd seen in Europe. The sky was vast and empty – I kept thinking how everyone talked about the massive skies of Africa and they were right, a shimmering blue in the heat; a haze around the sun. We passed a truck overloaded with bolts of cloth, some of which were flapping in the wind. We passed a small pickup stacked with wooden crates that were stuffed with oranges and lemons: I could hear Charley singing the nursery rhyme through my helmet.

The traffic leaving Tunis had been heavy yet orderly; one lorry, however, was dragging a sheet of plastic in its wake and I slipped into the other lane to avoid it. The bike felt good, though Charley had commented on the suspension, the front in particular being a little hard for the knobblies. It had been set up for the road and when we hit gravel it might not be forgiving enough.

The two of us chatted away as we rode, wondering what the day would have in store. I wasn't sure what to expect in Tunisia, what threats we might face, what adversities. I'd always considered it a sort of tourist destination, package holiday country, but there had been terrorist attacks here and Al-Qaeda had planted a bomb that killed a group of Germans a few years before. Historically I knew the country was pretty moderate, they'd gained independence from France in 1956, and the subsequent president kept a lid on Islamic fundamentalism and made sure that women had rights. I wasn't certain what kind of wildlife we might see: someone told me that Hannibal had bred war elephants in centuries past and the Romans kept lions, of course, so two of the big five must have been here at one time. I think the country is renowned for birds more than anything, though.

The road was so smooth I was really enjoying myself, and thinking it would be nice if it was like this all the way to Cape Town. I felt calm, everything felt calm, perfect for our first day on the continent, and I gabbled away merrily as the buildings dwindled and the road opened onto flattened landscape, scrubbed sand right and left of the tarmac.

CHARLEY: We pulled into a town for lunch. The buildings were mostly single-storey and constructed from sandstone, canopies draped the windows and people waved and smiled as we passed. We found a cafe and followed the cars that seemed to use the chessboard concourse for parking. We eased the bikes right up to the tables, the orange plastic chairs, where we could keep an eye on them. Not that we necessarily needed to, Tunisia felt very peaceful. We could hear a kind of low wailing – music coming from inside. A waiter came over and we spoke to him in our limited French. He showed us a rack of lamb's ribs then set to with a massive chopper, like some medieval axe. He barbecued the meat and we ate it with salads and this really spicy garlic sauce, washed down with bottles of water.

'Nothing like a nicely hung lamb, Charley,' Ewan observed.

God it was hot. Our first day in Africa and I was melting already, my legs were roasting, the vents in my trousers not creating much airflow, all the air seemed to sweep over the tank. Even off the bike and sitting in the shade I could feel the sweat sticking to me.

I tucked into the salad and dipped bread in the sauce. We'd been told to avoid salad and washed vegetables because of the water, but I figured we should eat what the locals eat and where; we'd probably more chance of getting sick in some fancy hotel or restaurant. All the time we were eating a solitary sheep tied to a large pink flowerpot looked on and baaed at us.

'Hey, Charley,' Ewan said. 'There's someone's lunch or dinner right there, or the mother of what we've just eaten, maybe.' He paused then for a moment. 'I'm feeling a little lonely, you know what I mean? Maybe I'll trot over after.'

'Ewan,' I said slowly, 'maybe we ought to leave conversations about sheepage on the cutting room floor.'

After lunch we headed south towards an ancient coliseum at a place called El Jem, some hundred and thirty miles south of the capital.

We discovered an ancient amphitheatre with most of the seats intact. Climbing to the top it was fantastic to gaze across an arena that once had been host to the games. They claim the place seated up to thirty thousand people, more than the population of El Jem itself.

'Can you imagine the noise, Charley?' Ewan murmured. 'Just imagine it.'

We walked down the banks of stone seats and paused before massive ruined arches that still dominated the place. We could see the catacombs and passages below ground, where the gladiators would have waited, where the lions were kept together with the poor souls the Romans used to feed to them. The place was still in pretty good condition considering it was seventeen hundred years old, and we were told it would have been better still if it hadn't been blasted by local tribesmen.

It was baking now, I'd never felt anything like it. 'You know, Ewan,' I stated, 'we need to leave really early every day because between three and five in the afternoon it just gets ridiculous.'

He nodded. 'You're right. We need to be in the shade or else riding very quickly.'

Back on the bikes we made our way through the town of El Jem where hundreds of people seemed to be on the street. Out of town we were back on smooth, flat carriageway and beetling south towards Libya. We fuelled the bikes at the next town where the people were very friendly and market stalls bulged with fruit and vegetables. We were looking for a place to camp, somewhere away from the road where we couldn't be seen, where we could light a fire and find flat ground for the tents.

We found what we thought was the right place, and leaving the bikes we scouted the area on foot. It was safety first; as Ewan pointed out we didn't want to just wop our tents up anywhere. It was getting dark and we were still too close to the road. Then I noticed a clearing beyond a small hill. It was surrounded by narrow-trunked trees and low stubby bushes, a prickly kind of green. We walked over to take a look and found the ground baked as hard as concrete.

'What do you think?' I asked.

'I reckon it's all right. It's clear of brush and that means less "buggage", doesn't it: less "snakeage".' Ewan was nodding. 'I reckon we might have cracked it, Charley.'

EWAN: We brought up the bikes, the track rutted with wheel marks. Charley was right, the front end was overly hard and we'd have to damp it down.

'We can absorb much more if we do,' Charley was saying. 'And we won't fall off as much.'

'Which is nice,' I added.

My feet were killing me, sweating so badly they seemed to be vaporising. Taking the lid off one of my panniers I used it as a sort of tray to stand on, whipped my trousers off and washed my feet. The skin was broken and flaking, itchy; finding some powder in my medical kit I coated them.

Charley was looking on: 'That must feel nice,' he said. 'One of the pleasures of life out here in the cuds.'

'Athletes foot powder, but good for any old foot rot.'

Charley was kicking away stones and mussing the dirt to make our beds softer, bemoaning again the fact that he'd still not invented the half-rake, half-shovel he'd promised to patent after Long Way Round. Maybe by the time we did Long Way Up, he would. The ground was rock hard and breaking up the surface meant our beds would be a little softer.

We couldn't see the road from here, though we could hear traffic. The clearing was surrounded by tall trees, beyond them coarse looking bushes that drifted to a flattened horizon. I got my tent up and parked the bike right next to it, dragging all my gear inside. I left the inner zipped to keep creepy-crawlies out but opened the bell ends to generate some airflow. Then I gathered wood and set about making a campfire. It was our first fire since leaving home and it was brilliant. Charley made Bovril drinks to replace some of the salt we'd lost and we sat down to cook dinner with the sun sinking like a fireball, the sky a hazy gold and the trees casting insect-black shadows. I looked across at Charley. 'Today was great, wasn't it? I'm chilled out, relaxed. I'm not nervous about anything, Charley; dangerous combination really.' I paused for a moment and added. 'Having said that, I reckon the camera team must laugh at us fiddling around like we do: I mean they spend all their time in Iraq or Afghanistan, they must look at us like a couple of ninnies.'

Charley shrugged. 'Maybe, but at least we're doing it.'

The birds slowly stopped chirping and the sound of cicadas took over. I loved that sound, louder and louder the darker it got: the strains of the heat, the desert.

Charley was sipping Bovril. 'Have you ever camped in Africa before?'

'Yes, once. I spent a night in the sand dunes in a Bedouin tent in Morocco with a bloke called Azadine; he drove me around when I was making *Black Hawk Down*.' I was smiling now, remembering. 'We went into the desert, just the two of us, and he drove like a maniac. All the way he was discussing Muslim belief and if Allah decided it was your time, it was your time. I was sitting there going: Oh God, but that means when it's your time it's also mine because you're driving like a lunatic.' I laughed. 'Anyway, I survived the drive and we camped out and I left the tent door open. I remember Azadine telling me to close it. No, I said, I wanted to look at the stars. Charley, I woke up at four in the morning with sand up to my chin.'

CHARLEY: It had been a brilliant first day, the two of us camping together and having a real laugh; we'd been to El Jem and seen ruins that were in much better condition than those in Rome because everything was so dry here. We'd been told that twice a year they held concerts, classical recitals, in the coliseum and I was trying to imagine what it must be like to play music, to listen to music in an arena where people had been thrown to the lions. We'd also had more opportunities to just sit and chat to people – we'd met a lovely guy who'd spoken to us about his life in the country. Kids came up to us all the time and if they got too much, which they rarely did, the older guys would sort of shoo them away. But they weren't a hassle; we liked them coming over, they were generally interested and just sort of hung around.

The next morning we were up early and on the road with every vent in our gear open and the jackets all but unzipped. Last night we'd spoken to the others and there was talk of maybe getting to Libya today instead of tomorrow, which we thought was pushing it. Ewan in particular was acutely aware of the desire to rush on all the time. It annoyed me too, but I was always conscious of the huge miles and the fact that we had to make the ferry next Saturday. Ewan and I are very different personalities; it's the same with Russ and David and I suppose when the four of us are involved in something as complicated and hazardous as this it can become a little tense. Four strong-minded and very forthright people: Russ is a problem solver, he sees the situation and sets about finding whatever resolution is required, like making the time we needed and pressing on. I'm like that myself, seeking the destination so to speak; I suppose it's the racer in me. Ewan, on the other hand, is more circumspect. He's a thinker who comes to the table with a different mindset completely, as does David. Already that dynamic was becoming apparent and bringing with it the attendant tensions.

EWAN: I didn't come here just to get to Cape Town, I came to experience Africa on a motorbike, something I'm not likely to do again. The deadline was the ferry, however, at the bottom of Egypt, and we were committed to making it or we could lose a week. But I was worried about just pressing on and on and not seeing anything. I was determined to take the time to really soak up the experience.

Our second day in Tunisia, we headed for Matmata. This was where George Lucas filmed the first *Star Wars* movie, what became episode IV, specifically Luke Skywalker's house carved into the rock. The air was livid with the heat. I would have loved to have ridden in just T-shirt and jeans but you can't do that, not on a long trip and not if you value skin and muscle tissue.

Coming to Matmata we parked up and sat for a moment just gazing across an amazing desert vista of low hills and stunted bushes. Since the last town the road had been much more interesting, quite twisty and we'd been climbing. Low walls banked the asphalt and hills grew up in layers of sandstone like great piles of pancakes abutting the side of the road.

Planning the route: Avonmore Road, January 2007.

Eve's bike is delivered to the workshop. Ewan is still in plaster after his accident.

With producer/directors Russ Malkin (*left*) and David Alexanian (*right*). They made it all possible.

(*Left to right*) Cameraman Jimmy Simak, security expert Jim Foster, and Dai Jones, our medic. Although we would be surviving on our own a lot of the time, it was good to know we had such a great support team.

The Long Way Down team gave us a fantastic send off.

At John O'Groats, our official starting point. We're both looking in the wrong direction, which doesn't bode well!

Wishing each other luck on the start of our 15,000-mile journey.

Ewan and William at Rachel House in Kinross.

Charley and John.

Ewan's brother Colin (*far left*) invited us to Erskine Hospital for injured or sick army veterans. Alex Lees had been involved in the Great Escape during WWII.

Testing the bikes at Silverstone. Later we camped for the night right by the track.

Contemplating a change of wheels in Siena, Italy.

In heaven at the Moto Guzzi factory.

On the way to Sicily, and enjoying
the tarmac while we can.

We both took a moment to reflect on the journey ahead as we left Sicily for Trapani in Tunisia.

Going through the medical kit with Dai at the Tunisian border.

Eating dinner in the dark with Russ (*left*) and Claudio (*right*).

In the cuds in Tunisia. Ewan would like to point out that he often got his tent up before Charley. Charley would like to point out that not only is his tent up, he is already starting supper.

The incredible ancient city of Leptis Magna in Libya.

I mean, what have the Romans ever done for us?

In Libya, we were forced to ride several hundred miles through a sandstorm.

Ewan washes sand from his eyes at the end of another gruelling day.

Handsome devils.

At the Libyan–Egyptian border.

An Egpytian market seller.

In a café in Egypt, watching a news report on the unfolding tragedy in Darfur.

Fwan with a little boy in Egypt.

With the temperature rising, it was no surprise that these ice-cream sellers were so popular.

An amazing experience – riding right up to the great pyramids in Alexandria, Egypt.

We took a quick detour by plane from Egypt to Aswan in Kenya to meet with the incredible workers for Riders for Health.

We met this lad who spoke English while we were having a coffee and he offered to be our guide. Lots of people had made such an offer but he was mellow and laid-back. He took us to the caves, first pointing out a couple of flat rock slabs with metal hatches set into the surface. Opening one we realised it was a well. We could smell the water, see our reflections fifteen feet below. He explained that there were more than a hundred troglodyte houses dug into the soft sandstone, people had lived here for seven hundred years and they still collected their water. We gazed down on an amazing courtyard with arched portals cut into the rock; it must have been twenty or so feet below ground level and climbing down we found an old woman who invited us into her home.

Inside it was light, airy and surprisingly spacious; flat bronze plates hung on the walls as ornaments and she sat us down in alcoves laid with ornamental blankets. She boiled tea in a large kettle, pouring it from a great height and finally stirred in spoonfuls of sugar. She told us that in summer the heat in town got to some fifty degrees and it was much cooler here. Our guide explained that the most ancient house was indeed seven centuries old, the original cave dwellers being Berbers, a race of people that dominated much of north Africa. The walls were pearlescent white and we drank tea in the relative cool, watching another elderly woman winding the handle on two enormous mill stones.

We found the *Star Wars* set, which was effectively a replica of the place we'd just been, though more touristy. It was decked out with sections of old drainpipe that had been painted in terracotta, with the inners from hair dryers (would you believe) set into the walls. Just like the old woman's house, the entrances were whitewashed arches cut into rock. There was a massive door with a seal and lean-to shelters for animals, the interwoven sticks of the roof faded grey by the sun.

There were tourists all over the pink steps that led up to the entrance to Luke Skywalker's house. There was a market selling

Star Wars as well as Tunisian souvenirs, complete with old photographs showing how the place had looked thirty years before.

CHARLEY: Ewan was really enjoying it. *Star Wars* was such a big thing to have done, although he'd not been involved in the original series, he'd been *just* a little too young. But he'd been in episodes I-III and to come back here where it all began was, for both of us, very impressive. Tongue in cheek, I have to mention he was a little miffed, mind you, that nobody recognised him despite the fact he was wandering around in a Long Way Down T-shirt with 'McGregor' emblazoned on the back. He told me that he 'rather arrogantly' thought he'd be mobbed.

Normally I hate touristy things, especially on a trip like this, but today I didn't mind. *Star Wars* was history and Ewan was a part of it: I was really glad that we'd come.

We returned to the bikes and Ewan told me he fancied taking a teabag and squeezing it into the water bottle he carried on his back – he might as well have boiling tea to sip instead of boiling water. Leaving Matmata we rode out; the roads were great with plenty of sweeping bends where we could really get cranked over. The towns and the buildings we now passed looked almost biblical.

The roads were pretty empty and we raced along tipping into the corners; speed was the only way to keep even vaguely cool. Pretty soon, however, we left the main road and headed onto a single track tarmac that became dirt and then gravel, some of which was pretty deep; it was littered with rocks and stones and was our first real off-road experience on these new bikes. We drove deep into the desert, drifting between the hills and heading eventually (we hoped) for the town of Medenine. We passed an old car and a tiny village: a cluster of buildings where people in traditional Arab dress waved to us. We came to a junction and didn't know which way to go but then a couple of kids seemed to pop up from nowhere (something that we were to discover happened a lot in Africa) and we asked them in French and they gave us directions.

Again we thought we were lost, so we stopped at a camp and an older guy came over and we talked to him as best we could but he spoke only Arabic. We tried to find out how many kilometres we had to go, but he pointed back the way we had come and we knew that wasn't the way. We rode on and the deeper we got the less sandy the landscape became, the less desert-like, everything was suddenly greener. Finally we met a young guy with his son; he was carrying four or five baguettes, one of which he was chewing. We showed him Medenine on the map and he pointed us in the right direction.

EWAN: We camped again and were up early and I was still thinking about that mountain section; it had been the first time we were off-road fully loaded with camping gear. There'd been a bit of deep gravel that could have been a bit dodgy but on the whole the bikes were fine. It had given us a real flavour of the country and we'd passed herders with their families, tents and livestock; real Bedouin stuff. We'd got lost and you know what, it had felt strangely good to be lost on a motorbike in North Africa. The *Star Wars* set had been great, though it had been weird to be there even though I'd not been involved when that episode was made. I had filmed at Tozer, however, and it had been funny walking round with nobody recognising me.

We were heading for Libya and though it had been brief I'd really enjoyed Tunisia. Yesterday we'd mooted the idea of taking the dirt road that New Zealand forces had constructed in World War II and I'd been surprised when Charley initially plumped for the tarmac. He's the one who's really into the dirt biking. Apart from one day in Wales, the last time I was off-road was three years ago when we made *Long Way Round*. I told him, at the risk of sounding like his mother, he had to forget about pushing on and remember to enjoy this. It's why we were here after all.

But now we were pushing on. We had to. I was thinking about the border crossing and if it took a while I had my book and I'd try and find some shade. We were on asphalt again and drifting through small towns, where the sky was massive and the horizon low and dramatic. Town after town, squares and roundabouts, market stalls and mosques; every now and then we'd hear mullahs calling the faithful to prayer. There were children everywhere, wide-eyed and waving to us; people zipping about on mopeds. It was still very hot but the skies were no longer clear, instead they were laced with cloud. We seemed to have raced through Tunisia and yet we had seen some amazing sights: we'd been off-road, we'd been on the set of *Star Wars*, we'd visited troglodyte homes and we'd seen the ruins at El Jem. Now dead ahead were two white buildings, and strung between them a red and white barrier. I felt a shiver of anticipation. On the other side of the border was Colonel Kaddafi's Libya.

10
Here's Sand In Your Eye!

EWAN: Six hours later we were beyond the border and riding into a sand storm. I could feel the heat, currents of hot air burning my throat. We seemed to have the world and his wife escorting us: whatever we wanted to do in Libya, we'd not be doing it alone.

Leaving Tunisia had been complicated by the fact that David and Jimmy had gone off to catch a plane. They were flying to Geneva then Cairo and inadvertently they left us with a vehicle problem. David had the Tunisian authority for one Nissan stamped into his passport and therefore we'd nothing to certify that the truck had ever been allowed in. There was a mini drama, quite a bit of jiggery pokery, but between them Russ and Jim managed to smooth things over.

In the end we were through and immediately everything altered. All we'd done was travel a little further down the same stretch of tarmac but the landscape looked different; it *felt* different, as if with the man-made boundary the land itself knew to change. The wind had picked up and it brought the sand, hot stinging grains; I'd never felt that kind of heat on a motorbike before. It was like driving into a blast heater.

The people were friendly but the driving went rapidly down hill – most of the cars we encountered made even the Italians look careful. They seemed to stick to the back wheel, nosing us along; it was scary at first but after a while sort of fun, if challenging.

This country was poorer, a dictatorship, an Islamic state with borders that had been closed to westerners for many years. There was a distinct military feel. We were in convoy, heading for Tripoli and we had no choice but to follow Nuri, our fixer.

The land was flat, the sand still swirling around in the wind. I made out a passing truck loaded with onions, another packed with fruit. Charley was muttering in my ear about a 'good set of melons'. Electricity pylons dominated the skyline; they drifted into the distance in a way I'd not noticed just a few hours before. The trees were short and looked half-grown and still sand filled the air.

We followed the cars to some ruins – the ancient town of Sabrata. For a while it wasn't clear whether we would be allowed to film – the guides seemed to want us there to help promote tourism, but at the same time they told us that filming was forbidden. The old shackles were very much in evidence, used to being yoked to an absolute system they now seemed weighed down by indecision. At one point they said we could only film from the cameras on our crash helmets, which would have meant keeping them on as we toured the site.

In the end they overcame their concerns and we passed inside. It was worth the toing and froing with the guides – it really was magnificent; another massive Roman amphitheatre with huge pillars and what looked like Botticelli cupids scrolled into the stonework. Looking closely Charley reckoned much of the place had been restored with concrete though our guide insisted it was exactly as it had been. It did look restored, but it could have been from Roman times because as far as I remember they were the first people to use concrete. It was hard to figure out and our guide was the man from the ministry and not a local expert.

We climbed the steps into roofless, doorless rooms that were cut in sandstone. We came to a small courtyard and Charley suggested it might have been for concession stands or where they sold beer maybe: immediately I went into bartender mode.

CHARLEY: Ewan wanted to know if Romans had beer and I had no idea. He was serving though and I leant on the imaginary bar.

'What'll it be, sir?' he asked me. 'What can I get you?'

'A flagon of wine and, er, a glass of sherry for the wife.'

'Right, sir, coming up.' He was pouring from an imaginary pump. 'Come to see the lions, have you, sir?'

'Naw, here to see that famous Charley Boorman gladiator.'

'You know,' Ewan said, 'he's not all he's cracked up to be. Sherry, for the missus was it?' He poured a glass. 'I mean he's not bad, but he's not all he's cracked up to be.'

'He's the only reason I came,' I said sourly. 'Got any crisps? Actually forget the crisps; I'll take a bag of pig's ears instead.'

'Got some in the back, sir,' Ewan sought pig's ears. 'Yeah, he's all right that Boorman, but he's not all he's cracked up to be.' He handed me the bag. 'That'll be fifteen Roman shekels.'

We climbed to the top tier of stone seats and got a fantastic view across open ground to the shore. We could make out where the rest of the buildings had been now – the stumps of pillars, the last layer of stone blocks: the place must have been enormous. Down below we checked out the acoustics and even now when you spoke or sang out the sound seemed to ping right back at you, like having a speaker or stage monitor there in front of you.

It was getting late and our guides had booked hotel rooms for us in the capital. A few miles with crazy drivers, absolute nutters all around us. Like Ewan said, they were right up your bum and much worse the closer we got to the city. We passed under a massive metal arch and were really in Kaddafi country now; his picture was everywhere: on billboards, buildings, in the hotel lobby. I noticed he was always looking up, chin thrusting, kind of arrogant. We decided it was fortunate we had guides after all, certainly as we came into Tripoli, because the road signs were telling us nothing and the road systems, Jesus; we'd come to what we thought was a roundabout and the next thing we knew it was actually a dual carriageway.

Finally we got to the hotel and by now I was knackered, the sand still sticking in my throat. Ewan and I set about unpacking our bags. 'I'm glad we decided to crash here,' I said, 'instead of pushing on.'

'Me too. We'd only wear ourselves out and have a horrible accident or something. Another hundred and thirty clicks to wherever it is, not worth it. Pity we didn't know anything about that last place, wasn't it?'

I was smiling. 'So we didn't know the name. Hey, after a while one set of Roman ruins starts to look like another. You know what I mean, it's like join the dots, isn't it?'

Ewan was killing himself. Claudio on the other hand was filming and he piped up from behind the lens as he does now and again: 'It is a little embarrassing that you don't know anything about the place,' he stated.

'Shut up, Claudio.'

In my room later I put my boots on the balcony, squeezed the damp from my pillow and sorted through my bag. It really was very busy outside and it was a relief to arrive in the dark and cooler air; we'd have a nice surprise when we woke up tomorrow with the city laid before us. It took a day at least to figure out a country, the roads in particular. Here we were in Libya with 2500 kilometres of coast road ahead of us. The drivers had been crazy and I hoped that the further away from the capital we got the better they might become.

As we'd left the ruins earlier I'd seen a couple of young sisters, hand in hand and dressed in matching clothes. I'd had a pang for home – Ollie used to dress our daughters in matching clothes and now I really missed my family.

Again I studied the text my wife had sent me; she was right, enjoy it, Charley. That's what I had to do. I thought about

Claudio's comment. OK, so Ewan and I weren't overly aware of the history. I wonder how many people actually are given this is Libya and they have fewer tourists in a year than the Isle of Wight does in a week. It didn't make it any less inspiring and besides, this venture wasn't supposed to be a history lesson. I enjoyed just soaking up the sights, learning as we went along. Anything we weren't sure about we could always ask, or check up later.

I started thinking about David and Jimmy taking off in darkness and driving back to Tunis, sorting the trucks in the middle of the road, gear here, gear there, what they needed to take. Looking back I think Ewan and I might have seemed a little blasé, like it wasn't a big deal the two of them not being allowed into Libya. If that was true, we hadn't meant to. We were genuinely upset, but we had spent four months trying to find a solution, and in the end we'd had no choice.

We'd see them again in Egypt. We had a long way to go before that. My mind began to race through what lay ahead, how little time we had, how many miles we had to do . . . and that was just this country. We had to make the ferry in Aswan next Saturday or we'd lose a week and we couldn't afford that because we'd made a commitment to UNICEF in Ethiopia. I mustn't think about it, not now, not after riding all day. Ollie was right, forget the bigger picture. Wake up, Charley. For Christ's sake wake up and smell the coffee.

EWAN: We *were* blasé about David and Jimmy, a little nonchalant I suppose, that two members of our team had to go. They had been gutted, and I think our attitude had only added to their upset. It was something I regretted, and I sent David a text to let him know we were thinking of them both.

I was equally worried about making the ferry that would take us the length of Lake Nasser. The cars and bikes had to be there on Saturday and we'd not sail until Monday. I hated the idea of the vehicles travelling outside our supervision. I also had no idea how we would do the mileage and the thought of racing on and on all the time was beginning to piss me off. We had only six days and we were still in the north-west of Libya and there was every chance we'd be held up at the Egyptian border. Even if we weren't we still had to get all the way down the Nile. Fuck, it annoyed me; the last thing I'd wanted to be was a slave to the clock. I'd accepted it in Europe but now we were in Africa and nothing had changed.

CHARLEY: Riding through Libya following a van full of official people makes it very difficult to meet anyone, and perhaps that influenced our decision as much as the time pressure we were under. We'd left Tripoli at eight o'clock and it was already thirty-three degrees. Ewan pulled alongside me. 'Hey, Charley, only thirty-three. Christ it's fucking freezing.' We had a laugh and he indicated the back of the Nissan. 'Take a look, Jim Foster, taking Jimmy Crankshaft's place.'

Camera in hand, Jim was straddling the spare wheel wearing shorts and T-shirt with his legs apart; first thing in the morning it was not a pretty sight, especially given the fact he had the shaft of a shovel sticking up between his legs. Next to him, stuffed behind the straps that held the second spare, were the underpants that had chafed Ewan's arse. They'd been there a few days now and if they didn't fall off maybe we could auction them in Cape Town.

There were buses everywhere – minibuses crammed with people they just seemed to pick up from anywhere. Tripoli's not high-rise, in fact it's a pleasant, atmospheric city, and we rode through the centre, coming to Green Square where an old fort overlooked a lake. The buildings were two storeys, white mostly, though some of them with a splash of minty green. We were in the old part of town and I could pick out a few coffee houses but the city seemed all but untouched by tourism. There were some signs of modernism, mind you, like mobile phones and a few decent cars. It's easy to forget that even under what we'd consider oppressive dictatorships people do what people do, they go to work, they go to the coffee shop, there's beach life. I even saw merry-go-rounds.

Out of the city we could see warships at anchor just offshore. The land was flat, the trees short and bushy and everywhere I looked there were thousands of plastic bags, plastic containers, just dumped by the side of the road. After the cleanliness of Tunisia it gave the whole place a down at heel, ugly feel. It appeared that if you had something to chuck away you just did, whenever and wherever you pleased.

Once you got away from the city the quality of tarmac declined considerably with potholes and sand encroaching from either side. The whole place had a parched feel, the air hot and dry. Apparently there are no natural rivers in Libya only wadis: valleys that hold water after periods of heavy rain. The lack of natural flowing water was evident in the atmosphere; there was not even a vague sense of freshness even though it was early morning. As we went deeper into the country we passed more farmland. We saw fruit growing, rows and rows of small trees that looked like nurseries. A few miles further on, we passed a horse in the back of a pickup. A low pickup, car-sized; the horse was just standing there.

EWAN: We'd seen a camel in another pickup, on its knees with its head facing the upcoming traffic, nonchalantly chewing the cud; a camel and now a horse. I guess they had to be transported somehow.

The litter was oppressive and with it that insistent odour of garbage. It didn't bother me too much; it was as it was and I was excited about the city we were heading for. Not just any city, an ancient city. Our guide was called Iystiri and for eight years he'd been showing people the magnificence of Leptis Magna.

He told us it had been established about 1100 BC, but it's

mainly known as the city of Septimius Severus. A native of Leptis Magna he became Emperor of Rome in the second century and died in York, of all places. Just as we'd ridden the Appian Way, Charley and I now walked a road that led from the great arch of Septimius all the way to Alexandria: in the other direction it had stretched to Carthage. The arch itself was incredible – it had been smashed into pieces centuries before, but in 1920 a group of Italian archaeologists had excavated the stones buried in the sand and reconstructed them. The road itself was exquisitely paved and stretched as far as the eye could see about six feet below the level of the sand. Some of the stones were decorated with images of Septimius and his sons – copies apparently, the original pieces in a museum in Tripoli. There were also huge triangles and our guide explained that they were in fact Venetian from a much later period, put there to keep evil spirits away. There were eight Corinthian pillars with eight Gods, palm in one hand and crown in the other, and four spread eagles, the ancient symbol of power. We could see ramparts, remnants of the old walls and discovered that in the city's heyday they had run for three kilometres. We saw images of the Gods, Diana in her short skirt and Apollo completely naked.

'Well hung,' Charley commented quietly. 'Well, he is a God after all.'

Some of what we were exploring had been discovered as late as 1962 and the excavation was still going on three years ago. Charley was shaking his head in wonder. 'Imagine finding it,' he said. 'Digging it up and realising what you had: it must have been incredible.'

Iystiri pointed out that the middle stones in the street had a camber to them and told us that in the old days water flowed under them; it came from the wadi of Leptis Magna three hundred metres away. Wadis supplied the whole city with fresh water, for drinking, bathing and sanitation.

'There used to be shops here,' Charley said, 'right here. And houses, business places and people.'

'Not so many mopeds though,' I put in.

'No, right: I bet they had those little chariots to tear about in, the kids I mean, you know, drawn by greyhounds or something.'

CHARLEY: We came to a corner where our guide pointed out another cosmic battle; this time the defender of the city was a winged penis. Yes, that's right, a winged penis doing battle with the evil eye. According to Iystiri the penis fought the eye to keep the same evil spirits away. The piece of limestone where the battle was captured had been there since the second century so we just *had* to press a palm against it for luck. Ewan looked sideways at me. 'Well, mate. We've touched a penis in Libya. Not what we set out to do perhaps, but a winged penis at least.'

'It was placed here in communist times,' Iystiri told us.

Ewan and I exchanged a puzzled look. 'Communist,' Ewan said, 'in the second century? Jesus, really, I just don't know anything about anything.'

It didn't make a lot of sense. Surely communism was Marx and Lenin: Russia in World War I?

'Did he really say communist?' Ewan asked again.

A voice lifted from behind the camera. 'I think he means Commodus,' it said.

We came to an open, grassy area. It had been a kind of sports field where people wrestled and messed about. Across the street were the remains of the public baths.

'Turkish baths,' Ewan reminded me, 'from Long Way Round, remember?'

'Where we were beaten to a pulp,' I said.

'Scrubbed to within an inch of our lives,' he was shaking his head with a smile. 'Imagine it, having a bit of a wrestle with your mates then coming over here for a bit of a bath.'

The wind had picked up and was bringing sand, very hot and hard on the eyes – a warning of what was to come. The guide led us through the baths, which he referred to as Hadrianic – I suppose from the time of Hadrian whose wall we'd already been to. The Romans were really muscling in on this trip now, weren't they?

Iystiri showed us the outside pool first, the floor of which had been mosaic, the sides marble. We could still make out great slabs of stone, plinths where statues had once stood. He took us to what he called a 'Hot Room' where there had been additional pools, or basins, as he called them. He showed us where the pipes came in – one for hot water and one for cold; the hot water heated by massive furnaces. Above each was a cistern holding water from the wadis and slaves worked all the time to keep the fires burning. Hot air was captured and pumped through tiles in a flue system that was covered over with marble. Heated walls and floor, it was amazing. The engineering was incredible and to think this all went back to the second century. Some of the people brought their own slaves to the baths to massage their masters with olive oil. They'd start in the sweat room, have a massage then go to the hot room to clean the oil with scrapers. After that it would be the warm room before finally plunging into the massive pool in the open air. Ewan made the point that little had changed over the years: in Leptis Magna they had a bit of a wrestle then went to the baths for a swim and sauna; at home we might go to the gym and have a bit of a workout then go for a swim and sauna. The only difference was the cost of membership.

There were dressing rooms and everything and anyone was allowed to use the baths though the wealthier people also had them at their villas. It was so forward thinking; they even had a sewerage system complete with communal toilets. In the open air Ewan and I perched on a stone bench with lots of keyhole-shaped apertures punched through it.

'So Ewan,' I said with concentrated effort, 'how're the slaves?'

He took a moment to squeeze. 'Fine, fine. I got a right good new one the other day.'

'I had a hell of a time at the vomit bath the other night,' I told him. 'You know, the one we saw in the street; must've done it three times, but then I did have four meals.'

Underneath your bum running water passed through a trough so your doings were swept away as soon as you'd done them. In front of your feet was another trench: you did your business then scooped with your hand and . . . well . . . you can imagine.

'You have to watch for the bloke further up, mind,' Ewan said pointing. 'Make sure he didn't double-scoop, you know what I mean?'

'No double-scooping. Right. You don't want corn in your scoop.'

Iystiri took us into the forum or marketplace that had pillars running the perimeter in a rectangle. There had been a portico built above them housing lots of stalls, shops and arcades; the central area had been open to the air. One wall was intact and it gave us a tremendous sense of how it would have been: the hustle and bustle of trading cloths, fruit, spices, incense maybe, even livestock and slaves. The entrances had been decorated with the heads of two gods, one of which was Medusa with the snakes in her hair. From the forum we went to the Severan Basilica, originally the law courts but, after the Romans converted to Christianity, this place had become a church decorated by stones carved with griffins, one of which lay smashed on the ground at our feet.

EWAN: The basilica really made an impression on me. I loved the griffins, who had the body of a lion with the head and wings of an eagle. Iystiri told us they symbolised eternity. I found it moving, the thought of this ancient civilisation, long gone, painting images of things they believed would last for ever.

The whole place was amazing, so unexpected and moving, and as near a glimpse of everyday Roman life as you could get. I had such a vivid image of the people of Leptis Magna going about their lives. I was reminded again of how important it was to stop and take time out from the journey and from racing on ahead.

Back at the bikes, we had a major discussion with Russ about what we were going to do next. The choice was either to stick to the coast road and see places like Benghazi and probably not make the Aswan ferry, or speed across the desert road tomorrow. The ferry took us to Sudan and it only went once a week. If we missed it, we would be turning our schedule upside down.

Charley was mulling it over: 'I know we're rushing, but what choice do we have?' he said. 'Of course we'd like more freedom here and in Egypt, but we have the whole of Sudan ahead. Once we're done with the boat in Egypt there isn't anything to stop us.'

'Except we have to think about the UNICEF visits,' I put in. 'Yes, of course we should try to make the ferry, I'm not upset about that. But if we hoof it like this all day long, we're on the motorcycles all the time, and I'm afraid we'll miss things.'

Russ shook his head. 'We just have to find the right balance between doing the miles and getting off the bikes. At least we're talking it through here.'

'What if we don't get the ferry?' I said. 'Maybe there's a possibility of renting our own boat. It's such a rarity to be in a place like Libya at all, it's a shame to blatter right through it.'

Charley cut in again. 'We're going to have that issue of how much time we spend in each place the whole way down, aren't we?'

Russ pointed out that with minders around all the time, it was much harder to break free and meet people in Libya. He was also aware that simply riding 420 miles through the desert in the scorching heat would be a challenge in itself. 'Ball breaking stuff,' he added.

I shrugged a little wearily. I had to concede that he had a point. 'Well, we've got to try and make the ferry, I suppose, so we should just do it.'

'Look, let's talk about it tonight when we camp. If we decide then we'll go for it tomorrow.'

The discussion went on a little longer, I was knackered and we'd been riding without a rest for days. It's hard to describe just how exhausting that was, particularly in the heat we were experiencing. We'd had a break on our boat crossing to Tunisia but that had been a tense affair, what with everyone's nerves and the altercation between David and Charley. I was reluctant, though I could see the logic in what they were saying. I kept worrying that we might miss out on the experience if we weren't careful. But then again we had seen the coliseum, the caves at Matmata and now Leptis Magna. The other end of the desert road was Tobruk and war graves; and Russ was right – riding that way would be an experience in itself. We just had to hope the wind kept off: the last thing we needed was the kind of storm we'd ridden into yesterday.

We headed off and still I was mulling it over, either miss the ferry or head across the desert in forty-five degrees of heat.

Charley spoke to me over the radio: 'Whatever happens there'll be a story there, Ewan.'

'Yeah, yeah. I know.'

'Adventure whatever happens – that's the spirit of the thing, isn't it?'

CHARLEY: We left Leptis Magna under dull and overcast skies, yet the heat was still ridiculous. It was hard to imagine what it would be like tomorrow if the wind really blew. Already it was beginning to pick up; it had been whistling through the ruins and that was ominous. It was busy, mad drivers everywhere, and still I was thinking of what lay ahead. It was a toughy, it really was; stupid ferry and only six days to get there. The thing was that if we missed it, then our trip to see Riders for Health, plus three UNICEF visits, would turn into a bit of a nightmare. It was crazy, but then again it was crazy following a white van all day and stopping every couple of miles at army checkpoints. It was crazy that we couldn't read a single fucking signpost. And I have to admit the thought of rattling through the desert was pretty cool.

The driving seemed even more erratic now it was getting dark. There were lorries all over the place, in the middle of the road, slowing down and speeding up, so we had to take great care overtaking. Every time we did we were buffeted hard by the wind. For a few seconds you're protected and then it really gusts, hitting the bike so hard you can weave into a tank slap or completely lose traction. The land here was empty, desolate; a hell of a contrast after the splendour of Leptis Magna.

We stopped for fuel and the attendant splashed petrol over Ewan. We exchanged a glance, both reminded of the last trip when twice petrol got in his eyes; once was my fault and I'll never forget thinking I could've blinded him.

'See that, did you?' he said as he pulled alongside. 'The old eye burn in Kazakhstan.'

We nearly missed the campsite; well not so much a site as a collection of flat-roofed buildings – half a dozen maybe, just the door and one window in each of them – hugging a dirty beach. Ewan and I rode down a concrete causeway all the way to the water. We took a long look at the sea then, turning the bikes, we parked up and I grabbed my tent. The wind was howling, really loud, whipping my hair across my face and though our decision had now been made this didn't bode well. We had a huge day ahead of us; really big miles and judging by tonight the conditions might not be that favourable. I wanted to get my tent up, have a swim and get something to eat. I found a spot close to the buildings and whipped up the inner. Fly sheet attached, I secured the ends by fastening the guys to a couple of massive blocks of stone.

Ewan was still getting his gear from the bike, in good humour now. He told me he'd enjoyed the last stretch of highway. The driving was nuts, of course, but it made the ride interesting; you had to be on your mettle and that appealed to him.

'How the fuck do you do it?' he asked me.

'Do what?' I was securing the last of the guys.

'Get your tent up like you do. I'm getting gear off my bike and yours is up already. It's always the same, always has been. I've camped a million times more than you and always you're ahead of me. It's pace,' he decided. 'Your internal rhythm is much quicker than mine. It's fucking irritating.'

'Yeah, but Ewan,' I was on my feet now, 'I'm the guy who's there at five to when everyone says we'll meet at the pub for eight. I'm still sitting there on my own at eight thirty.'

He was shaking his head. 'Your tent's up and I'm still unpacking and I don't know how you do it. Fucking cut it out, yeah?'

'Sorry, sir,' I mumbled.

I was looking for a quick-drying towel so I could take a dip. It was dark, but I didn't care; there was no shower and I just needed to get wet. 'So here we are again,' I said. 'From a silly talk in a pub a few years ago, here we are with our entourage of secret service men recording every word we're saying.'

'Like Russia and Kazakhstan, and to cap it all I've had a petrol flashback.' Ewan looked at my tent. 'Once,' he said. 'The only time I got mine up before you was at that Shadow Hawk training camp.'

The wind didn't let up all night and I doubted any one of us would get much sleep. My tent was flapping so hard I could feel the pegs pulling out. Lying there with my head torch on I could see how bent the poles were and I was worried about them snapping. I decided to move the tent, and shifted it between two of the square buildings. Earlier I'd noticed the door of one building was unlocked and I thought maybe I should just kip in there. I didn't though. I moved the tent and as I set it down I swear I saw a huge black scorpion running across the sand. My heart was in my mouth – that would really put the lid on things getting stung by a scorpion. Anxious now, I shone my torch into every nook and cranny. I went through all my gear, boots, clothes, sleeping bag.

No scorpion, maybe I'd been seeing things. I put it to the back of my mind and concentrated on getting the tent shifted. Using my boot I hammered in the pegs. I whacked the back of my hand but ignored it and carried on. A little while later I was still hunting scorpions when my hand began to hurt. It wasn't like the pain of being whacked, it sort of stung, and now I convinced myself I'd been stung by a scorpion. It really got hold of me, the sand, the night, the howling wind. Tiredness, I think, and the prospect of our 420-mile slog tomorrow. For about five minutes I swore I'd been stung and it took all my powers of logic to work back to the moment when I'd hit my hand with the heel of my boot. That was why it was hurting. Scorpion or not I'd had enough, and taking down my tent I slipped into the open building.

EWAN: All night the wind gusted and the tent would billow to the point of the poles almost breaking. I lay there with my feet pressed to the sides and my arms spread, using my weight and doing anything I could to stop the tent blowing away. The sides rattled, no longer a flap but a terrible racket as if someone was shaking stones in a can.

It got louder and louder and, grabbing my head torch, I saw the bell end whipping wildly. My boots and tent bag were covered in sand. Sand had crept into the tent, the finest grains in a thin layer that coated my bedroll, sleeping bag and clothes.

I had a bit of a tent emergency going on.

Working my way round the outside I checked the pole footings and re-fixed elastic guys, burying the pegs while the hot wind dragged my hair so hard it hurt. I decided to check on the others. I made my way through the maelstrom to where I could see Russ's dome literally squashed under the weight of the wind. As I got closer I could see his face peering into the lamplight from a partially unzipped inner. The sand swirled in a blizzard only it was hot and the particles stung when they hit you.

'You all right, mate?' I called, trying to make myself heard over the cacophony.

'Fine,' he said, 'I'm just lying here trying to hold my tent down.'

I could see the impression of his knuckles gripping the tent where the inner met the ground sheet, pressing his weight along the floor for all he was worth. 'Sort of worked loose,' he said, 'and you know what?'

'What?'

'I was playing J J Cale. Can you believe that? *Anyway the Wind Blows*. That's when the tent went flat.'

I must have slept because I woke up. The first sound I heard was the wind, my first thought the fact that we had 420 miles to cover today. My face ached, eyes itchy and bleary. Everything was coated in sand – tent, sleeping bag, every stitch of clothing.

We got going by eight, heading for Tobruk – a name that conjured images of war and war movies. We hoped to be there by about six or seven in the evening, but in this wind and with sand drifting on to the asphalt I wondered. In a way, though, I was exhilarated, looking forward to the challenge in the same way that I'd kind of enjoyed last night, lying in the tent, desperately trying to stop it blowing away with the wind screaming and sand flying, knowing the one thing I needed was sleep if I was going to cope with today.

And what a day it turned out to be: hour after hour and the land didn't alter; bleak to the point of depressing. Police checkpoints, military, always following the white van driven by Nuri and the man from the secret service. I was filthy, my stuff was filthy, sand everywhere. It's funny how when you start out on a trip everything is meticulous, the way you pack your gear, tent, your clothes. After a few weeks everything was just stuffed into the bags whether it was dirty or not.

Mercifully it was cooler. Yesterday it had been thirty-three degrees as we were rolling out of Tripoli, this morning it was a pleasant twenty-four. I prayed it would stay that way as I couldn't imagine riding through this flying sand in temperatures hitting the forties. We rolled on and on, nothing but telegraph poles and desert, the perpetual wind that bent the bike to weird angles, pushing it down, willing it to tip over; a wind that came from behind and forced my head to the side so I had to strain every muscle to keep upright. The ache was dull; it was getting hard to concentrate.

For the first time I passed a sign written in English: *Africa constitutes one nation of a thousand tribes*. I'd try to remember that.

Camels wandered loose off to my left and I imagined what it would be like if one lumbered across the road in the swirl of nothingness created by this storm. Terrifying. As if to accentuate the point I saw something up ahead and slowed to a stop. Charley came alongside and together we inspected the carcass of one such beast shredded by the side of the road. Its flesh had been picked clean; the skull exposed and tipped back, the neck bent. We could see smashed ribs and where its stomach had been, a pile of half digested grass.

We rode on and the road kill got worse; more camels, a cow, dogs, sheep . . . you name it, it had been killed on this road. That was the theme of the day: the flying sand and the amount of road kill. Sand was blowing across the pitted asphalt now, like some kind of whiteout, only this was a sandout or brownout – I don't know what you'd call it. The desert seemed to close in as if it would envelop us completely, only a few low bushes demarcating the road. It was spooky and exhausting; my eyes stung, my neck ached, all my muscles were working. Whenever we passed trucks or trucks passed us it was all I could do to keep control of the bike.

But despite all this, it was exhilarating, too. We passed an oil field, flames snaking skyward from some massive chimney. Against the sand it was bitter, stark, the kind of image I'd only seen on TV before, during the first Gulf War. We stopped at yet another checkpoint and as we pulled away, as if in defiance of the elements, Charley hoiked the front wheel. The sand swirled, wrapped around us, cutting the bikes off from each other so that even though he was only just in front of me I could barely make out the red of my mate's tail lights.

It was so cool though – almost mesmeric. With every gust of

wind the bike would try to crash: wind would catch in the panniers, weigh against the massive fuel tank, swirling about the bars it would try to tip me off. Incredible, this desolate fantastic place that was Libya.

CHARLEY: We passed a car lumbering along on the wrong side of the road, the driver with no idea what the fuck he was doing. We passed lorries with no lights that just appeared from the sand fog to create wind blast that shook the bikes and threatened to dump us on the tarmac. My neck ached, I was cranked over, the sand was everywhere: the crack of my arse, my scrotum. It was almost four and we hadn't eaten since breakfast. I was hungry, tired, pissed off. All I could see was sand, dust and fucking plastic. The stench of rubbish carried on the wind. The fun of it, the challenge was dissipating and I was fed up with being battered. I was sick of sand getting under my visor and into my eyes, of cramping hands where I was gripping so hard my injuries from the Dakar plagued me. I'd had a gutful of the smell of garbage and dead animals.

We were in and out of small, deserted towns. Nobody on the street, who could blame them in these conditions? But it was weird, as if they'd been abandoned – ghost towns from some mad sci-fi movie.

It grew steadily darker: the sun just a hazy reddened ball. Most of the time I couldn't see a fucking thing and this was getting dangerous. Yet I was picking up speed, blatting through with bugger-all visibility at speeds of more than seventy. I suppose when I think about it, it was some kind of fun. I thought, yeah, it's ballsy and whatever happens, happens. We were in the lap of the gods; I just hoped they were shining on us.

By seven o'clock it was almost dark and the world just seemed to shut down. Fuck a duck, this was crazy. The weather had closed in so badly now our speed had dropped to below 20 mph, at times no more than fifteen. What were we doing, riding this road in a sandstorm and possibly into the night? There was a petrol station ahead and we made for it, determined to stop there and camp if we had to. I passed a pile of broken toilets right by the side of the road. I couldn't believe it: a great load of smashed porcelain that some trucker had just tipped out. I almost didn't see it and in those conditions you crash into that and you're toast.

At the fuel stop we took shelter from the storm and debated what to do next. Ewan sat astride his bike, resting his arms on the tank bag.

'Interesting weather, Charley. Shit, my eyes are scratchy.'

'What are we going to do, carry on at night?'

Jim Foster came alongside us. 'Can't,' he said, 'it's too dangerous. We're on the limit of danger now.'

Ewan had his helmet off, his eyes bunched, and he shielded them from the wind. 'Just have to stop here then,' he said. 'Or when it gets really dark pile in the trucks or something.'

'We've still got two hundred miles to go,' I said. 'But we don't know if it's like this all the way, do we? We could ride ahead and flag down a car, ask them what it's like further on.'

We found out there was another petrol station a hundred clicks up the road and after a change of visor which took for ever, we were on our way again. By 8.15 it was pitch black, the wind still blowing but no sand. It was clear and for the first time that day luck seemed to be with us. But it didn't last long. Dai noticed black smoke kicking out of Russ's Nissan. They started losing power and we all pulled over. Within minutes Jim had his head torch on and was crawling over the engine. The air filter was clogged with sand – he knocked it clean against the running board. They had been using snorkels to ram air through the turbo but instead they were actually sucking the sand in. Ewan, neck tube half covering his face, twisted the snorkel round so the intake faced back instead of forward.

We hoped a clear filter might do the trick and got going again. But it was short lived; they were still losing power and had to pull over a second time. Now 'Mr Fix-it' was working on the connections for the turbo.

We'd been on this road for thirteen hours and after another thirty minutes we got moving a second time, though Russ and Jim could only pootle at forty-five. I heard that Russ had been on the phone to an RAC man back in London and he'd given them a few tips on what might be wrong. He wasn't planning a roadside recovery mind you.

EWAN: The adventure was wearing thin. I mean what are we doing this for? If a camel crossed the road now we'd plough right into it. Fuck, I thought, if I get hit by a camel someone make sure they tell my kids it was so very important that I get to Tobruk tonight.

Nuri, our fixer, was trying to get a mechanic organised, someone who could come to the hotel when and if we finally got there. If the Nissan was out of action then this mad dash for the ferry would be in vain. I couldn't believe the weather, so much sand. It was in my face, my hair, every orifice in my body. Charley was alongside me. 'Did you hear Russ spoke to the RAC?' he called across the radio.

I nodded. It was weird to think of some RAC man back in England getting a call from Russ in a sandstorm in the Libyan desert.

'He's amazing in situations like this,' Charley added. 'He stays incredibly calm and never gives up.'

I felt sick with muscle ache but ahead of us at last were the lights of Tobruk. With the end in sight I brightened. It had been pretty exciting. We had ridden the desert trail in a monster sandstorm and still reached our destination. It felt like a huge achievement – really exhilarating after everything we'd been through.

It was after eleven when we finally got off the bikes. I dragged my helmet over my head, my eyes running from wind and sand. Charley was loosening his tank bag. 'Deserve a little shower,' he said. 'Don't we?'

Nuri came over and told us he'd found a mechanic who was prepared to come out as soon as Russ and Jim got there. We'd left them on the highway maybe twenty minutes behind.

Nuri wanted our passports. 'I tell you,' he said, 'I've never seen sand storming for twenty-four hours. The miles we covered in those conditions, it's amazing.' He smiled then and taking the passports turned to go inside. 'Yeah,' he added. 'The Force is strong with you guys.'

11
Ice Cold In Alex

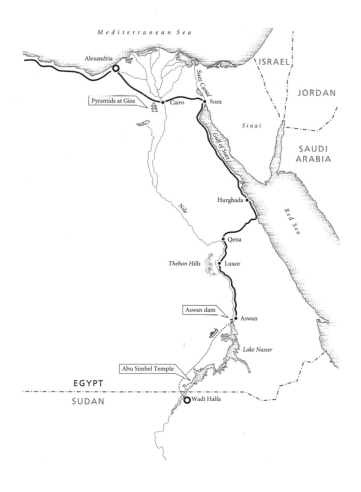

CHARLEY: I woke up feeling worse than when I went to sleep. It had been a marathon of a day – we'd ended up riding more than five hundred miles. I suppose I did feel some sense of satisfaction, but it was tempered by the danger we'd put ourselves in. I wasn't sure if it had been worth it. I wasn't sure at all.

I took a moment to look around my room; the walls filthy, paper peeling, the torn strips of lino on the floor. Tiles were missing in the bathroom and a coating of rancid-looking grime caked the bath. I had quite a view, mind you – the contrasts of Libya, perhaps – in the distance the massive Tobruk power plant, in the foreground a terrace and the crystal blue of the sea. I stared at myself in the mirror. I looked exhausted, despite a full night's sleep – puffy around the eyes. The sand, I guessed. I kept thinking about the crosswind, the incessant pounding, my head being buffeted all day. Jesus, no wonder my neck ached.

At least the Nissan was fixed. Last night before I went to bed I saw Jim under the bonnet again and he told me a pipe had slipped off the turbo. With that in place everything should be working as normal. God, what a journey. Looking back I know I'd seemed enthusiastic but that was only because we had to get the ferry. Having said that I suppose it was a sort of *Ice Cold in Alex* moment, and our destination had been Tobruk where the Allies held out against overwhelming odds. In 1941 the army had been pushed back to Egypt and the whole area, save Tobruk, had been under enemy control.

I'd been through so many emotions yesterday. I'd switched from being exhilarated one minute to really fed up the next. Eating late hadn't helped; we should have learned by now that we had to eat properly. We needed all the energy we could get.

I changed my visor back to a dark one; it was much easier here in the hotel room than it had been in last night's tempest. There had been times when I didn't think I could cope with the wind, the sand and the dangers of riding at night.

This morning I was still full of apprehension. The latter part of the ride had been really depressing, not just the elements but the towns had been real shit-holes. I remember one that looked as though the inhabitants just walked out their front doors and dumped their rubbish in the street. It was piled everywhere and blowing everywhere too. God, I really had the collywobbles this morning. I was thinking of the miles, the bigger picture, how everything was going to be. I think it was exhaustion, we'd had no real rest day and it was manic: today we were crossing the border to Egypt and that alone could take all day.

EWAN: Both Charley and I were emotional enough already after yesterday's epic ride. We hadn't prepared ourselves for how the war graves at Tobruk would affect us.

I had spoken to Eve earlier in the morning. I spoke to my daughters too. Sometimes it's really easy to have a laugh and mess about with them on the phone; but other times like this morning it's really hard. I was absolutely exhausted, and speaking to my family just made me want to be home.

The cemetery was in the middle of nowhere, a massive place with beautiful sandstone walls and a pitched roof portico at the entrance. It was a tranquil place tended by an elderly Libyan man who acted as our guide. Through the gate we were greeted by a path of baked earth that led to the first of three memorials. There was one for Australians, another for Poles and a third for Czech fighters. Our guide told us that British soldiers lay here as well as New Zealand, South African and Yugoslavian forces. They occupied what he called the commonwealth cemetery, and lying next to them, with their headstones facing Mecca, were Muslim dead from Libya, Algeria, Sudan and India. I gazed the length of the stillness to low walls and the flat envelopes of desert beyond. The place was beautifully kept with cactus growing in spiky flowers between the silent graves. We came to one where a Private Edmondson from Australia was resting: he'd been awarded the Victoria Cross after saving his friends from a German position whilst taking the bullet that killed him. We came across many plots whose occupants were unknown, the same inscription on all of them: 'Soldier of the 1939–45 war, known to God'.

Everyone had been someone's son or husband, somebody's father. Charley pointed out another inscription that had resonance for both of us. 'Our Loving Son, loved by all. Peace, perfect peace.'

I found a young man called T P Lawson and that intrigued me. He was from Ladybank in Fife, and had died when he was just twenty-seven years old. He shared his name with my grandmother on my mother's side. I took down all the details, his regiment and serial number. It was possible this man was a relative and I'd ask my grandmother when I got home.

Sitting in the cemetery, I felt a deep sadness close in. So many young men, so many families bereaved. Being in this place with so much loss brought home the conversation I'd had with my children in a big way; it made me almost angry: with myself, the time pressure, the fact that long days and hideous miles put us in situations where accidents were more likely to happen – the theme kept recurring.

CHARLEY: Some of the inscriptions had been written by the wives of those who'd died, or by their mums and dads and they were so touching. I walked among the stones, trying to imagine the men who lay there, who they'd been and how they'd died, how their families had learned of the tragedy. I saw one man from Waterford, an Irish soldier who'd also been awarded the Victoria Cross. I wasn't aware any Irishman had won it and this was close to home, Waterford being the neighbouring county to where I grew up. I thought about my own mother and father, their loss, and how any parent must feel when a child is taken from them. Russ had also been moved by what we saw and said that seeing all those fallen soldiers lined up together made him realise how important it is, especially in modern times, that we all unite and stick together.

Back on the bikes we set off for the border and all I could think about were those young men who'd died so gallantly – it touched my heart hugely and riding along I was teary. I thought again about Telsche, my sister who died eleven years ago. I missed her so much it hurt; it was almost as if I was reliving the grief by being in the cemetery. She'd been so young, so beautiful. I've said before I felt her with me on Long Way Round, the Dakar too, and I knew how those soldiers' families must have felt. I could imagine their pain and riding along I cried my eyes out, blubbering away in my helmet on the flat, dusty road to the Egyptian border. I always think about Telsche but especially on these trips, when I'm on the bike and strained physically and emotionally. I just wish she could be here, could have seen what I've done. I knew she would have been so proud of Long Way Round and the Dakar. I wish she could have seen my children grow up, but more than anything I just wanted to talk to her.

EWAN: We stopped for lunch not far from the Libyan–Egyptian border and found the BBC news playing on the TV in the corner. The report was about the horrors in Darfur; the Bush administration using the term genocide to describe what was happening. George Clooney was speaking; I have always admired the way he stands up for what he believes in, and isn't afraid to speak his mind. We caught the tail end of the piece. He was talking about the millions who would die if what he called 'real and effective measures' weren't put in place. It was a complex situation, but when the populations of entire villages were raped and killed, the bodies of the dead thrown down the drinking wells, it ceased to be complex and just came down to a matter of right and wrong.

The fighting has been raging in the western part of the country since 2003. It was like some kind of old-style range feud only with political overtones; on one side there's a militia called Janjaweed whose members are mostly camel-herding nomads from the north. On the other is the Sudanese Liberation Movement, and their fighters are mostly farmers – land tillers or sod-busters as they were called in the American West. Whilst publicly denying it, the Sudanese government has funded the northern militia and joined in with attacks on the tribes from which the Liberation Movement is drawn.

Russ was concerned about the effect any overt American pressure might have on David and Jimmy's presence when we tried to cross from Egypt. In Libya they had been victims of circumstance, the US made it hard for Libyans to enter America so Libya reciprocated. It was tit for tat and happened in various guises all over the African continent, not just with America but also with former colonial powers like France. Hoop jumping, Russ called it; simply as retaliatory action.

CHARLEY: It took five hours to cross into Egypt. Not too bad really and I pulled the obligatory wheelie. Telling me not to do so is like being told not to drink for six months. And I don't mean alcohol.

We were in Egypt and although the landscape looked much the same, we had crossed to another country and it felt like it. The difference was as discernible as it had been when we passed from Tunisia into Libya. I'd enjoyed Libya, the people had been very friendly and, given how restricted we'd been, Nuri had managed to make sure the presence of ministry officials hadn't been overbearing. But here in Egypt, everything already looked fresher, cleaner . . . wealthier.

We watched some women about to cross from Egypt into Libya, hoisting their skirts up then taping up the knees of the massive bloomers they were wearing underneath. It was the oddest thing I've seen at a border crossing. Once the tape was in place they stuffed box after box of cigarettes down their pants in full view of us, the guards, everyone. They'd cross into Libya and sell them for ten dollars a carton then come back for some more – capitalism at work all of a sudden.

Egypt was clearly busier; the towns we went through were bustling with shops and markets, open-air stalls packed with produce. The cars were better quality too, though still very crowded and not a lot safer. We passed one pickup with a canvas hood where a kid was perched on the tailgate. The buildings seemed fresher and better kept; we passed a few mosques and some isolated hotels and apartment blocks. The roads started to become more interesting; climbing higher we hit some bends, a welcome distraction after the arrow-straight and windblown tarmac of yesterday. We were still on tarmac, had been since we left home except for that one dirt road in Tunisia. Strangely enough I was looking forward to some real riding. In Sudan for example, the road was pretty grim and I was eager to pit myself against it. I'd done the Dakar; I'd trained off-road for a year and this (albeit potholed) asphalt was becoming a little boring. I love off-road riding; it's dangerous and unpredictable but massive fun. Watch the Steve McQueen movie *On Any Sunday* and you'll see what I mean. A bunch of mates with the same passion working on dirt bikes all week then clearing off at the weekend to race and win, or pitch off and break arms and collarbones. Then laugh about it.

EWAN: We'd met up with David and Jimmy and it was great to have the whole team together again. I'd apologised to them both for being flippant about the Libyan affair and they were cool about it. We were off again, in convoy with the trucks sitting in line astern the bikes. I thought I saw black smoke coming from Russ's truck and he tested it by flooring the throttle a couple of times. In the end it seemed all right.

Egypt certainly had that different feel; the buildings were built much closer to the road and the towns were more vibrant and colourful. Alexandria was 506 kilometres away and we'd be there for lunch tomorrow. Lunch in Alex: that would be good. I'd always wanted to go there – the old black and white movie where

Sir John Mills arrives after crossing the desert is one of my all-time favourites. I don't drink, but I love that image of him sitting down at that bar and watching condensation glisten on an ice-cold lager. I felt more upbeat again: another country, another adventure, a whole new world to ride through.

The climb into the twisty stuff was invigorating, a beautiful bay in the distance and once again the kind of bends where you really don't want to make a mistake. It was now getting dark, we were an hour beyond the border and Charley and I rode two abreast. I couldn't quite believe we'd ridden to Egypt, and what that meant: the pyramids, the Nile, the Red Sea. Alexandria, Cairo, Luxor – they were names to conjure with. Equally, I couldn't believe we'd only been on the road a couple of weeks: we seemed to have travelled so far it was hard to imagine we had at least two months to go and that thought was both exciting and intimidating at the same time. At the border I'd spoken to Eve again and she told me she'd ridden a hundred miles the day before. She was really getting into it. I couldn't wait for her to come and ride with us, husband and wife in Africa together at last.

As we passed through the towns I noticed there were no pavements, just sand stretching to apartment buildings and market stalls and people saying hi. Men in robes would wave and nod, and beyond the town into the desert a full moon hovered above the highway. It was really quite beautiful and I thought, God I'm riding through Egypt and there's nothing to my right and nothing to my left and the bike is upright, not at forty-five degrees. The sky was purple and blue, no light pollution, and as darkness took hold the blend of colours was amazing.

We rode into the night, something we'd vowed we wouldn't do. An hour before sunset to recce a camp spot was how I remember discussing it. The best laid plans, eh? Lights flickered on the horizon now, the town of Marsa Matruh was just ahead, and I was thinking of the night before. I'd been completely out of it by the time we stopped. I'd dumped my gear, stuff strewn everywhere when normally I'm a bit anal about folding everything away. I didn't care; I just carried the bags in and conked out.

CHARLEY: The following morning we were on our way to Alexandria, Cairo and the pyramids. I was a little grumpy and I detected a similar mood in everyone. Almost immediately we were stopped by a motorcycle cop; a bit of the road coned off as it had been so often in Libya. He was riding an old FZ750; the bike clean enough but aged. I reckoned it must have done a few miles. I think I irritated Ewan because he was getting his passport out to show the cop when I jumped in with my driving licence; his space, my invasion. It was indicative of the way we were feeling.

He roared off and I followed and once more the land was flat, the road straight but at least it was bordered by trees. We were close to the sea, sand drifting onto the asphalt now and again, the sky above a hazy kind of blue.

Up ahead we saw a couple of men driving donkeys pulling flat-bedded carts; as if someone had attached a pair of wheels to a wooden fence. Claudio wanted a shot and he pulled off into the dust and got his camera. Ewan and I were further along, still on the bikes and looking back. The donkey drivers were none too happy and hands out, angrily demanded money.

EWAN: We were kind of surprised although our Egyptian fixer, Ramy, had told us that one in five people here was associated with the police, and those that weren't liked to get involved anyway. He had warned us that people might be touchy about being filmed and for the first time in Africa the situation felt tense. Not only were the donkey drivers demanding payment but also a car pulled up sharply. Two men jumped out. They were yelling at us, waving their hands and making faces that asked the question: *What the fuck do you think you're doing?*

They started across the road. 'No photos, no photos.' The first bloke, heavy-set with a moustache was wagging a finger.

'OK,' I said. 'OK, that's cool. No photos, sorry. No more photos.'

His mate bent to the road and picked up two dirty great rocks. It was time to leave; Charley spoke to Claudio over the radio and told him to get back on his bike and get the hell out of there. The guy with the rocks was weighing them in his hands, ready to pitch them at us, when suddenly the other guy was all smiles and handshakes. It was a total transformation: a moment before he'd been shouting, now he was joking about football, asking Charley his name and where we were from. It was weird; a complete change of mood, though I noticed the other bloke held onto the rocks a little longer before finally ditching them. It was definitely time to go, though; our mood had been sour enough without this. Gunning the engines we took off again.

That incident really pissed me off. I don't deal well with that kind of aggression, never have. A mix of fatigue and the riding, the constant race we were in, coupled with people shouting and threatening to lob stones. I fell into silence, no desire to talk, either to Charley or into the video. I hunched in the seat, clicked gears and stared straight ahead. I guess you can tell from all this that the general mood in camp was pretty dour. And it was; the radios quiet for ages, every man jack of us feeling grumpy.

We were in three lanes of motorway now and the massive sprawl of the city loomed on our left. To our right, in contrast, there was the stillness of a bay where the water looked almost pink. And far in the distance, spindly towers like derricks marked the horizon. The traffic was manic, a white van heavily loaded screamed past and Charley and I now spent all our time warning each other about the next nutter approaching.

All of a sudden it swamped me – the heat, the traffic, the rush. We passed a horse and cart lumbering along and the pace, the contented nonchalance, just seemed to mock me. We had to get to Cairo this afternoon because tonight we were looking at a pyramid, tomorrow Luxor; incredible to be doing it and yet so madly rushed. I wanted to stop and kick back, to really absorb what we were doing. I'm not complaining, believe me: I'm only too aware that most people would give their eye-teeth to be where we were, but the pressure had been on since the get-go and I'd be lying if I tried to sanitise how I was feeling. For seventeen days we'd been on the move and, places like Leptis Magna notwithstanding, we always seemed to be racing the fucking clock.

Finally we found the others. Time for lunch then off we'd go again. Lunch in Alexandria, Egypt, our first city and that was it: what was the point? I pulled alongside Jimmy Simak and immediately he pointed a camera at me.

'How we doing?' I mumbled.

'Good, how're you?'

I had to think about that for a moment. 'Good,' I replied through my teeth.

CHARLEY: I think the donkey episode really finished us off. I was on my bike in this heaving metropolis, hot, knackered and really fed up. I knew I couldn't go on like this much longer.

We sat in traffic getting hotter and hotter then slowly made our way into the city. I barely noticed the surroundings; the tower of a mosque maybe, and the sea. We headed along the shore where small boats shaded by palms were beached up by the road. Some part of my brain was telling me it was all very pretty, but I was just too tired and pissed off to care.

I killed my engine and looked at Ewan.

He looked briefly at me.

Ice cold in Alex? It felt like my brain was on fire.

12
Pyramids & Porn

CHARLEY: Russ and David joined us for lunch. Sitting down at the table, I think my face said it all – I was pensive and agitated and it showed. Across the table Ewan folded a piece of flat bread and dipped it in some sauce.

He was quiet, I was quiet. Russ looked sideways at me and finally I shook my head.

'Can't do this,' I said. 'It's too much. Too many miles, not enough time . . .'

Russ hunched his shoulders: 'Then let's change it. We came here to do what *you* want. *You* tell us, you know: we're trying to follow *your* lead.'

I drew a breath, glancing at Ewan who chewed the bread in silence. For a few moments no one spoke and, hungry as I was, I barely picked at the food. My brain was numb with exhaustion.

Ewan gestured. 'We've just ridden to Alexandria and we've no sense of the place: it's already three o'clock and we've got to get to Cairo. When we get there we probably won't see anything because it'll be too dark.'

Russ sighed. 'So we can add a couple of days if you want.' He paused for a moment. 'All I'm saying is there's a ferry on Saturday and if we don't make it we wait a week.'

David was sitting further down the table: 'I think we should just stay here tonight,' he suggested. 'I mean we talk about racing from one place to the next. The ferry actually leaves on Sunday if we want it to. We can get to Cairo whenever you want tomorrow then get to Luxor and Aswan. The rush was to get to the ferry for Saturday – if we don't have to rush for that, now, it takes the stress out of it.'

While we had been in Libya, David had flown down to Cairo and arranged for another ferry to leave with us on Sunday if we wanted it to. The problem was we desperately wanted to go to Nairobi to meet up with the charity Riders for Health. Because Nairobi was so far south the trip added a further three days on the bikes, and in order to alleviate that Russ thought a better idea would be to fly down now instead. It would mean that when we did get to Kenya later we could concentrate on the north of the country and take more time. But that meant catching the ferry on Saturday.

None of us knew what to do. It was sheer exhaustion, five thousand miles on a motorbike, another ten thousand to go. The cumulative effect of having no days off compounded massively by fourteen hours in a sandstorm.

'Look, it's 520 miles to the ferry,' David said. 'Depending on the riding we can take two days if we want to. We're on schedule: it's tight but you're doing it. Russ's point is to get the Riders for Health visit in now, but we can do it later.'

Russ cut in again. 'I just want to stress that I only ever try to do the right thing by you guys.'

'We know that,' I told him.

'We've talked about it.' Ewan sounded a little agitated. 'We're trying to now work out what we do so somebody doesn't end up having an accident because he's fucking tired and fallen asleep on a motorcycle.'

For a few moments Russ was quiet. 'Well, looking at the mood in the camp you're knackered and need a day off.'

Sensing the atmosphere, David tried to put a positive spin on things. 'Look, we're at the north-east corner of Africa now and we're going south all the way from here. What do you think of that? We made the north-east tip of Africa.'

Neither of us said anything.

'Listen Russ,' Ewan said, after we'd spent some more time exploring our options, and basically going round in circles. 'We totally appreciate you were only trying to work out our plan. We totally get that. I think we were tired and upset to be riding into Alexandria for just five minutes and not see it.' He grinned a little sheepishly. 'I suppose I wanted some sympathy for being on the bike all the time.'

I was mulling over everything that had been said. 'I think . . .' I started. 'See how you feel, Ewan, but I'd like to try and get to Cairo tonight.'

Russ glanced from me to Ewan and back again. 'If you do get there tonight and you see those pyramids, that'll pick you up, I bet; that piece of energy. I do feel sorry for you guys,' he added, 'getting caned on the bikes all the time.'

Ewan made a face. 'Yeah, but endurance is as big a part of this as anything else. I just want us to be careful, that's all. That sandstorm, it really knocked us on our arses.'

EWAN: We left after we'd eaten. Given the Riders for Health situation it was the best course of action, though I was tired and I'd really wanted to see the city John Mills made famous in that old war film. On the way out of Alex we passed donkey carts and tractors, the obligatory trucks loaded to the gunwales. We hit serious tarmac and really put the hammer down; four lanes of high speed traffic. I couldn't believe my eyes when a truck crammed with people rumbled up the hard shoulder going in completely the wrong direction. It just cruised by, the driver taking it as normal and heading towards Alexandria.

Charley was on my outside and I rode with one hand on the

bars and one in my lap; the asphalt true and grippy. For a while it seemed the land was greener, farming country perhaps, but before we knew it there was the sand again – the rubble, piles of rock littered across the horizon.

I'd been in a very bad mood and it was only just beginning to ease. There's no doubt when I arrived in Alex I just wanted to blame someone and I suppose I blamed Russ and David. But it wasn't their fault; it's not them but me and Charley who're ultimately calling the shots. We'd chosen the route. I wasn't quite sure how our planning had gone so awry; it hadn't been like this when we rode round the world. I don't remember this level of tension either; we'd had our moments but this time we seemed to go from one petty squabble to another. I knew Charley was thinking we could maybe cut out some of what we had planned in the future, like northern Ethiopia, for example. It was a thought, and the four of us would have to sit down and try to work out what we needed to do because, despite some amazing experiences, none of us was enjoying it as we should be.

Giza came up quicker than I expected, so preoccupied was I with my thoughts. All at once the driving worsened, the cars came thick and fast and we were on the outskirts of the town. Cars were hooting, kids yelling from donkey carts and bicycles.

And then there they were. Just a glimpse to begin with, they seemed to grow up from the middle of the town itself. It took a moment to dawn: the pyramids. My God, I'd ridden my motorbike all the way to the great pyramids of Egypt.

Excitement gripped me. We funnelled into traffic; the buildings stained a dirty yellow; apartments, stalls; people everywhere peering at us and waving. We came to a checkpoint and stopped. It was early evening, the sun just beginning to set.

People wandered over to look at the bikes; mine was hot and sounded pretty gnarly. I switched the engine off.

'Hey, Ewan,' Charley said, 'there's a golf course over there. Imagine having a round of golf with the pyramids as your backdrop.' I could hear the enthusiasm in his voice. Suddenly all the tension seemed to lift. There's nothing like witnessing one of the great wonders of the world if you want to put your troubles into perspective.

Moments later we were moving up to a chequered barrier and the pyramids were right ahead of us and not quite as deep in the town as I'd thought. The road was wide and dusty; it snaked a few hundred yards to where the massive stone structures dominated the skyline. As I passed his truck, Ramy, our fixer, was standing there in his Indiana Jones hat.

'All yours,' he called.

Initially I didn't understand what he meant. Then I realised – the area was closed off for the evening, and we were the only visitors. I couldn't believe it. Not only had I ridden my bike to the pyramids, now we had them to ourselves. Two colossal structures, they lifted from the desert with Cairo on one side and an ancient expanse of nothingness on the other. I was speechless, standing on the foot-pegs as if in homage.

As I rode further the third one came into view. It was breathtaking. I still couldn't believe we were there on our own and as Charley pulled up I just thought how inordinately lucky we were. I looked down at the tiny video screen on my bike which tells me what I'm filming and there was Charley Boorman and behind him a fucking pyramid.

CHARLEY: The petty irritations just faded away. I couldn't get my head round the fact that we were actually here. With the pyramids ahead I pulled a monumental wheelie.

'Can you believe it, Ewan?' I called. 'It's just incredible.'

The desert was huge and empty, the sun sinking, the sky hazy; it was a fantastic time of day to be there and I knew I'd have to come back soon with Ollie and the kids. We could see the lights of Cairo, a massive sprawl and such a contrast with what stood before us.

We moved into the desert so we could see this wonder from a

vantage point where there was no road or city to compare it with. The light was fading quickly now and the desert had an eerie chill to it. The pyramids were shadowy, almost spooky, and the sun seemed to bury itself, throwing up a dusty glow like a sandstorm across the horizon. It was an experience I'll never forget, standing with Ewan at the great pyramids of ancient Egypt, five camels being led nose to tail not a hundred yards in front of us.

Of course the bikes got stuck. Well, they would, wouldn't they? I spun the back wheel, burying it in deep sand and we had to haul the bike to one side then fill the hole and drag it out. Jesus, it was heavy.

Riding in sand is a bit like water-skiing – you have to give it your all to get upright and then really go for it. Same on a bike: you dump the clutch and pin the throttle and let the bike do the rest. We finally made it back to the car park and it was fully dark now. Once we'd taken off our helmets and jackets, Ramy took us inside.

I mean inside the pyramid.

No one was allowed in at night and yet here we were. Ramy asked us if we were afraid of spirits. We climbed to the entrance and stepped into a dimly lit tunnel, walking on metal runners and holding hand rails. Floor lamps cast shadows across the stone and Ramy took us up ladders into the grand gallery. He told us there were three burial chambers. One was actually underground and carved into the bedrock; the second was referred to as the Queen's chamber but was never intended for any of Khufu's wives – it had actually contained a statue of Khufu himself. His burial chamber was in the very centre of the pyramid and the only way to get to it was from the grand gallery.

Ramy told us the pyramid took about thirty-five years to build and I told him it had been built by aliens. I was joking of course, but it is a theory because to this day no one knows how the pyramids were constructed or how the builders could so accurately get them facing magnetic north. So it had to be aliens, didn't it?

Ramy told us it wasn't aliens and it wasn't slaves either. It was a group of very skilled men, such as stonemasons and architects, who worked directly for the king and lived together in construction villages.

EWAN: The kings of Egypt cared more about the afterlife than they did this one: the pyramid would be their house for eternity and it was their life's work to build it. According to Ramy, the king would oversee the project personally, visiting many times during the period of construction. They used two different types of limestone; one for the main blocks and another finer stone for the topmost decorative skin, what Ramy termed the crust. He explained that much of that stone was missing from this pyramid but you could see it in other buildings around different parts of Cairo. He pointed out that over the centuries, particularly after Islam came to Eygpt, people just viewed the pyramids as old buildings and reclaimed some of the stone for new construction.

The limestone was local but the red granite inside Khufu's burial chamber wasn't found any closer than a thousand kilometres away. We saw holes in the walls where logs had been placed as runners and the massive blocks of granite hauled across. There was a theory that as the pyramid ascended so did a sort of mud ramp, and it was on that ramp that all the materials were transported.

'But how would you know you were on the right line?' I wondered. 'In the construction, I mean, if the whole thing was covered with mud and sand?'

'No one knows how it was done for sure,' Ramy told me.

'We'll try to figure it out then, before we get to Cape Town.' I nodded firmly. 'Charley, what do you think? You reckon we'll come up with an answer?'

'*I* probably will.'

'How come?'

'It's in the Charley book of everything, page seventeen.'

Before we left I stood before the great Sphinx, carved from bedrock in front of the second pyramid, Khafre's. It was like greeting an old friend I'd never met and yet known all my life; I'd been aware of the pyramids and the Sphinx for as long as I'd been aware of anything. I had to pinch myself so I'd know that after everything we'd been through in the last few days I really was there, standing in front of them at last, and this wasn't some kind of dream.

The evening had been spectacular and all my worries and gripes had been washed away. But stupidly, they were back the next morning. I got my bike gear on and went down to breakfast. The others were all lounging at the table and Russ asked me why I was kitted out so early.

'We're not leaving till twelve,' he said.

'Well nobody told me!' I snapped at him. I bit his head off for no reason then laid into him about the schedule all over again. I spat the dummy, I don't know why and I was out of order. None of this was Russ's fault; I knew that, but I couldn't help myself, I lashed out and off we went again.

CHARLEY: It seemed Jim Foster and Jimmy Simak were at loggerheads at the moment, and I got the feeling that Jim and Dai were frustrated generally by David and Jimmy, and equally the reverse was true. And poor old Russ was caught in the middle. We were riding beside the longest river in the world and last night we'd been inside the pyramids, yet still there was this kind of unrest in the camp: it was fucking stupid.

This really was a scabby river; worse for litter than anything in Libya. Up ahead I was amazed to see not only some kids swimming in it but a couple of horses too.

We left the city and hit the bigger roads. With my jacket open it was nice to have some air rushing over me. We were following the Nile now with the city on our left and the gloriously lush delta to my right, palm trees and green meadows and beyond them sloping hills. The Gulf of Suez was behind us, the Red Sea on our left where hundreds of massive ships lay at anchor. Across the Gulf was the Sinai Desert, Israel and Jordan.

We followed the river south and the world opened up again with scrub and sand and a horizon marked with electricity pylons. We passed wind farms and the desert grew rockier and much less sandy. I couldn't believe how much building was going on; blocks of apartments going up all over the desert. We hit a dual carriageway where the opposing lanes were located a hundred yards across the open scrub. I was rattling along at 80 mph when a car came beetling towards me in what was our outside lane. I had to pull across sharply to avoid hitting it head on. I waved and shouted but the driver just waved back, grinning away as if everything was normal. Which for driving in this country, I suppose it was.

EWAN: We took photographs en route and then, leaving one beautiful spot, we really stepped through the gears. I watched the speedometer rising: eighty, ninety, a hundred, a hundred and five, ten; a hundred and fifteen. All at once the bike went into a weave. For a few seconds (that felt like hours) I was convinced I was coming off. Jesus, it was scary. I held my nerve though and didn't shut the throttle. I knew if I did that I would crash; the slap would get so bad I'd be off before I knew it. I tried to accelerate out of it but that only made it worse. So very gradually I eased back and oh-so-slowly the bike settled. It was one of those adrenalin-sickening moments when your heart is in your mouth, and all you see are images of bones breaking as you bounce across the tarmac.

We stopped on the Red Sea, a sort of lay-by where rocks overhung the road. Charley and I discussed the driving, one bus in particular that had been hammering along faster than either of us and had a habit of overtaking on blind corners. Crossing the road we found what looked like a private beach. There was a reed and palm lean-to and another smaller structure like a grassy sun canopy. Charley whipped off his clothes and raced down the beach, Jimmy catching his 'ass' on camera. I stripped off and followed him, the water cool and relaxing; I could see ships dotted on the horizon. It was great – just what we needed after the perils of the road.

Back in the lay-by we found the crew talking to an English couple who lived in Cairo. They'd been watching our progress on the internet and thought they'd try to find us. I loved the fact that people were interested enough to do that.

We chatted for a while, and when they were gone David and Ramy came over. They were in fits of laughter, not about the English couple but what had happened just before they arrived. This was indeed a private beach – a military beach. Seeing the bikes, a couple of soldiers had come down to investigate. They wanted to know what was going on and when they saw cameras and two guys frolicking in the surf naked, they thought we were making gay porn movies. It took a while for Ramy to explain but they were eventually placated. Can you imagine the headlines, a whole new career for me and Charley?

CHARLEY: The checkpoints pissed me off, there were hundreds of them all the way to Luxor and I saw no reason why we needed to be stopped and asked for papers or our gear inspected quite so often. It's not as if we'd crossed any borders. I'd lost the licence thing they'd given me for the bike when we entered Egypt, though, and it was bothering me. I'd stopped to change the map on my tank bag and it must have fallen out. I'd need it to get my bike on the ferry at Aswan and the last thing I wanted to do was put any additional pressure on the team.

We'd picked up a police escort (as all tourists have to in this part of Egypt) and I was reminded of being in Kazakhstan. We stopped for something to eat at 8.30 and didn't hit Luxor until after midnight. I was shagged out, yawning, my eyelids drooping; at one point I almost barrelled into Ewan. The streets were heaving with cafes open and people going about their business as if it were the middle of the day, not the middle of the night. I passed a couple on a moped, weaving in and out of the traffic. The guy was driving; his wife sat side-saddle behind him holding a newborn baby.

In the morning I woke to a fantastic view of the Nile and beyond it the slopes of pinkish rock that marked the Valley of the Kings. I was worried about Russ, he was still very quiet. Ewan had spoken to me about it and Russ leaving was the last thing he wanted. As we headed for the Valley of the Kings he told me it had been bothering him all night.

EWAN: I'd thought of nothing else. I should never have spoken to him that way, but in my frustration I just lashed out and now I hoped to Christ he wouldn't leave. There was no question there were significant psychological differences within the team. As with Long Way Round, it was always best when Charley and I set off on our own. But in Egypt, with a police escort, this was not only difficult, it was actually against the law. I was also aware that Charley and I often approached the journey in a fundamentally different way. Charley might say he was tired all the time and couldn't carry on like this, but at the same time he was always thinking of getting to the next place. It's the racer in him. And much as he says I can alter a mood when things don't go my way, the fact is that more often than not Charley gets his way.

And yet despite some of the frustrations, we had already enjoyed some amazing moments, like at the pyramids yesterday. And now we had another extraordinary experience ahead of us – the Valley of the Kings. For five hundred years the rulers of Egypt's New Kingdom constructed their tombs there, west of the Nile in the Theban Hills. It's most famous, of course, for the discovery of Tutankhamen and the curse of the pharaohs.

We crossed the Nile in a small boat with the hills and dunes lifting before us, and that in itself was amazing. We walked pathways between the sloping hills, grey in shadow and pink in the sun; the burial chambers cut deep into the rock.

Ramy took us to the tomb of Seti II, which gave us a great insight into the construction process. As a man, the Egyptian pharaoh was thought to be the embodiment of Horus, God of the heavens and protector of the Sun God. When he died he became Osiris, King of the Dead and the next pharaoh took on the mantle of Horus. Seti II only reigned for four years between 1203 and 1197 BC, and his tomb demonstrated as much; the square corridor to the burial chamber was only partially plastered and decorated with hieroglyphics. There hadn't been enough time to complete everything before he died. As we made our way to the burial chamber, we saw unfinished walls and the chamber itself just hewn from the rock. There had been no time to personalise the place because as soon as the king died his path to the afterlife began and he had to be mummified right away. Ramy told us that the bodies were never cut; the organs were removed through the dead man's nose.

'Not his bottom?' I whispered.

'No, his nose.'

'Are you sure? I would have thought it would be easier through his bottom.'

'No,' Ramy insisted, 'it was always the nose.'

Charley gestured. 'I'd have thought . . . you know . . . if there's a hole, use it.'

Ramy explained that the first part of the king's journey would be to stand before the judges, the Gods. Judgement was simple. The king's heart was placed on a set of scales, with a feather on the other. If the heart was heavier than the feather then the king would go to hell. But if he had been a good king and the cares of his heart were few it would be lighter than the feather and he would go to heaven.

Ramy showed us the burial chamber, the empty granite

sarcophagus and in the lid the image of a beautiful goddess. 'To look after him,' he explained, 'on his journey to the afterlife.'

'Of course.' I looked at Charley. 'I think we should all have one, don't you, a nice goddess to look after us in the next life?'

Apparently when robbers raided the tombs they took away the mummies and kept them together carefully in a cave. They didn't want to destroy them because whatever damage was done to the body in this world would be how that body would appear in the next. Not good for them then when it came to the afterlife, not if they snapped a king's legs, or poked eyes out, or sliced off an ear by mistake.

'So you had a cave full of kings all kicking around together?' I shot a glance at Charley. 'I imagine there were a lot of arguments, don't you?'

13

Riding Bikes & Saving Lives

CHARLEY: It's true I am the sort of person who thinks about the destination, but at the same time I did feel aggrieved at the pace we were travelling. But you do get a sense of place on the bike, a sense of the people. Ewan knows what I mean. Riding through is riding through, you're exposed to the elements, you smell things, hear and see things that you just don't experience in a car.

Leaving Luxor we managed to get to Aswan while it was still daylight. Even so I was yawning into my helmet, eyes as heavy as they'd ever been. The city is perched at the top of Lake Nasser and it's from Nasser that we would cross to Sudan. I was a little apprehensive – another country and another set of circumstances. It was not knowing what to expect that always got to me; that and the fact that I'd lost my bike document.

All I wanted to do was take a shower, eat and crash. But I had to file a report with the police which I could then give to customs. I went up to my room, dumped my gear on the bed and splashed cold water over my face. Ewan came in, looking relaxed and with that old sparkle back in his eyes.

'You OK, Charley?' he asked me.

'Fine, mate. What about you?'

'I'm good.' He smiled now. 'Have you seen your view?'

'No, I've not had a chance.'

'Take a look at your view, Charley.'

Pulling back the curtains I opened the window and was greeted by one of the most beautiful sights I've ever seen. The dark waters of the lake sparkled in the sunshine; the hotel was perched on a rocky outcrop overlooking single-sail boats with canvas canopies. On the other side a dozen or so more boats were in the shelter of an inlet lined with palm trees. Beyond them I could see another massive ruin, pillars and sandy steps leading down to the water. I could make out ancient roads and walkways, and dominating the whole thing a mass of rolling sand dunes.

Together we leant on the rail and Ewan started singing: 'Ruins to the left of me, ruins to the right, here I am, stuck in the middle with me!'

We fell about.

'You know what,' he said, 'we've been to the pyramids and the Valley of the Kings We've made it to Aswan and I'm determined we're going to get over this little hump. For my part I'm not going to snap at people any more. I'm going to think before I speak and when I'm tired I'm just going to button up and get on with it.'

'You're right; if it gets bad it gets bad and we just have to suck it up.'

'I'm sorry for my part, Charley.'

'Yeah, so am I.'

'From now on we just get on with it, make every effort to enjoy it. This is the trip of a lifetime and we're not going to waste it.'

Slipping my arm around his shoulders we hung out of the window, just gazing across the beauty of the lake. I noticed the open air restaurant on a little promontory where a table was set with a white cloth. 'Let's have dinner there,' I suggested.

We had a great dinner, a real laugh, and everything was back to normal, relaxed, happy; apologies offered and accepted. I still had to sort the paperwork for my bike, mind you, and after dinner

Ramy and I went down to a tinpot police station with peeling walls and wires hanging from the ceiling. We had a cup of tea with the top man, decided which report we needed, filled it in and then Ramy ran down the road for a photocopy. While he was gone these younger cops were cracking on to me in English, about drugs and sex and whether I did drugs and was sex easy to find in England. Very strange.

Still waiting for Ramy, I watched as first four people all handcuffed together were brought in, then a few minutes later three brothers who had been fighting. One of them had called the police and the sergeant was disgusted that they should be fighting in the first place and that they expected the police to sort it out. Three brothers – he told them they should be ashamed of themselves. By the time we had resolved everything it was past one o'clock in the morning, and I was due to be up again at five.

EWAN: Saturday dawned a little cloudy and we piled into a minibus for the airport. We were headed for Kenya and Riders for Health, leaving Jim and Dai to repack the cars and get them and the bikes down to the ferry. We had a plane waiting, and though we were much more relaxed we still had a schedule to keep.

I knew about the charity through the film director Mark Neale, who made the two Moto GP documentaries I narrated. This was Charley's deal really, though; he'd been introduced to the organisation by racer Randy Mamola and was more involved than me. I was very interested in their work, however, and couldn't wait to get down there.

We got to the check-in desk only to find that customs wouldn't let us fly out because according to our passports we had two Nissan trucks and three BMW motorbikes registered to us. We explained that we were coming back tomorrow but it wasn't enough. As far as customs were concerned we could have sold the vehicles and they needed to physically set eyes on them before they'd let us board the plane to Kenya. We took it all in our stride and returned to the hotel, collected the vehicles and drove them back to the customs compound.

I was really excited about Kenya. By making this flying visit we'd see some of the Masai Mara and then when we returned to Kenya after crossing the border from Ethiopia on the bikes, we would be able to take more time up in the north. Meanwhile Russ was talking about how he'd once been in a sort of plane crash. This was great timing: a 'sort of' crash when a 747 'sort of' crash-landed. Inspiring really, as the ground fell away beneath us.

We landed safely at a very lush and green-looking Nairobi airport – in fact much of the country we'd flown over had been green and I wasn't sure if that was the way it always was or because we'd just come out of the rainy season.

We were met by Andrea and Barry from Riders for Health who guided us to a puddle-jumper – a small plane that would take us to the unit we were visiting not far from Mount Kilimanjaro. We'd see for ourselves how motorcycles were taking life-saving resources to terribly sick people in remote places. Barry told us that this was the first facility of its kind and a groundbreaker in Kenya, a model for how the idea could work elsewhere.

The plane landed on a red clay airstrip in the middle of the Masai Mara; lion country. Indeed a handout on the plane instructed us to remain in the compound at night and to always remember that plains animals such as zebra and antelope were prey to carnivores, and if we got close to them we might be also getting close to some predator lurking in the underbrush.

From the plane we drove across green savannah and low scrub to the Mbirikani Group Ranch Clinic, a fenced compound where the seriously ill were treated. A series of water towers dominated the gates, and inside open sheds protected a line of 200 cc dirt bikes from the elements. They bore the Riders for Health emblem on the front mudguard, the same emblem I'd seen on leathers in the Moto GP paddock.

We were met by Dr Mariti, tall and smiling and at thirty-two years old one of four doctors who worked full time at the clinic.

Later he told me he'd actually wanted to be a pilot but the college he'd been sent to didn't do flying lessons. He became a doctor instead, thankfully.

The idea for some kind of bike outreach had started back in 1988 when Barry and Andrea, together with Randy Mamola, raised money for Save the Children. Invited to a project in Somalia they discovered a pile of disused motorcycles that they were told were out of commission. As bikers they saw that with a little care the bikes were anything but out of commission and could easily be put to good use, and it was from there the idea of remote access transportation was born. Cutting a very long story short the Mbirikani Unit opened in 2003 with a mobile caravan calling at five separate stations, but the HIV epidemic was so great the need for a permanent facility was obvious. Its permanence, though, is only half the story.

CHARLEY: The idea was to use motorcycles as a method of transporting healthcare to people who'd otherwise die. The principal killer was AIDS but they also dealt with more easily remedied illnesses like dysentery and malaria. The advent of antiretroviral drugs and the fact that they were finally being manufactured in Africa meant that in principle more people could be treated. Not if they had to walk seventy kilometres to get the treatment, though, or, in the case of HIV, three hundred. Before Riders for Health got involved in this area, the nearest HIV treatment had been Nairobi, and most people were either too poor or too sick to get there.

The sight of abandoned and rusting bikes in Somalia had eventually led here to Kenya where sixteen community health workers were trained to ride the most inhospitable roads in the world. Some of the health workers were lab technicians, some trained in public health, others were nurses, but all of them rode bikes and without them literally thousands of people would die. Their basic supplies are simple: mosquito bed nets, blood-testing equipment, the required drugs and a 70/30 corn and soya food supplement – it's pointless administering life-saving medicine if the patient still suffers from malnutrition. The health workers are backed by fifteen nurses and the four doctors, as well as four full-time lab assistants. Mbirikani is totally self-contained, the compound made up of a number of Nissen huts with paths running between them, and the whole placed enclosed by a wire fence. We wandered over to the bikes and the workshop where they were maintained. This really cool guy in a white shirt and thick black braces was in charge and Ewan and I were in our element.

These bikes had been modified slightly with twin side stands and crash bars on the engine casing and handlebars, as well as reinforced metal racks to carry the top boxes. The workshop carried every spare imaginable and all the riders were trained in basic maintenance.

Mounting up we followed our guide out of the compound and a few miles up the dirt road to a small cluster of huts dwarfed by Mount Kilimanjaro. I'd never seen Kilimanjaro before and, as we pulled up, images of Hemingway and Stewart Granger movies filled my head.

The huts had thatched roofs and the walls were made from mud or animal excrement. We were there to see Agnes and she came out to meet us, a woman in her thirties, hair plaited; she was wearing a sand-coloured dress with a brightly coloured bracelet on her wrist. She was surrounded by half a dozen smiling women, all dressed in vivid colours with a mass of laughing children at their feet. Agnes was the first person to have been treated by the clinic at Mbirikani; infected with the HIV virus, she was bedridden and helpless. She weighed forty-six kilos when they found her and, like thousands of others in Africa, she had effectively been left to die. Now she weighed sixty-four kilos and looked terrific. She was happy to stand there with cameras and chat about what had happened to her. I thought she might have carried some stigma maybe with the other villagers but in fact the reverse was true. Most people had known her when she was dying and here she was, proof that the medical facility was working. Instead of being stigmatised she was the inspiration for hundreds of other people to come forward and be tested for HIV. She remains on antiretroviral drugs, of course, which are brought to her by a community health worker on a motorcycle. That means she doesn't miss her dosage which is absolutely critical: if she did her blood levels would be affected and the virus would mutate and overcome the drug.

Our guide was one of the community health workers who'd grown up in this village and he told us the unit dealt with five hundred outpatients, all of whom were visited on motorbikes. They don't just treat HIV or tuberculosis – they also bring simple sanitation equipment that means the difference between life and death, like the plastic portaloo we could see under the shadow of the mountain. Ewan commented that this had to be the world's most scenic toilet. 'Imagine that view,' he said, 'Kilimanjaro in snowy splendour after your morning doings.'

EWAN: Agnes looked fantastic and so did the guy who strode round the side of the hut towards us. He was clearly the head man, and most likely the husband of all the women and father of their children. (Being a Masai warrior has its advantages.) He was tall and elegant, wearing a heavy orange blanket over one shoulder and the long red skirt of the Masai, a massive machete thrust like a sword in the sash. He nodded and smiled and went on his way and we could only look after him and sort of gasp.

It had been a privilege to meet Agnes, an amazing woman and living proof that the project was successful. HIV was one thing – I've been involved in Malawi and seen the devastation it can cause – but what amazed me most was the simplest of things. The project covers a seventy kilometre radius and when it started they'd encounter perhaps two to three hundred cases of malaria each year. The introduction of bed nets had reduced that rate to almost zero. Incredible to think that a net costing no more than a couple of quid saved so many lives each year. It wasn't just a case of handing them out, mind you; it was bringing the washing solution to make sure they were re-treated, it was showing people how to tuck them in so the bed was secure, it was follow-up visits to make sure the nets were working. The health workers didn't just call on the patients either; prevention being better than a cure, they visited schools to educate children; they spoke to mothers, young women, village elders.

Back at the ranch I spent time with Dr Mariti. He showed me their labs, which although extensive were in the throes of being extended. He explained that they could test for just about anything right there on the premises: renal function, liver function, and of course HIV and TB. I asked him about counselling: I'd witnessed a woman having an HIV test in Malawi and seen her reaction when she was told it was positive. The doctor explained that there was both pre-test and post-test counselling; the patients who arrived at the visitor centre, those who weren't sick but wanted to know if they would be, were counselled before the test. If they were positive they went to see a doctor immediately and received more counselling afterwards. Those who proved to be negative were counselled on how to ensure they remained negative. It was comprehensive, even those who were brought in so ill that they needed immediate care were properly counselled once they'd been stabilised.

Prevention was the key. Dr Mariti explained that every morning one of the health workers would have a group education session there in the clinic, before getting his or her bike and setting off for the outlying areas. They had a total of 2500 patients in the HIV programme, 1800 of whom were on antiretroviral drugs, while seven hundred were yet to develop full symptoms. On discharge from the clinic all patients became the subject of visits from the community health workers, who made sure they took their medication, kept up with sanitation and where necessary received food supplements.

I spoke to Dr Mariti about pregnant women and the way HIV is often passed from mother to baby. In Malawi women were treated with antiretroviral drugs early in pregnancy but were told to breastfeed their babies when they were delivered, because the water was so bad any formula feeding would be impossible – the HIV virus could be passed through the mother's milk. Here the Prevention of Mother to Child Transmission Protocol was completely different; they advocated that formula milk should be used and once the baby was weaned they would move on to a sort of porridge. The health workers carried water-purifying sachets and as long as these were used when mixing the baby formula there was no risk of waterborne disease. The doctor told me that since the clinic opened they had successfully delivered 110 babies, who didn't carry the virus, from HIV positive mothers. In fact the only babies they'd 'lost', so to speak, had already been born when their mothers came in.

CHARLEY: My mate in the white shirt and thick braces was showing me the bikes in detail: 200 cc was the right size machine for the terrain and what they were carrying, light enough to be manoeuvrable yet with enough power to cope with the dodgy roads. There was one road in particular that had just about every kind of hazard a biker could think of, ten times worse when it rained. Apparently riding in the rain here was like jumping in a lake.

Each health worker was not only a trained medical professional – they were up on bike maintenance as well. They had to be: this was the Masai Mara and not the Old Kent Road; there was no AA man at the end of a phone. Every morning before setting off for the day the riders do what my man called PLANS, which was a basic bike check: Petrol, Lubrication, Adjustments, Nuts and bolts. The S was for Stop, i.e. the brakes and tyres. They had fuel facilities on site and made sure they had enough in the bikes for that day; they oiled and greased working parts like the gear shifter and back brake pedal; they checked engine and gearbox oil. They tested front and rear brakes and meticulously scoured the tyres for cuts and nicks. More than once a health worker had ridden past a herd of elephants or a pride of lions only to get a puncture. They carried tyre levers, inner tubes and repair kits and I could only imagine the speed you'd fix that puncture knowing a pride of lions was watching you. Each morning they'd check the chain for movement – a maximum of 20 mm play was the marker. They checked nuts and bolts because they worked loose almost every day given the harsh country these bikes were ridden through.

The training was taught by Riders for Health, starting with the basics like balance and throttle control, moving on to braking safely, emergency braking, cornering and dealing with the likes of gravel, sand and mud. They taught defensive riding – how to deal with errant minibus drivers, for example. We were told about one young nurse who saw a bus coming for her, shifted the bike off the road and parked. Somehow the bus still hit her, breaking her leg, the poor soul. Recalling the handout we'd been instructed to read on the plane, I asked about the wildlife and the attendant dangers. My guide told me that lions were a problem, but because the Masai warriors hunted them, they were as afraid of humans as we were of them. Buffalo were the most dangerous because they'd attack without provocation. Fortunately there weren't many of them, but I could still imagine the terror of being out there with a flat tyre with two tons of angry wild bull bearing down on me.

It was a brilliant day, really informative and relaxing. I was in my element, so delighted to be there after all I'd learned from the racing fraternity. The work is invaluable, the most effective answer to the problems of reaching people in remote areas; I could see it working all over the world. The bikes last five or six years because they are prepared properly and well maintained, whereas normally a bike would last about six months on these kinds of roads. That in itself was a major achievement and meant that once a machine had been donated it was sustainable.

I was hugely impressed with the Masai people; tall and elegant, confident and incredibly well spoken. Most of the riders were from the local area. It was a real community thing; they were saving lives, riding bikes and creating jobs. It had been the highlight of the journey so far for me, and I know that Ewan was just as moved and inspired.

The following day we met up with Richard Branson who was in Kenya donating motorcycles. It was because of him that we'd been able to grab a plane in Aswan. We had lunch at an old colonial house with wild boar and a giraffe called Lyn in the garden. We chatted about all things African and people kept coming up to me and asking if I was Richard's brother – must be the beard. He, of course, told them I was his brother, his elder brother in fact. Ewan and I gave him a quick lesson in bike craft and the three of us rode around a mini dirt track for photographers. The end of a fantastic couple of days and Ewan and I were buzzing. One of the great privileges of doing these trips is being able to witness first hand the achievements of the charities we're involved with. It's humbling to find so many people so keen to make things better; humbling and uplifting, hopeful when you contrast it with the news reports we'd seen from Darfur. For every warmongering, power-hungry psychopath there are hundreds of normal people going about their business quietly ensuring the human race retains some dignity.

EWAN: Back on the plane to Aswan we were talking routes again. Sudan was coming up and that would throw in a whole new set of possibilities. Before we got there we had twenty-four hours travelling the length of Lake Nasser and I was really looking forward to that. We'd had a text yesterday from Jim and Dai telling us that the trucks and bikes had been loaded onto the ferry. I was really grateful to them, working away while we took off and did this. The truth is the whole mood had changed; everyone was positive and upbeat and really looking forward to the rest of the trip.

We got the maps out and discussed what we'd do in Sudan and Ethiopia. As it stood we were coming into Ethiopia from Famaka, which was well north of the capital Addis Ababa but well south of where we were due at the Eritrean border. Charley was questioning the roads, the mileages; he didn't trust the maps or how long they claimed the journeys would take us. It would be a lot longer than we had forecast, that's for sure. We were determined not to make any mistakes this time. I remembered what the community health worker had said when he showed Charley and me the contents of the top box: 'If you're well prepared your goals are much more easily realised'.

We had two choices in Sudan: what looked like another desert road with not a lot on it in terms of settlements, or the road that followed the Nile. From either we could make our destination and cross to Ethiopia. There we had another set of circumstances to consider: we could stick to our plan and go north from Gonder then head for Addis via Lalibela, maybe. Or we could go across country and skip the northern bit altogether. I wasn't sure what to think about it; certain places on these trips feel special, the potential nirvana if you will. Before we left on Long Way Round it was Mongolia for me and that's how it turned out when I got there. This time it had been the Ethiopian Highlands and I had a sneaking feeling that I shouldn't miss them. Having said that, as Charley pointed out, missing one thing might mean coming across another; we never knew what was around the next corner so we shouldn't think of route changes as missing out. He was right of course, we'd have to see, but before we came to that decision we had the sand of Sudan to negotiate.

14

The Stuff of Dreams

EWAN: Two days later I walked the flattened landscape acutely aware of the stillness. I could feel sand underfoot and it took a few moments to fully come to terms with it. Darkness was falling and tonight I'd bivouac in the desert. This was the stuff of dreams, a boy's adventure and I could only think how lucky I was. I recalled the previous morning on the boat. Looking up from a dozy state at breakfast, I thought I was on a film set where the extras had broken for lunch; so many faces, voices, so many different costumes.

We'd been at the docks by 8.30. I was finally witnessing what I'd hoped to find when we steamed into Tunisia. A medley of vehicles, people, boxes, packing cases, sacks of everything imaginable; one truck so overloaded the wheel arches scraped the tyres and the load itself was the size of another lorry. A man stood on top shouting orders. Everywhere it was bedlam; a mass of buses and cars, pickup trucks, noise and colour – at last I'd found my scene from Indiana Jones.

I saw family after family carrying what looked like their entire houses; they stepped gingerly across the barges to the ferry as we had done. I watched as they grabbed a space on deck or disappeared below to the racks of seats that made up some kind of steerage.

We 'rich white travellers' had cabins, fortunate compared to most, and though they were cell-sized with twin bunks, they had a porthole that opened fully. I was delighted at that; I wanted to be able to smell the lake, the land as we crossed the border.

Charley came in, looking as excited as I felt.

'Fantastic, Charley, isn't it?' I said.

'A boat to Sudan. It's brilliant! My cabin's next to the ladies' toilets though, so it's a bit sniffy. But then I suppose that's better than Dai and Jim, they're next to the blokes on the other side.'

We were told there were no keys to the cabins and that bothered me initially as we had a lot of expensive filming equipment. But as we said goodbye to Ramy he told us the gear would be perfectly safe. He'd been great and, considering we'd no choice but to stick with the back-up, he'd made it as unobtrusive as possible.

CHARLEY: The boat was chaotic and yet at the same time strangely organised. Noise everywhere, people shouting, the loading haphazard and so much stuff; I saw people shifting fridges end over end when you're not supposed to turn them upside down. They were piled on top of everything else and everything piled on top of them and I could only imagine how crushed the stuff at the bottom would be by the time we got to Wadi Halfa.

We'd boarded at 11.30 this morning and now it was 5.30 and still we'd yet to pull away from the wharf. I asked one of the crew when we were leaving and he told me this was African time and to leave that watch behind. He was right; everything here worked its own way and in its own time and as I gazed across the dock to where people were still boarding, I had a real sense of adventure. I just knew that Sudan and Ethiopia were going to be amazing.

I could see the barge carrying our vehicles, together with another couple of monsters, one laden with lengths of concrete pipe. I could also see the triple-decked cruise boat that had looked so inviting when we first arrived. I'd thought it was our boat and that with deck chairs and everything this would be some journey. Then someone pointed out this metal hulk of a ferry and that brought me down to earth again.

The deck was heaving with bodies. We noticed a guy and girl who'd grabbed space under one of the lifeboats. They had plenty of shade and Ewan and I were a little envious at first, but as the deck filled up I was considerably less so.

Ewan was alongside me. 'I tell you, Charley, this is the highlight of the whole thing so far. It's excellent.'

People were still coming aboard, laden with beds and wicker chairs, TV sets and cases of soft drinks.

'I was talking to one of the crew just now,' Ewan went on. 'Apparently people come up from Sudan, they buy what they want and ship it back to Wadi Halfa. The trip the other way is really quiet.'

'It'll be nice to get to Sudan,' I said. 'After a few days off and all that asphalt I'm looking forward to the desert. I haven't ridden in sand since the Dakar. Did I ever tell you I did the Dakar, Ewan?'

We had discussed our route at length and decided we'd definitely take the road that followed the Nile: it was longer but there was far more to see that way. We'd also learned that the UNICEF girls we were going to meet had already left for Addis Ababa. That meant we were definitely travelling north when we got to Ethiopia.

We wandered downstairs, no cabins and few windows, just open compartments of benches where families were sitting together and you could smell food from the kitchens. The atmosphere was lively and infectious; the noise, the smells; the feel of the boat; the hundreds of different people. We chatted to people, we shook hands and told them our names and one girl in particular caught my eye; she was wearing a pink dress, dark hair tied in two plaits. For a moment she reminded me of home and my own children.

Finally we got going and on deck once more we leant on the rail between the rows of orange lifebelts as the horn blew loud enough to deafen.

'Chapter three, Ewan,' I said, 'the desert and sand in your arse.'

'I'm glad we decided on the Nile route,' he told me. 'Not sure about the heat though, what do you reckon?'

I shrugged. 'Just have to suck it up, I guess.'

'It'll be twice as hot as this probably; maybe thirty-five or forty. One guy told me it can get up to sixty-five in some places at certain times of the day.'

'We'll just have to deal with it.'

EWAN: Charley had a feeling that the riding was going to be a lot better in Sudan and Ethiopia – there would be no police escort and we would be able to get off into the cuds on our own. That was my sentiment exactly, and I couldn't wait to get started.

'President Nasser flooded this lake,' Charley said.

'Maybe he needed somewhere to swim.'

'I think it was his mausoleum, you know, his pyramid or temple; his everlasting mark on Egyptian history. They say the whole area was covered in ruins and artefacts: it was a real kick bollock and scramble to get it all out.' Suddenly he was smiling. 'You know, I can't believe we're leaving Egypt after having been in Kenya.'

'I know.' I rested my chin on my arms and gazed across open water to where the horizon drifted. 'I'm really excited about that now.'

'Did you hear that the UNICEF girls are already on their way to Ethiopia?'

I nodded. 'I think it's a good thing. If we'd missed out northern Ethiopia I think we might have regretted it. It'll be great, Charley. No one rides up there. No one rides a bike to the Eritrean border.'

We were up by the bridge and wanted to get back to the others, who were on the far side of the boat. The trouble was a bunch of Sudanese guys had their camp set up, complete with rugs and a hammock already hung. The only other way was through the open doors to the bridge but the captain had already he'd told us we couldn't go here and we couldn't go there and now he was shouting at his crew. Five of them were standing across the bridge, the guy at the wheel with barely enough room to move. The captain looked like something from an old Sinbad movie; old and gnarled, great thick fingers with calluses all over them. He was wearing a long white robe and white cloth wrapped around his head. He had fierce eyes, sharp like a hawk's, and his features were pinched and thin. He kept glowering our way and every time we approached he'd shout at someone and we'd back off. Nobody was in any kind of uniform but they were all talking loudly. The captain perched on a cupboard now, legs swinging; the helmsman was boxed in and one other bloke started swabbing the floor of the bridge.

'I think he's barking,' I said softly. 'The captain; quite the toughy, isn't he, a real salty old seadog.'

'Or not so *salty* maybe,' Charley said, 'given this is a lake. I reckon he's seen a few things in his time, though. Don't you?'

'Yeah. Like one too many freshwater crossings.'

We tried to pluck up the courage to ask if we could go through, but the bloke on his knees was still washing the floor and the others were shouting at each other now with another yelling over the loudspeaker. In the end we asked if we could film the captain and he just kind of looked at us and we made our way through.

Downstairs in a salon area we found Dave and Amelia, the couple who had been sheltering under the lifeboat. Dave was from Australia and was backpacking around the continent, Amelia was headed for Darfur and a summer of volunteer work. They'd just hooked up together as travellers often do. We spoke about Aswan and the unfinished obelisk. I'd heard it was unfinished because the stonemasons carving it discovered a crack which rendered it pretty useless, so they just left it. Amelia had been to see the Temple of Isis and we ended up talking about stuff in the British Museum and the little sarcophagus that had carried Tutankhamen's organs. Of course that brought us back to hooks and noses and bottoms and I was at pains to point out that your bottom is a larger orifice than your nose.

Later in my cabin I hung out the window. The sun was going down, the sky plum coloured and the water almost black. I watched as it grew darker and darker and then finally the sun seemed to hiss into the lake and for a moment the whole sky blazed gold. There was a sense of silence despite the engine noise and the hubbub from the decks – night on an old boat. I felt as if I was back in the thirties.

Lying on my bunk I took a moment to reflect and knew instinctively that there had been something really important about going to Kenya. I couldn't quite put my finger on what exactly, but I was inspired again, my batteries recharged, and I was itching to go on with the adventure. The village clinic had been unbelievable; wonderful to find people dedicating their lives to helping others. In many ways I thought the riders had the best job in the world, riding bikes to keep people alive.

CHARLEY: I just loved the chaos; the boat was full of so much colour and noise, so many incredible characters. There was a method to everything despite the bedlam and when we went to the cafeteria we just grabbed what we wanted to drink and then these waiters would appear in blue and yellow uniforms and food would be on the table in a matter of moments. When you were eating it was easy to forget where you were; you'd look up and be astounded by all the different clothes and hats, some people wearing turbans or bands of cloth like the captain, others in little caps, women completely shrouded. There were guys with marks on their foreheads from praying, and cool dudes in baseball caps and shades, smoking long cigarettes and saying nothing.

Waking early I knocked on Ewan's door. We were passing Abu Simbel and I really didn't want him to miss it. Ramy had told us that from the boat it would be something special.

It was on our right close to the shore, a couple of flat-topped bluffs the colour of the desert. The sky was a kind of thin blue, that early morning stillness about it. I knew it was going to be a really hot day. From a distance the structure just looked like a sloping hillside with tall shadowy portals cut into it. When you looked closer, of course, they weren't portals, but massive figures, four of them sculpted from the stone.

'Pretty cool,' I commented. 'Nice little resting place for someone important or someone of self importance maybe.'

It had been built by Ramasses II as a monument to himself and his queen. This wasn't the original site though; he'd built it in the thirteenth century BC, but it was moved lock, stock, and barrel in the 1960s just before Nasser flooded the place. Up on deck we took a closer look and saw that moored to one side was an old-style paddle steamer, real *Death on the Nile* stuff.

EWAN: We'd crossed a line of floating barrels that spanned the lake, the border I assumed, which meant we were now on Lake Nubia in Sudan, close to the port at Wadi Halfa. I could see the desert stretching away to the horizon. I knew that Sudan and Ethiopia, by their very terrain, would demand that we take more time.

We tied off at the grimy, oil-stained docks and there was the barge and our bikes and the trip was on again. Or at least we thought it was. It was 11.30 but by two p.m. we were still on the boat. We'd tried to get off but it was a rugby scrum and officials from Sudan made sure that despite the mass of heaving, sweating humanity it was paramount that a photocopier disembarked first. A couple of fuckwit cops were barking at everyone, really lapping up their bit of power. I retired to my cabin, somehow knowing we were in for the long haul. A few minutes later David appeared and informed me that the cops had got really irritated when they saw video cameras and word filtered through that they intended to take them off us. That was a little alarming. Charley came in shaking his head. 'This could be interesting,' he muttered.

Finally we did get off, cameras safe, and everything was unloaded. I noticed a couple of bull-nosed trucks already straining under the weight. It was five kilometres to the customs compound where the barge had docked and our vehicles were waiting. Along with about a hundred other people we jammed onto the bus. Sweat was pouring off us now, the heat like nothing I'd ever experienced; it had to be well into the forties.

At the customs yard we checked the bikes then settled down for the carnets to be worked through. I perched on a wall of rock, staring beyond the compound gates to a sand road that stretched into the distance. I had my scarf, my white keffiyeh, and I used it to shade me from the sun. Charley wandered over, sweat marking his jeans, and complained about a patch of damp on his bum.

'We need more wet wipes,' he joked.

'And an umbrella maybe. Remember in Ted Simon's book how he'd carry an umbrella and have a kip under the shade on his bike? He told us we should take umbrellas and we didn't listen.'

There were two massive customs sheds, lots of men in blue uniforms and one man who spoke English wearing long robes and a headscarf like the boat captain. He was an older guy and he smiled a lot, asking our names and shaking hands. It was almost six by the time we were finished and even then we weren't free to leave entirely: we had to come back in the morning for our passports and registration documents.

We went off to find a camp spot and I was thinking God, this is Sudan and a whole new chapter is opening up. We stopped to chat to some people, all of them incredibly friendly and the first two speaking English. Mambru wore a white cotton shirt and he asked me who I was and what we were doing. I told him my name was Ewan and we shook hands and I explained about Cape Town and Scotland. He wished us luck. I spoke to a couple of kids and then a wizened old fellow called Mohammed. He too spoke English and also wished us luck. Perfect, I thought; really good luck.

The road was hard sand, gravel almost, but I was a little discomfited when I noticed all the vans had sand rails fixed on the sides; they use them to get out of deep sand and the sight of them was less than inspiring.

CHARLEY: We camped beside one of the few hills dotted across the land. Apart from that it was sun-baked sand, rolling out endlessly in all directions. I'd been told that the road was dirt most of the way to Khartoum and that was nearly eight hundred miles. I couldn't wait to get started. First though, I adjusted the suspension settings on the bikes to make sure we had the play we needed, then reduced the tyre pressures. I hadn't decided whether to put my tent up or sleep on one of the bivouac bed mats as Ewan was planning. Dai, however, already had a hammock slung between the bull bars of the two Nissans and he was lying back clutching an inflatable sheep.

I burst out laughing. Russ came alongside, shaking his head sadly. 'A Welshman and a sheep,' he said. 'We should have thought about that.'

'Have you met Barbara, Charley?' Dai was in fits. 'I was keeping her till morale got low but . . . Anyway, she's ready and . . . We're going to snuggle up together later.'

I spoke to my dad on the phone. He was in good spirits having got the go-ahead for a film called *Hadrian's Wall* (those Romans again). He's such a talented guy and I was delighted for him. The sun went down, and gazing across open land I saw it disappear behind a mountain, its smooth sides suddenly serrated. This was it; sand tracks all the way to Khartoum, the Nile Road and who knew what we would encounter. A new adventure was beginning, and with it came a rush of excitement: sun, sand and sweat.

'Bring it on,' I muttered.

15
The Sand in Sudan

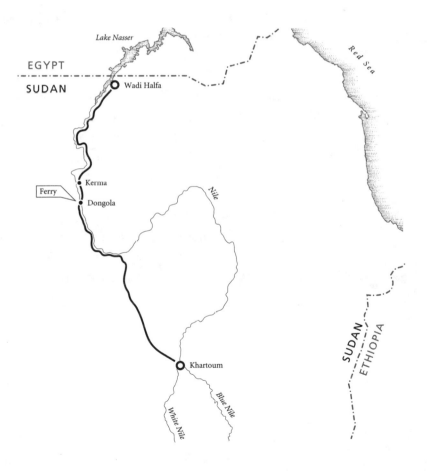

CHARLEY: I was up early and itching to get riding. No sooner were we on the bikes than Ewan hit deep sand. His front wheel started to wash out and he tried to save it. He almost did but the bike went down and he was off.

'Better here than out there,' I told him.

'Right.' He was checking the bike. 'My least comfortable surface, Charley. The only sand I remember is the beach in Wales when the police chased us off.'

'Remember what I told you: lean back on the pegs, dump the clutch and use the throttle. Look ahead as far as you can and if you get in trouble throttle your way out. If you come to deeper sand then lean back a little more. Oh, and avoid the tyre tracks. Always go virgin; once you get in the wheel ruts you'll be stuck. Cut across them to get to the smoother stuff.'

I really felt for Ewan. To put things in their proper perspective I'd trained for a year before I did the Dakar. Ewan doesn't even ride off-road for a hobby; he just overcomes his fears and gets on with it. If he falls off he gets back on again. Sand is different from any other surface, really hard to judge and you either love it or hate it. Ewan hates it, but hats off to him because he was in the saddle and sliding the back end all the way to the hard stuff.

We said goodbye to our fellow travellers Dave and Amelia, dealt with what we had to at customs and then we were off. Finally. God, it was hot, not much after nine and really beginning to boil. We weren't wearing jackets, just the inners with the armour attached and for the first time we were sporting knee braces. Standing on the pegs was tiring and the braces give support to the joint, stop it hyperextending when you're bouncing around all day.

We were headed for Dongola where we would cross the Nile and I can't tell you how good it felt to be off-road. I was enjoying myself immensely and it was cooler now we were on the move, of course, a little wind to ripple the old clothing. I played around, weaving this way and that, sliding from one side to the other looking for the smoothest line. The scenery was incredible – vast and empty, a sand-filled nothingness, it was beautiful. We had day after day on this stuff and had to look after the bikes so I found a nice smooth line right on the edge of the sand.

The road was barely discernible; the only demarcation the slight rise at the edges, otherwise it was the same colour, the same texture almost, as the rest of the scenery – a dusty floor that went for miles in every direction. Above it a sky so clear it looked as though it was melting.

Dust lifted in front of me: a truck, they were few and far between on this road. I came on it pretty quickly, weaving from right to left to try and figure out where it was exactly then keeping my thumb pressed to the horn. I checked my mirrors for Ewan.

EWAN: I think I'd already drunk most of the water in my camel pack. There's a tube attachment and you bite down then suck the liquid up. It was a good job we were carrying plenty in the panniers because we'd be supping it up all day.

I'd started well, hadn't I?

I've never pretended to be an expert in the sand and I don't mind admitting I'm not comfortable. Charley was great, though; helping me out and passing on the advice that had served him so well. I was doing it now, up on the pegs and leaning back and watching the road instead of my front wheel.

I'd been sorry to say goodbye to Dave and Amelia and I wished them well and hoped Amelia would be OK in Darfur. Hanging out with them was the nearest I'd get to backpacking, a gap year if you like; and it was great talking to them.

Maybe a slow speed crash early on was actually not such a bad thing, I decided. I was unhurt, the bike undamaged and my confidence undiminished. I'd just drifted too far right and into some big dips. I made it through the first couple then instead of throttling on I eased up. The steering went, a big wobble, and the weight of the bike tipped it over.

This was fantastic: truly Lawrence of Arabia country. I half expected Peter O'Toole to come riding across the valley on a camel. The knee braces felt secure, though they were creating a little extra heat. The road at least was hard – compact sand and grit – and much easier than the spongy stuff. I was used to the feel of the front now and was confident that with care it wouldn't wash away without some warning at least. I followed Charley past the truck and Claudio followed me. We were climbing; the look of the country very different here, the sand was changing colour and there were more rocks. It was infinite, so very empty; emptier than anything we'd seen in Libya.

The road felt like a washboard, narrow ruts running across, it was a real boneshaker. I could feel the bike begin to vibrate and made a point of staying loose and relaxed. We climbed higher and up on the pegs I could feel my feet burning – really hot like they were being boiled in a bag. The discomfort however was negated by where we were; it made me tingle just to look around me.

Ahead I saw Charley wobble, on his arse, his feet were off the pegs. Seconds later I was on the same patch of loose stuff. The bike wagged its head savagely but I held my nerve and kept the throttle open. Yes! I was through, adrenalin pumping, suddenly exhilarated.

Fifty yards further Charley pulled to the side. 'Claudio's down,' he said.

I looked round sharply and saw Claudio's bike lying on its side and pointing back the way we had come. He was on his feet, though, thank God.

'Typical.' Charley had his helmet off and started walking back. 'He always did like to crash in spectacular style.'

When we got to him Claudio was checking the patch of sand. 'I was too close to you,' he stated matter-of-factly. 'I didn't see it. Look, it's so fine, it looks like concrete dust, really.'

'Fesh fesh,' Charley said. 'Really deep fine sand. It just sucks you in and there's nothing you can do about it.'

'Are you all right, Claudio?' I asked him.

'Fine.' He slapped his right thigh. 'I landed here. The bike though, she's looking in the other direction so I don't know what happened.'

'You're lucky you're not hurt,' Charley commented gently. 'That was fast, Clouds, could've been really nasty.'

Claudio had broken the camera leads on his helmet and his panniers were bent. He'd scraped the guards on the engine casing and I noticed the bottom of one of the panniers was shredded.

'It's a nasty bit of sand right enough,' I said. 'Are you sure you're OK?'

'I'm fine. It's astonishing it doesn't hurt you any more, though, falling off like that.' He shrugged. 'When it got soft I gave it more power but it didn't help.'

Typical Claudio, he just took it in his stride. But we'd been shifting along and it must've really spat him off. I know what a crash does to you psychologically, especially a big one.

Charley looked at the bike, checking for any damage other than what was obvious. But there didn't seem to be any, the controls were all working, the fluid reservoirs intact. Taking a big rock he set about knocking the really bent pannier back into shape and pretty soon the lid fitted and we were ready to get going.

'Are you sure you're OK, Claudio?' I asked him again.

'I'm fine.' He was holding his tank bag. 'This is broken though.'

I looked closer and saw that the fixings that held it had sheared off.

'It didn't survive the crash,' he said. 'Never mind, we have cable ties.'

CHARLEY: We had to shift the bikes off the road before we fixed the tank bag because a bloody great double-decker was on its way and kicking up another cloud of dust. Claudio, of course, was back on the bike as if nothing had happened and riding along at the same pace like the trouper he is. I hoped his confidence hadn't been knocked too much; it was horrible to have that kind of feeling. It had been a warning, though, and with the dust and sand flying up, we had to keep a good distance from each other from now on. I'd had enough trouble with the fesh fesh and I was leading.

We came to a construction town; or should I say a few flat-roofed buildings in the middle of absolutely nowhere. There were tankers dotted around operated by a group of road workers who came out as soon as they heard the bikes. The section manager – the only guy wearing a hard hat – spoke English. He didn't look Sudanese, he looked Indian. He sounded Indian too, and told us his name was Mohammed. He invited us to join the men for lunch. Leaving the bikes, we ate bread and cheese and a tin of sardines apiece. Everyone wanted their picture taken. Before we left, Mohammed told us about construction further along the road and to be aware of both vertical and horizontal curves. I wasn't quite sure what he meant exactly but he said they were very dangerous.

We hit the road again and the heat was all but unbearable. I knew we couldn't ride like this, not day after day. I decided that tomorrow we needed to be away at first light and when the sun was at its highest we had to be off the bikes and in the shade drinking plenty of water.

We took our time, rode and stopped, rode and stopped, and around four we came to a tiny village made up of a couple of white stone houses and a sort of lean-to with a cloth curtain. There were three trees grouped together casting shadows on the otherwise parched ground. Ewan swung his bike into the shade and took his helmet off.

One of the buildings was a shop with an open front where mats were laid and a man in a white shirt was resting. Another couple of guys were lounging around; kids playing all about. When they saw us they came running over. They dipped wooden bowls into chipped terracotta urns that held drinking water. At the back of the shop was a chest fridge containing cans of soft drinks. We sat on the mat with the others, too hot for anything else, Ewan sipping every now and again from a can. 'You can't prepare for this,' he said, 'not this kind of heat. There's no way you could except maybe by riding your bike in an oven.'

After a while we went back to the trees and another group of kids came over. Dark-haired and bright-eyed, they sat and watched us, eating watermelon. Ewan glanced from them to me and back again. 'You want to see if can get us some melon, Charley?' he suggested.

I followed the boys to a house and found their mother squatting on the floor with her back to the wall; she was wearing robes and a shawl around her head. She too was eating melon. Normally the women we came across shied away from the camera, but not this one. She positively revelled in it, pushing the shawl away from her face and showing her best side. She indicated for me to help myself to the slices of melon that lay cut up in a bowl on the floor.

'Thank you,' I said. 'Thank you very much.'

She just smiled again, sat back and offered her face to the camera.

Back in the shade we ate the melon; cool and dripping, it was delicious. 'This is the hottest place I've ever been,' Ewan told me. 'And that road just now – like a washboard.'

'Yeah,' I said. 'We have to find the smoothest line, try and save the suspension.'

After a while he spoke again: 'I can't believe these trees. How does that happen? They must water them, I suppose. They're the first trees I've seen since we've been here.'

'Yeah, I know. You'd think there'd be more. We're supposed to be really close to the Nile here but I haven't seen it. It's just desert. If this is the Nile Road we might as well have taken the other one.'

EWAN: Back on my bike I was into the ruts, the road much nastier than before. It rattled bones; my legs were aching, my arms, the small of my back. The crosswise ridges were deeper, more uneven and they covered the whole road. I don't know how they get there, trucks or something, but it felt like the earth itself had shifted. I was being battered around like a football and when I talked I sounded like I was gurgling.

There was apparently some disruption in the camp and it really pissed me off; for Christ's sake this trip wasn't about our petty grievances, it was about the experience of Africa. My mood dipped considerably, not helped by the road. It was a shame because that last place had been wonderful. I'd been enjoying today, we'd been off on our own, and though Claudio had had a nasty crash he hadn't been hurt. We'd been on top of things, but now the road was shaking the shit out of me and we had this other business to contend with. Fuck this road, it was like being on corrugated iron. I was puffing and panting, so hot I couldn't believe it.

CHARLEY: Jesus, it was tough, a baking wilderness and I was going through water like you wouldn't believe. But we'd been having a great day up until now and I'd found a comfortable niche riding the soft stuff where the lip curled into the sandy edge of the road.

We were climbing again, the land getting rougher, more rocks and closer to the road. I saw Ewan in my mirrors bouncing around like a horseman trapped in a trot. That wasn't right; sweat was pouring off him, the bike smashing into the ruts so hard I could almost hear it.

Something was wrong.

He pulled up shaking his head and we took a look at the back of his BMW. The springs around the shock absorber were compressed, the adjustment knob cracked.

'Fuck it, Ewan,' I said. 'Your suspension is shot.'

We were in forty-eight degrees of heat, blazing sunshine by the side of the road and there was no sign of Claudio. He'd ridden on to set up a shot and he doesn't use his mirrors. Ewan was still inspecting the shock. 'It's completely collapsed,' he said. 'I can't ride like this, Charley. It'll wreck the bike.'

'We'd better try and get hold of Claudio and get him back here,' I said. 'Good on him, though, for carrying on. That fall didn't faze him in the slightest.'

Ewan tried calling him on the sat phone but there was no answer. 'We'd better tell the others,' he said.

I was pointing to a bunch of rocks. 'Let's move to the shade, they'll still be able to see us.'

'Just let me get through first.'

He spoke to Jimmy Simak and told him what had happened. 'Tell him we've got a spare shock absorber,' I said.

'Spare?' He looked incredulous. 'You put one in?'

I nodded. 'Last minute, I saw it and chucked it in. I don't know why, I didn't think we'd ever use it. It's the original BMW,' I told him. 'By the way, they're going to love this, aren't they?'

'Yeah, they are.'

He was right. We only changed the shocks in the first place because Ohlins had such a good reputation. Ewan told Jimmy where we were and we shifted the bikes to the shade.

'Not a great day, Charley,' Ewan stated a little bitterly.

'No, started well. This morning was good.'

'It was all good until four o'clock.'

Claudio got back just as the others arrived. He had indeed gone on for a shot and had been setting up but of course we didn't show up. The trucks found us and Jim came up with his tool kit. I noticed David was particularly quiet, a little apart, not his normal self at all. There was nothing I could do about it and in a way I was sort of glad we had a problem to solve.

Taking a considered look now I found the seals on the shock had blown and the nitrogen had been lost. There was no compression and the springs sagged; it must have been like riding an old hardtail across a river bed. No wonder Ewan was complaining of a rick in the small of his back.

He lifted the wheel while Jim and I took the seat off. Russ

climbed on top of the truck and dug around in the boxes until he found the spare shock absorber.

EWAN: Charley's a star. He'd been brilliant all day; not worried about the route or the pace we were travelling. I know he can ride three times as fast as me on this kind of stuff yet he pootles along never making me feel like I'm not up to it. Not only that, he was fixing my bike. I don't know why. I could have done it – it was me who replaced the shock with the Ohlins in the first place. But it was like something off the Dakar, he and Jim attacking the thing like a pit crew.

I had a word with David and he was very withdrawn. I really felt for him. It seemed that he and Russ were really getting it in the neck on this trip.

Charley and Jim got the new shock absorber fitted and the bike back together. We prepared to ride to a camp spot that our Sudanese fixer, Amir, said was particularly beautiful. He had a cook with him, something we'd never had before, and I was looking forward to some properly prepared food. Having said that, Russ and Charley thought we should talk the situation through all together and I have to say my guts were churning at the prospect.

Charley came over sucking a bottle of water.

'Hard day,' I said. 'More politics. Some might call it a chimp's tea party.'

'Yeah, a bit too much drama-queening going on. It'll blow over.'

With my bike feeling sound again I rode the few kilometres to a high plateau sheltered by a hill of black rock, lying in slabs like chunks of liquorice. The sand was a wonderful colour, a burnt yellow with boulders mottling it like little islands. Looking back I noticed Claudio lurching along as if his bike was about to fall over.

One glance at the back wheel told us all we needed to know:

his suspension was shot as well, the springs all but fused together. The second shock absorber to go and we had no more spares. I shook my head, reminded now of the last trip when Claudio's bike had to be freighted to Ulan Bator and he rode that little Russian motorbike we nicknamed the Red Devil.

Russ clicked into gear; problem-solving is his forte, and he's really good at it. I hoped that this new crisis might put things into perspective for everyone and shove any lingering emotional crap to one side.

Claudio was muttering: 'I can't believe the suspension has gone on two of the bikes in one day.'

Charley's bike seemed OK but then again we had no way of knowing whether it really was or whether it was about to die on us as well. He was the best rider, though, and always found the smoothest line. But we were still two hundred miles from Dongola and Claudio couldn't ride his bike so he'd have to go in the car. This really was one of our more eventful days. Russ was in his element, however – shirt off, phone out, he was taking care of business.

Off the phone momentarily he came over. 'Right,' he said. 'We'll get a truck from somewhere and load Claudio's bike onto it. He can ride in one of the cars. Charley, we get the weight off your bike and hope the suspension lasts. I've been on the phone for spares but we can't get them to Khartoum till Sunday at the earliest and even then there'll be customs issues.' He scratched his head. 'I've not figured the details exactly yet because we can't get visas for anyone to fly in from London.'

'So what do we do?' I asked him.

'Don't know yet. I'm working on it with Lucy back at the office. Now,' he went on, 'Amir reckons we can get someone out here with a truck and load up Claudio's bike either tonight or tomorrow. I'll go with him and get that organised. We can get the bike to Khartoum or, if there's a problem with spares, all the way to the Ethiopian border. Is that all right with you, Ewan. You and Charley on your own with Clouds in the car?'

'It's fine with me,' I said.

'OK, good. We'll be back.' With that he and Amir climbed into the Nissan and headed off down the basin.

I drilled some holes in my boots to try and reduce the heat. I was wearing solid off-road ones because I wanted the security after breaking my leg. When they were fully ventilated I left them and climbed the hill – mindful of scorpion burrows given I was in bare feet. I wanted some peace and quiet and I wanted to soak up the atmosphere. I love the desert; it's so beautiful and inspiring. I walked to the top of the rise and when I made the crest I stared out towards the horizon. Breathtaking. The sand drifted among volcanic boulders; a savage, staggering beauty, barren and uncompromising. Below me the trucks, the camp, the people seemed so small, petty almost, insignificant in the enormity of this place. I realised that if we weren't careful the personalities were in danger of overtaking the trip. I was sure that the best way forward was for everyone to concentrate on where we were and why we were here.

CHARLEY: What an amazing few hours. I walked away from the camp to watch my sunset. It was becoming a habit but then there's nothing like the sun going down on an African horizon.

It had been a good day despite the setbacks, but then as we'd so often been told it's the interruptions, the incidents, that create the journey. Ewan had been terrific after his spill, riding well in conditions he hardly favoured and Claudio was stoic as ever. For the first time the roads had been really challenging and it was kind of cool to know that if the need had arisen I could have blatted along at full chat. I would do the Dakar again. I had decided that for certain now. I had unfinished business and this was merely a taster.

My thoughts were interrupted by Russ coming back, a pair of headlights sweeping the desert floor. He and Amir had found a village and persuaded someone to come out with a truck. The chap only had a small pickup but Russ thought we'd get the bike on the back without too much trouble.

'Now as far as spares are concerned,' he said, 'I've been on the phone again and apparently people from Tanzania can fly into Khartoum, so we're getting someone from there to meet Robin.' Robin was one of our production co-ordinators. 'He's flying to Cairo with spare shocks and he can give them to our man from Tanzania. He can then fly them into Khartoum for us.'

'Fucking hell,' Ewan said. 'How did you organise that?'

'Not me, Lucy thought of it. Good old Luce.'

Then he showed us the Nissan, roof rack askew and a dent in the bonnet. 'The bad news is the roads we're hitting tomorrow are worse than what you were just on, at least for a good few miles anyway.'

He told us that they'd dipped into a deep rut so hard he thought they'd smashed the front. The roof rack worked loose, shunting forward six inches, the ladder was bent and the spare wheels fell off, whacking the bonnet and almost smashing the windscreen.

'Christ,' Ewan said. 'If Charley's suspension goes I could end up riding on my own.'

'Don't worry,' I told him, 'I'm going to nurse that puppy all the way to the tarmac.'

EWAN: That first day we'd only managed to get sixty miles south. The next day, once Claudio's bike had been shipped out, we put 120 under our belts and were completely wasted by the end of it. For some reason I'd woken up today not really looking forward to the ride. Weird, because apart from the last ten minutes or so I'd really enjoyed yesterday's ride: it had been hot and hard but I'd only peeled off in the really deep stuff, the fesh fesh as Charley calls it. Tonight we'd camp on our own.

I'd miss the cooking; this idea of someone preparing our meals was great and I was sure that's what happened on bigger expeditions. It was hardly hardcore but I didn't care, particularly when the chef was Sudanese and bloody brilliant. Charley suggested we throw him on the back of one of the bikes or have the fixer follow us lock, stock, and barrel, leaving the support crew to their boil-in-the-bags. They were having none of it, of course, so we thought about a call from the satellite phone, a takeaway in the desert. It wasn't going to happen, though in the spirit of goodwill Russ did take our order.

Last night the trucks had got stuck in the sand. I'd been unpacking my bike when I saw David sinking, and then Dai, trying to get it out, dug it in even deeper. Jim came in with the green truck to give them a tow and he got stuck too. I heard Russ yell out that they should use the winch. That went down well given he was sitting up in the rocks with Charley, though he was probably right.

With the problems of the dead camera bike taking over, the situation between David and Jim had settled down, thank God. They'd had a heart-to-heart and that seemed to clear the air. Fine by me; I never was one for group therapy and we'd managed to avoid it.

Charley and I rode out like the desperados we thought we were – him one way and me another until we realised our mistake and I dropped my bike as I tried to back down a hill. A great start and unfortunately the shape of things to come.

I caught up with him, though, and we headed off together, the trail every bit as atmospheric as it had been last night. But twenty minutes out I realised I'd forgotten the phone. So it was back to camp, grab it and off we went once more.

Finally we were off by ourselves, hard sand and gravel under the wheels. We passed kids who waved and shouted; all smiles and laughter. Last night a couple had ridden into the camp on a beautiful grey donkey; they were carrying a spray of wild dates still green and hard; sweet enough but not how you eat them at Christmas. Everyone in this country had been so friendly; it was hard to conceive that such horrors as Darfur were occurring only a few hundred miles north-west.

It was also hard to believe we were still north of Dongola and, like the lake in Mongolia on Long Way Round, getting there had become something of a mission. We had to make it and yet the closer we got the further away it always seemed to be.

We met a few cyclists on the road; a couple from Switzerland had joined us for lunch yesterday. We had been amazed to learn they'd been on the road for nine years. They were only heading home now because the woman's parents were elderly and needed looking after. They'd met in 1994 on separate bike trips in Argentina, of all places.

They had just come from Ethiopia and told us we'd have to watch for kids chucking stones. They told us they'd been hit a couple of times. We'd seen it here; now and then a bunch of kids would run into the road and lob the odd rock as we were passing. They also told us that the Kenyan roads had been a nightmare, deep gravel a lot of them. That was all I needed. I hate sand but at least when you pitch off it's a relatively soft landing.

Soon my early lack of enthusiasm lifted and I was riding along quite comfortably. Then I heard a clunk from under the bike. I thought it was the suspension again and my heart missed a beat. The next thing I knew the power dipped and the engine stopped completely.

CHARLEY: I was still thinking about food. A takeaway seemed like a great idea: phone up with the order and give them the GPS coordinates then sit back and wait for the delivery. Not going to happen, Charley, not going to happen.

I was looking forward to Khartoum, a name full of resonance and where the White Nile merged with the Blue. We planned to get there tomorrow afternoon.

I was a little concerned about how my shock would hold up; I had weight on the bike again today. We had a good way to go and it looked like the same kind of washboard we'd been on since Wally hazbeen.

Ewan was behind me when his bike conked out. I saw him stop in my mirrors and pulled over.

He told me he'd heard a bang and then the engine stopped. He said his heart was in his mouth as he thought the suspension had blown and he'd be squashed in a truck all the way to Khartoum.

Checking the bike, though, we saw it wasn't the suspension. A rock had smashed the sensor that tells the bike when the side stand is down. It's a safety device and as soon as you engage a gear the bike stops. With the sensor smashed the computer thought the stand was down.

The bike would start in neutral but if Ewan stepped on the gear lever it died. We looked over the assembly trying to see if there was a connection we could undo, tracing cable up towards the engine until we found one.

Ewan uncoupled it and tried the bike; it started fine but again died as soon as he put it in gear. We were in a bit of a spot; neither of us sure what to do. There was no shade here and it was blistering.

It was lucky we'd gone back for the phone: it meant we could call Steve, our mate from BMW in the UK. He was on his way to work and Ewan explained the situation. After a brief discussion he hung up then cut the sensor off completely. He stripped the cabling and exposed the wires. Red, white and brown, he twisted them together.

But the bike still wouldn't go.

We went back to Steve. He was at work now with another GS1200 in front of him and was trying to figure out why it wouldn't work. Meanwhile we were at the side of the road in Sudan. Crazy, really; as mad as Russ calling the RAC from Libya. While Steve was mulling it over I suggested to Ewan that maybe the brown wire was an earth and it was only the red and white we needed to twist. He was up for giving that a go but I was worried we might short the computer or something. We waited for Steve to call back and when he did he told us to twist just the red and white wires together. It used to be all three, he said, but now the brown was only there to earth the connection.

Bingo. Wires twisted, the engine went and we were off and running.

EWAN: Thank God for that, I really did have visions of being stuck in the car. Christ, it would've been a nightmare.

We were back on the desert road, weaving across the deep ruts, looking for the best line. An hour or so later we closed on the river, the sudden abundance of palm trees indicating its presence. Helmets off we made our way through the bulrushes and there she was, the sun on her back and flowing very fast . . . the wrong way.

'I'm serious,' Charley said. 'Isn't it supposed to be going the other way? It flows *to* Cairo surely, not from it.'

I didn't know, but it did look as though the current was going the wrong way, but that might have just been the wind gusting.

And then it hit me as sometimes these things just do.

'Charley,' I said. 'Do you realise you've ridden your motorbike all the way from John O'Groats to the Nile? What do you think about that?'

'Fucking stupid. What do we want to do that for?'

He started singing Madness songs and I gazed across the water to where an old fort dominated the headland. With grey stone battlements it looked like something from the time of Christ.

I looked at my feet. 'Can you see any crocs?' I said. 'This river's supposed to be teeming with them.'

Charley shaded his eyes from the sun. 'Why don't you throw yourself in and find out?'

Just love him, don't you?

We stopped for lunch in a town called Kerma, where kids were unloading melons from a donkey cart and old men sat in the shade drinking water from massive urns placed beneath the trees. We washed our hands using a tap on a barrel and ate rice and vegetables together with a sort of bean curry.

The Swiss couple yesterday weren't the only people we met – we'd spoken to a Japanese guy on his way north from Cape Town – but the coolest thing had been early yesterday. We were riding along the dirt road in the middle of the desert when up ahead we saw a cyclist approaching, towing a little trailer. Charley was leading and pulled over. The guy just cycled up, nonchalant as you like. 'Mr McGregor, I presume,' he said.

Charley told him he'd got us mixed up, but the guy'd been on the road thirteen years so you can hardly blame him. His name was Jason Lewis and he'd left Greenwich in 1994 – just when the Swiss couple were meeting for the first time. He was on his way around the world using human power only. He'd had a mate with him to begin with but he bailed out in Hawaii. They'd crossed the Atlantic in a pedal boat, then the USA on roller blades and another pedal boat to cross the Pacific. Right now Jason was heading for Wozzi hazzer and the lake. If he got permission he planned to kayak all the way to Aswan. It was amazing really, thirteen years – a record among the road-weary we'd met to date.

After lunch we got back on the bikes and headed out of Kerma. We were looking for the way to Dongola and, on the back roads where we'd been directed, we hit deep sand. We were still in the town with kids and donkeys and cars coming at us from all directions. My front wheel took on a life of its own and I could feel myself tensing up badly. My worst fear was hitting a child and here I was sliding everywhere in the middle of a town. Fuck, I hate sand. Really, I fucking hate it.

I managed to make it beyond the buildings without hitting anyone but back on the open road I had two or three falls. I just couldn't gauge the surface and the wheel would twist and shake me off the bike. I tried to implement all that Charley had told me about leaning back and powering on, but it all felt so alien to my body. I found myself stiffening up and as soon as that happened I was off. Picking up the bike in this heat was strength-sapping and I was becoming very tired very quickly. We rode on and I was OK for a while, my confidence slowly returning and gradually picking up speed. Then I just lost the front and the bike slapped down on its side.

It was a big spill, my foot catching under a pannier, the bike up on its wheels again to crash down on the other side. It really shook me up. It was only recently that I'd broken my leg and until you break something you don't actually realise that you break, if you see what I mean. Sitting there on the ground I had an 'I want to go home moment'. Who was I kidding riding through Africa? I just wasn't good enough, not experienced enough to judge where I could put the bike. Charley was really patient and very encouraging and I thought about Claudio the other day, how he just got back on. So I picked myself up, hauled the bike upright and rode on. If this was the only way to gain experience so be it.

CHARLEY: I really felt for him. Riding on roads like these is hard enough without coming off. Ewan must have fallen five or six times and pretty soon he was exhausted. That's what saps you, not just your energy but your confidence, your resolve, the will to continue. He looked knackered but he didn't complain – just carried on regardless. I really admired him for it.

Finally we hit tarmac and oh, did the black stuff feel good. It was nice to use sixth gear for a change, and for a few miles at least we were hauling ass. Of course it was too good to be true and pretty soon we were back on hard sand, sweeping south with the road forking every so often.

We went the wrong way.

We started heading inland and, given there was a car ferry at Dongola, we knew we should be closer to the river. Ewan was ahead, on the pegs and negotiating the corrugated stuff really well. A car came by and I flagged it down, yelled Dongola at the driver whilst pointing the way we were going.

'No, no. Dongola.' He pointed back the way we had come.

Ah shit. I set off after Ewan. He was really motoring now and

I had to pin it to catch up then get his attention by hitting the horn incessantly.

'I thought so,' he told me when we stopped. 'It didn't feel right, did it?'

After an eight-mile excursion we finally rode into the sandy town, wide streets and single storey buildings, cars and trucks all over the place. I was following my nose, the smell of the river and finally we came to the quay where cars were lined up waiting for the ferry. The boat was midstream and we parked the bikes alongside old Peugeots and battered pickups to wait. Everyone was dressed in white, most wearing some kind of turban, a couple of drivers squatting side by side at the edge of the water.

The boat docked and the cars backed on and it was only when we were half way across that Ewan pointed out the cars were now facing the right way and us the wrong way.

We met a lad from England, Tom Wilson, who'd been working his way north from Cape Town. His sunglasses were broken, one arm missing, but he wore them anyway. He drank water neat from the Nile, no purifier or anything to kill bugs. He said he was all right on it. He was glad to talk to us because travelling alone could be lonely and he'd not had a decent conversation in weeks. It wasn't long till he returned to the UK now, though, and he was looking forward to a ham sandwich and packet of ready salted crisps.

He filmed us leaving the boat and riding up to the heaving market where people and cars, donkeys and camels mingled in one monstrous mêlée. We wished Tom well and hoped he enjoyed his sandwich and then we left him. It was really nice to meet up with other travellers, find out who they were and what they were doing. Generally they were coming the other way and could give us the lowdown on the condition of the roads. According to Tom it was tarmac most of the way to Khartoum.

It was mid-afternoon now and the hottest part of the day. We parked under some palm trees and rested, Ewan really hanging after being on and off the bike for much of the day. He was still there, though, no one was carrying him and he was more worried that he was holding me up.

'Mate,' I told him, 'the pace is irrelevant. We're going the pace we're going and we're seeing the country.'

'I just can't deal with the sand.' He was beating himself up again. 'I can't get used to the steering wobble and just powering through. The only thing keeping me upright is the thought of Claudio the other day.'

'Your crash just now was as bad,' I told him. 'You're doing the same.'

'But we've got deep gravel to come.'

'Not till Kenya. And it'll be fine. Remember in Russia, bits of Mongolia; we had that deep stuff. We started out about five or ten miles an hour and in the end we were doing sixty-five.'

EWAN: He was right, but in this heat and being this weary I didn't feel any better. We'd had our first really strange encounter a little while back. We'd been fixing a loose tank bag when they came up and were yapping away, touching our stuff and one of them had his hand actually in Charley's bag. Very strange and in your face when up until then everyone had been so friendly.

We were thinking of calling it a day and finding somewhere to camp. We'd seen some open shelters in a couple of the towns and I thought we could throw our sleeping bags down and be close to the bikes. The river was relatively nearby, though (or so we thought), just the other side of a small town, so we headed over that way to see what we could find. The answer was nothing really; the town a bit fleabitten and passing beyond we made for the palms and a spot down by the river. We got to the green stuff and the trail wound on but there was no sign of the water. There were massive thorns everywhere, big enough to puncture tyres. The river was still about half a mile away.

'Let's go back to the road,' I said, 'bimble on a bit and find a quiet spot.'

Charley agreed and we swung round and headed back the way we had come.

We camped on what looked like moon rock or the ocean bed; a dune of pebbles sheltering us from the road and nothing to break up our horizon but the bikes and setting sun. We were thirty kilometres south of Dongola and we spoke to the others; still on the road and about to stop for the night. We needed petrol and we'd hook up with them in the morning somewhere. We cooked boil-in-the-bag food, and talked about riding in sand and falling off; we talked about our wives and kids and home. I really admired people like Tom, Dave and Amelia; people who took off on their own with no satellite phone or back-up and no one to call when they met trouble.

The following morning we were back on shiny black tarmac. Yee-haw! I loved it, smooth as butter after the trials of yesterday. Don't get me wrong, I enjoyed the challenge and we'd have plenty more to deal with before we got to Cape Town, but I do my riding on the road and I'm not even bothered about going that fast.

We were heading for Abu Dom and then Khartoum but we needed to get some petrol and intended to turn off the road at Ad Baba. The desert opened again; it was so varied and here it was yellow with a sort of burnt crust. We slowed to a stop as a herd of camels ambled across the scrub, the last one ridden by the herder. I lifted a hand and he came ambling over, an elegant man in a white peakless cap, sitting almost side-saddle with a quirt in his hand. He walked the beast into the middle of the road and sat there looking as if he could have come from any period in history. With nothing beyond him but desert it made for a great picture. We gave him water and tried to explain where we were going and then set off in search of petrol.

We found Ad Baba a little further on, another small Sudanese town with sand roads and square buildings, houses, shops, people milling around and children waving and smiling. The children were incredible. I thought back to the other day when Charley and I stopped for lunch and one little boy came up to me. Taking my hand he held it all the time he spoke to me. I didn't understand him, but he didn't realise and he chatted away wide-eyed and all the time kept his wee hand in mine. I managed to get him to tell a man who spoke some English what he was trying to tell me, and the man explained he just wanted me to know his name and where he lived, basically who he was. It was a special moment, the darkened interior of a Sudanese cafe; just me and the child. It reminded me how much I missed my own three girls.

CHARLEY: We'd had three hard days on the dusty stuff; even I was delighted with this delicious tarmac and we started to eat up the miles. Sometimes I think we forget how lucky we are. For the people out here a twenty-nine-hour bus ride at ten miles an hour, sitting on hard metal benches while others squat among your luggage on the roof, is normal.

We saw a few of those big buses crammed to the rafters. We also saw a lorry with a bunch of people sitting on the roof of the cab, their legs dangling down in front of the windscreen. Imagine the driver braking hard: they'd slide off and he'd run right over them; made me shudder just to think about it.

This was a real adventure now. What with all we'd been through since we left the boat, it felt like three weeks, never mind three days. The riding had been tough, the roads pretty nasty and I have to say it was great to be back on asphalt.

We passed a dead camel in the middle of the highway; recent road kill, maybe only moments before. It was stretched out; head tipped back as if its neck had been broken. The way the light was and with the flatness of the land it would have been so easy to come on it at speed and not see it. Fortunately truckers coming the other way waved at us to slow down.

I was looking forward to a shower; we'd not had one since Aswan and that was days ago. It was forty degrees and the dirt clung to me; sand in my hair, my eyes, itchy against my skin.

Past lunchtime and we came to Abu Dom – a sprawling

madness, an everlasting town that just seemed to go on and on. We were directed into a market place, where cars and vans and buses were all jammed together. I asked a tuk-tuk driver if it was the right way to go. He indicated another direction so off we went again and still the town went on. In the end we were pulling up at junctions and both of us yelling across at drivers, 'Khartoum? Khartoum?'

From Abu Dom it was pretty built up all the way, and as we came to the outskirts of Khartoum I noticed much newer cars and decent looking buildings, green spaces and no desert, walled gardens and parks even. There was a lot of construction, demolished buildings leaving sand and rubble and piles of bricks making way for new places to go up. We crossed the Nile on an old iron bridge with a soldier watching from a shelter beside the road. He was just sitting there with his 50-calibre machine gun, cool as you like, chilling out in the shade.

We were both tired now and the deeper we got into the capital the more excited I became. Ewan was full of it; the traffic, the roundabouts, the crazy mad junctions when the world and his wife seemed to be coming at you. Thank God for the traffic cops in white uniforms perched on their little islands.

Ewan yelled across how he loved cities and I knew what he meant – after three days in the desert it was great to be among so many people; the hubbub, the noise, even the smell of diesel. The skyline was dominated by a weird looking white building with mirrored glass. It reminded me of a sail or, as Ewan put it, a twisted egg: the Al-Fatih Hotel. It turned out we were staying in a hotel next door. We pulled up, parked the bikes and hauled our gear off. Ewan said he smelled like a badger's arse and went off to have a shower.

The following morning we wanted to film the place where the White Nile meets the Blue, so we grabbed Claudio and a camera and headed off to the Hilton Hotel. Apparently the best place to view it was from the hotel roof.

We arrived in a cab and were met by a guy in a yellow

With David and Russ – supporting us all the way.

Our boat trip across Lake Nasser to Sudan was a great chance to meet people and prepare for what would be one of the most challenging sections of the trip.

At the start of a long and arduous trek through the desert.

Afternoon tea, Sudan style.

It took a while to get used to riding on sand, but the desert landscape and the fantastic people we met along the way more than made up for it.

In Ethiopia – very green after the deserts of the Sudan. It was always the kids who were the most curious about us.

Believe it or not, this was one of the better stretches of road we encountered that day.

Fixing Claudio's shock absorber. By the end of the trip we could change one in about ten minutes flat.

Zalambessa, Ethiopia – near the Eritrean border. The first of our three UNICEF visits. We were given a tremendous welcome.

Thousands of mines were laid in this area during the war between Ethiopia and Eritrea. Here we are being shown the incredibly dangerous and painstaking task of de-mining a small patch of earth.

Tesfu lost his leg when he stepped on a mine that had been buried on his doorstep. He was determined not to let it destroy his life.

It was an emotional visit, but we left the village filled with hope for the future.

We spent a lot of time in Ethiopia, and were met with fantastic hospitality wherever we went. *(Above)* Charley gains a passenger and *(below)* a young woman roasts beans for our next coffee fix.

It rained a lot in Ethiopia, hence the umbrella.

Jimmy would often film from this position. He claims he didn't suffer from 'chafing', but we didn't believe him.

We exchanged mud roads in Ethiopia . . .

. . . for countless miles of rubble in Kenya.

The bikes were holding up but their riders were a bit worse for wear by this point.

We were lucky enough to be invited to spend the night with the Samburu Tribe – a fantastic experience.

Wet or dry – the conditions as we rode through Kenya were always challenging.

Two pivotal moments – *(above)* reaching the Equator, and *(below)* arriving at the Tropic of Capricorn with Claudio, the third amigo.

Ewan meets Lola,
a baby black rhino.

A new border crossing, from Kenya to Uganda.

We had an amazing day meeting school children with UNICEF in Gulu Amuru. Some were former child soldiers, and their stories affected us very deeply.

Don't try this at home.

SECURITY vest. We introduced ourselves, told him what we wanted to do and showed him the filming permits. He wasn't sure if we would be able to, but took us into reception.

We asked again and the two guys there didn't seem very sure; they were very friendly and had no problem with the camera but again asked to see our permits. They put us in touch with another guy in a yellow vest, complete with walkie-talkie. He inspected the permits then said we'd have to wait, so we sat down and ordered Turkish coffees.

Twenty minutes later he came back with an older man called Sami. He told us that there was a problem because the hotel was packed with government security men as the vice-president of Iraq was staying there.

Now we were beginning to understand.

Sami told us he'd have to speak to the general manager. Off he went and we waited and waited and finally the manager appeared. He explained the situation and said he'd see what he could do. We remained in reception and after a little bit more negotiation he came back and told us we could go up.

A few minutes later we were in the lift with another security man heading for the top floor. We came out and turned left, a large door facing us. Seated on a bench outside were two huge guys in dark suits who immediately got to their feet. Very deliberately they stepped in front of the door. We turned for the stairs with a nod and a smile, but they said nothing, their features blank, bulges under their jackets where their Uzis were slung. We found out that this year alone there have been twenty-seven attempts on the vice-president's life.

'Twenty-seven,' Ewan was aghast. 'Maybe they need to increase their security. I mean we walk in off the street, three guys they don't know, one with a camera and backpack. An hour later we're outside his door and not one of us has been searched.'

We had the roof and the view to ourselves. Although it was spectacular in its own way, it wasn't quite what we'd expected. There were two rivers, one a little muddier than the other, and there was a massive grassy island between them. I'd been told it was designated for a business suburb, all high rise and mirrored glass. But the confluence wasn't that special. I suppose we wanted blue water thundering into white. And crocodiles, lots of Nile crocs basking on the sandbanks. A romantic idea I know; this was a city, of course, and the only crocs we came across were the crocodile skin shoes worn by some the guests we'd seen downstairs.

16
Kalashnikovs & Customs

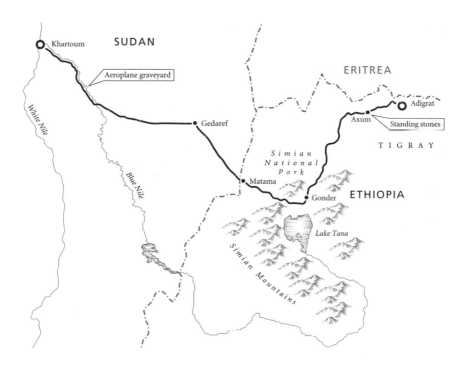

EWAN: After a week in Sudan the sound of rain rattling my tent was amazing. Earlier, lightning had struck in jagged bolts and thunder rumbled above us. Rain after so long, rain so heavy it would churn the ground into mush.

Yesterday in Khartoum I'd begun to think about the highlands. It would be cooler for sure which was a blessing – the average temperature this time of year in Sudan was forty-four degrees and in northern Ethiopia it was less than half that. I'd had enough of the heat and was looking forward to some cooler mountain air.

We rolled out of the city around two in the afternoon, the sweat sticking to me. Even on open road at sixty miles an hour there was no respite: normally I'd keep the visor on my helmet lifted and allow the wind to cool my face, but this wind was on fire, way worse than when we crossed into Libya. I've never felt anything like it; it sucked my energy and no matter how much I attacked the water in my camel pack I felt more and more dehydrated. I was feeling shitty generally; Charley too for that matter. Later he told me he could quite easily have thrown up his lunch. Never eat from a buffet, that's the old adage, isn't it; especially when it's a hotel buffet in the heat of Africa.

Three hundred and fifty miles to the border, tarmac all the way and I was keen now to get on with it. Yesterday we'd had a lazy afternoon and a relatively lazy morning, but I'd not got to bed before two a.m. and was awake at five thinking about Ethiopia and the pedestal status I'd apportioned it. Those cyclists had kept going on about kids chucking stones and for some reason now that bothered me. The Sudanese had been terrific, waves and hellos wherever we went and when we stopped they'd not crowd or hassle us at all. The north in particular had been great with those pretty sandstone towns and the magnificent brutality of the desert. I was less impressed down here, though, beyond Khartoum. It seemed there was just the road to the border and the manic men that drove it.

CHARLEY: I should have stayed in last night, gone to bed early and caught up on some sleep. Of course I didn't and I was knackered this morning and the heat wasn't helping. My hands were hurting: the injuries from Dakar. Day after day in the saddle it was beginning to take its toll. There's a nub of bone sticking down where I broke my left wrist. The surgeon welded it that way so I could ride a motorbike. It's fine most of the time but constant riding hour after hour and it really begins to ache. On top of that the muscle at the base of my other hand sort of seizes up and every now and then I have to reach across with my left to use the throttle. The weirdest thing I've noticed, though, is how I have so little strength in the ends of my fingers: it makes things like doing up buttons, or undoing my wife's bra, really awkward.

We wouldn't make the border tonight, it would be around lunchtime tomorrow, I reckoned. We were travelling south-east towards the town of Gedaref; the road straight and dusty, full of mad bus drivers and road trains, and trucks with enormous trailers hauling everything you can imagine.

The scenery was rocky, not much to look at until we came to an aeroplane graveyard. You know, like the proverbial elephant's graveyard only this one had planes in it. There were loads of them, ancient heaps that weren't rusting so much as shredding. The fuselage would be intact but the wings were peeling. The skin hung in strips that fluttered in the wind.

Amazingly we found a whole community living there; they had little shacks and fires dotted among the old aircraft. The planes were pretty old, different types – one had clearly been Russian. Ewan said they reminded him of the plane on *Casablanca*.

Climbing inside an old crop duster we found a life jacket discarded on the floor and a large internal tank with pipes leading off it. It was surreal: all these dead aeroplanes, their wheels overgrown by sand and those tatters of wings billowing in the wind. A group of men were sitting round a fire brewing tea. We shook hands with them and went back to the bikes. It struck me more forcefully than ever how so much of the world is nothing like what we're used to in the West. Most people live way below the poverty line. The things we take for granted just don't figure in their lives. I'd seen it in places like Kazakhstan and Mongolia and now I was witnessing it here.

The driving was getting worse, oncoming buses three abreast would bear down on us so hard we had no choice but to get out of the way. I began to wonder how many accidents there were on a road like this. It didn't take long to find out; a few miles further and we came upon two wrecked vehicles. There was a great crowd of people gathered beside them and stopping the bikes we asked what had happened. The accident had been earlier that morning and the people had been there ever since. They bunched around us, a hubbub of men having a great time talking up the crash. Using sign language we learned that the driver of a lorry (the cab of which no longer existed) had fallen asleep and careered into an ancient long-nosed truck coming the other way. Amazingly the driver didn't have a mark on him. The other truck was so badly smashed it was hard to imagine anyone surviving, yet it appeared no one had even been hurt. The weird thing was the trucks themselves though; they were so old the wreckage looked as if it had been there for years.

We were trying to find somewhere to camp and it was getting darker by the minute. We stopped at a village called Wadermazoo, or at least that's what an English-speaking brickmaker named Carlos told us. It wasn't a village on the map – rather one of many brickworks we'd seen this side of Khartoum. Carlos suggested we pitch our tents in their camp then checked with his boss. He said it was fine. But when we asked the Arab owner he wasn't having any of it.

No problem. We'd find somewhere further up the road – that's if we weren't wiped out by crazy drivers who got crazier still as darkness began to fall. We passed through a couple of small towns and were back on open highway with buses hammering by when the cops pulled us over.

They wanted to check our papers and the senior officer, a sergeant maybe, wanted to check out the bikes. Ewan and I were talking to another cop about where we might camp when we looked up and saw the top man sitting on Ewan's bike. Like an idiot I showed him how to start it and the next thing I knew he was high-tailing across the sand. Ewan looked on aghast but helpless: I mean what was he going to say? Hey, copper, get the fuck off my bike!

EWAN: Yeah, right. What was the worst that could happen? He'd drop it; well I'd done that plenty of times already. He brought it back safely enough and suggested we camp at their little compound, but I didn't want to sleep by the side of the road with a bunch of rozzers. They told us that a bit further along we'd come to a bridge, beyond which was a place where we could pull off.

It sounded great. Charley led until the lights were well behind us and a couple of miles later he turned off the road. We rode into the darkness and deeper into the desert. Hardcore camping, just the two of us: fantastic. We found a good spot away from the road and I could smell the Nile. Familiar now, I knew the river well – we'd crossed her many times since we landed in Egypt. Amazing – a month ago the Nile was the river of the pharaohs, now she was an old friend.

We were up with the sun and as we packed the bikes we saw we were being watched by a young man wearing a T-shirt with a sheet wrapped round him. Then a few more heads appeared and we discovered we were camped by another brickworks and decided to check it out. First the mud was hacked out of the ground, then softened and watered down. Then it was carried by wheelbarrow to a sort of rocky sink where it was pummelled and washed, then fashioned into blocks which were stacked to dry in the sun. Once dry they werc piled up and logs were lit, to fire them into bricks.

We were well beyond Gedaref now and heading towards the border. The land was greener with more hills, more trees and, in places, much rockier.

Monkey, monkey, monkey!

A troop of baboons crossed the road right in front of me. Now I knew we were heading south. First camels and now these little creatures; the changing wildlife an indication of just how far we'd come.

As we approached the border the country was greener still. We passed a dead cow and thatched huts with holes in the walls. I could see a metal arch ahead and a herd of goats crossing. We left Sudan, crossed into no man's land and ahead lay the village of Metema. I could see the Ethiopian flag, red, green and yellow, and above it someone had erected a banner: 'Welcome to Ethiopia Charley Boorman, Ewan McGregor and the Long Way Down team.' Our good luck just got better. I might have to talk to my agent about that billing, though.

As with every border everything suddenly changed. There was the smell of rain in the air, everywhere was green and the town was heaving with people. Everyone seemed to be on the street; on foot or riding donkeys or on little carts drawn by donkeys. The houses and shops were higgledy-piggledy and hunched together as if that was the only way they'd stay standing. They seemed to be made of everything you could imagine and were painted in bright colours, green and purple and red. The whole place seemed thrown together and was really vibrant, a real frontier town.

I realised that Sudan had been the colour of sand; the low, open towns blended into the landscape, everyone wore white, and whenever we'd stopped it was only the men who'd come over. It was an Islamic state and the women were covered and very much in the background. Here everyone came to see us: men, women, young boys and girls; the place had a tangibly freer feel to it.

At passport control – a mud hut painted green and purple with one wall of corrugated tin – we were entertained by a tiny girl in plaits and a pink T-shirt who laughed and laughed like a kookaburra. So much for stones, eh.

I shook hands with Charley. 'Well mate, here we are. We crossed the desert. Can you believe it? We crossed the fucking desert!'

'I know, I can't believe we survived the heat. Libya was nothing, was it, compared to that?'

And now it was night and hammering down with rain. The air was cool and refreshing after Sudan. It was so weird, I've said it before, but it really does seem as if with the lines drawn on a map the land almost knows when to change.

What I've not mentioned yet is that we were thirty kilometres from the border in a compound enclosed by barbed wire with three Kalashnikov-toting guards on the gate. They weren't there to keep people out; they were there to keep us in.

Getting through immigration had been simple, so easy in fact that David had tempted fate: 'This could be real quick guys,' he'd said. 'I mean real quick.'

We thought we were done and were about to get going when our Ethiopian fixer, Habtamu, explained that we'd been assigned an armed guard. He accompanied us to the next village and the customs compound. By the time we got there it was almost six and customs, of course, was closing. But they'd seen our carnets, how detailed they were and told us they wanted to make a thorough examination of our gear. Everything would have to come off the trucks. It would take hours and it would have to wait until tomorrow. So that was it, our first night in Ethiopia courtesy of customs men and Kalashnikovs.

17
A Cup of Ginger Tea

CHARLEY: It made me wonder about the carnets, whether in fact they were too detailed and that's why customs were so interested. Maybe if we had less on them we'd be through quicker, but as Ewan pointed out if they searched and found stuff not listed they might think we were trying to sell it.

Anyway, we were up at six and gone by ten – the usual four hours. The guard, the gun-for-hire, stayed; not with Ewan and me, but with the support crew. Apparently travellers needed an armed escort as far as Gonder.

We went on ahead, picking our way out of the village, careful to avoid the hundreds of people on the street; not just people, the cattle, goats, donkeys. I couldn't get over how different Ethiopia was; almost to the border Sudan had still been pretty arid and brushy, and any trees we saw had few leaves. Across the border the first thing I sensed, apart from the sudden swathe of colour, was rain.

It had rained all night and I'd been wondering how that would affect the roads. I've said it before, it takes a day or so to get to grips with how a new country works. Sudan had been dry and empty; this was mountainous, much cooler, with the world and his wife on the street.

The rain had stopped, but the cloud hung like a fog. We were back in our jackets now and after last night I had my waterproofs handy. We were heading for a town called Adigrat and eventually the Eritrean border. Tonight we'd camp at almost three thousand metres.

We were on a high plateau, the land green and cultivated. I could see farmers on their terraces trailing ancient hand ploughs behind teams of skinny oxen. The bulls had massive bow-shaped horns and I was reminded of Sean Connery at our place one time in Ireland. He was with my dad and they were injecting cattle when this bull just turned on him. Sean was knocked down and trampled, his ribs, his hand, his nose broken. He was tossed around a bit and he's a big bloke. I've had a healthy respect for bulls ever since. No doubt so has Sean.

The villages were so different from anything we'd seen in Sudan. Close to the border the houses were circular – a mesh of poles with wattle and daub between them, the roofs pretty roughly thatched. Deeper into the country, however, the structures began to change – they weren't round but oblong and they had roofs made from sheets of corrugated iron. We crossed bridges that spanned streams, streams that would become torrents, I guess, in the rains. It was June, of course, and the rainy season was supposed to start at the end of the month but already we'd seen the first signs.

EWAN: A completely different world. Just a handful of vehicles and hundreds of people walking or driving cattle, sheep and goats. We passed herders ushering donkeys laden with goods, donkeys that wandered all over the road. Kids would pop up from nowhere with their hands out: 'You, you!' they were yelling. Big kids, little kids, tiny boys with shaved heads and top knots, little girls in scruffy dresses, bare feet and shawls. We rode past a watering hole where a man had his animals, another guy hunched on the bridge carrying a couple of leather gourds round his neck.

I was overwhelmed; uplifted. The desert had dried me out, I think, and now I felt invigorated.

We bumped into a guy from the Red Cross and asked him what the roads were like further on. He told us they were OK, a bit potholed and lumpy but nothing the bikes couldn't handle. No sooner had we pulled over than all these kids appeared. Charley was still on his bike and they flocked around him, their hands out asking for books, pens and money.

We stopped in Gonder for a lunch of cake, coke and coffee. Gonder is the regional capital, and it's a bustling town. A group of teenagers descended on us and one wee man in a striped T-shirt recognised me.

'You make movies?' he said in English.

'Yeah.'

'Why don't you arrive in a big car? Why did you arrive on a motorbike?'

'Because I'm doing a motorbike programme.'

'Ah,' he said. 'Do you have a bodyguard?'

I held up all of my fingers. 'I have ten,' I told him, then pointed to the rooftops, 'all around, so be careful.'

This was a noisy, bustling place; plastic tables and chairs, waitresses in orange tops, the smell of coffee, people gabbling away on mobile phones, and dozens of kids watching us. Charley was trying the different types of cake, his jacket over the back of his chair. It was much cooler now, not even in the twenties.

'I noticed this morning,' he said, 'my brake lever and clutch were cold: first time in ages.'

After we'd finished our cake I wanted to change some money so we went looking for a bank. We passed a group of women crowding onto one of the blue and white minibuses, vans so full no one had room to breathe, let alone sit properly. I saw a couple of boys shining shoes in a doorway and beyond them a shop where they changed currency. I asked the lad serving what the rate of *birr* to dollars was. Eight point five, he told me and I prepared to hand over fifty dollars in tens. He then told me the exchange rate was different for smaller notes. Didn't I have any fifties?

'No,' I said, 'just tens.'

'Then it's different.'

'What're you talking about?'

'The banks,' he insisted, 'give us a different rate for smaller notes. I can't give you eight point five.'

'Different rates for different notes?' I half lifted an eyebrow. 'Come on.'

'No, it's true.'

'I tell you what, I'll change them somewhere else then.'

I found a clothes shop a few doors along and they mentioned nothing about different rates for different notes, they just changed the money.

CHARLEY: We were going north now. The clouds swept in low and dull and it was suddenly misty. We passed stands of eucalyptus and acacias. This was a poor country, I knew that. But most people's image of Ethiopia is from Live Aid in the eighties, whereas this land was tilled. The farming methods may be archaic but the terraces were turned and the soil obviously rich – it was that dark moist colour, such a contrast to the sand of Sudan.

We kept stopping for livestock; the road would be blocked by sheep with fat tails, little goats, or skinny cattle. The higher we got the more the clouds swamped us and it was damp now with the hint of rain in the wind. We'd climb and climb and then the land would plateau and it would be positively cold. We passed a mass migration of people all wearing the same colour shawls and driving their animals ahead of them. Ewan suggested it was one tribe and did I ever get the feeling we were going the wrong way? Everyone seemed to be passing us, not us passing them.

Up here the road was muddy; pot-holed and littered with puddles. We picked our way carefully and I was beginning to think about a campsite. It wasn't raining yet but it would be soon and I wanted to have my tent up before everything got soaked. We found a clearing a little way off the road that was sheltered by eucalyptus.

Ewan got his tent up before me. I know it's unheard of, especially on this trip, but I was confused about where to camp and faffed about trying to find the right spot. I wanted to make sure if it rained I wouldn't get washed away. I avoided the slopes and channels and finally pitched the tent under the trees, but by the time it was up Ewan was all but settled.

There were three children at first – in this country you're never very far from them – three girls wearing long dresses, one with blue flat-heeled city shoes, incongruous out here. The other two were in bare feet and all wore shawls round their heads. They were quiet initially but as time wore on and Ewan's jokes got worse, they grew steadily bolder.

One little thing with a gap in her teeth was the cheekiest by far. We nicknamed her Ruby, because in a funny way she reminded Ewan of Ruby Wax. They had been on a Comic Relief trip to South America together a few years back. We gave them water and they loved the plastic bottles. We passed out the empties we were carrying. The three became four, the four five, and six, then seven and so on. I noticed that each one who arrived was a little older, a little bigger than their predecessor. They crowded around us so closely I was worried someone would get burned by the primus stove I used to heat water. It was raining and I'd set it up on the rack of my bike. We heard the first rumble of thunder and I knew we were in for another downpour; two wet nights in a row, it was so strange after the heat of Sudan.

The children were fascinated by the camera; they kept running right up to the lens and blowing raspberries on the backs of their hands. Eventually a man appeared, tall and elegant. He was the father of some of them, certainly, and he ushered them off home.

Only now did we think about food and we ate boil-in-the-bag, standing by the bikes, head torches on as the clouds rolled in. More thunder, the first spots of rain. Claudio was bemoaning our lunch. 'We should do better than cake in future,' he said, 'really. If you want I shall act as guinea pig with the local restaurants. I'll go in and eat; half an hour later, if I'm not green, you can join me.'

EWAN: It rained all night but was clear again in the morning. Up at dawn we wandered across the hill and a field of rocks where cattle were grazing and sheep skipped out of our way. We wanted to see where the kids lived and came across a sort of village, or cluster of huts anyway. These were pole-walled; the gaps filled with wattle and daub and the roofs thatched. We saw little Ruby first and she was all giggles and laughter. Her family invited us in for breakfast. There were two women, who we guessed were Ruby's mother and grandmother, and a guy in a blue jacket, wellies and a scarf. He was the head man, the chief; and we recognised him from the night before. He sat down on a canvas bench, ushering Charley and me to take a seat while the older woman ground some kind of root on a smooth stone. There was a little fire going, the circular room dark, though with the door open and the windows there was enough light to make out a zigzag pattern on the walls and hand prints made by the children. Shelves had been cut and held various pots. Charley pointed out beams in the roof, blackened from a thousand fires.

The root smelled of ginger, and once it was mashed the older woman (who kept smiling and laughing) added it to water she was heating in an ancient black kettle. Ruby came in with a chipped basin and some water and we washed our hands. Her father set down a plate of sour bread together with a spicy garlic paste, that we found out later was berbere, and indicated for us to dig in.

All the time we were eating a cow stood at the window, dogs barked outside and every now and again a cock crowed. It was very peaceful; the family so gracious and generous. We'd arrived unannounced and they just opened their home.

Every now and then we'd hear a cracking sound from outside,

almost like gunfire. Earlier we'd seen a lad herding goats, whirling a great whip around his head and snapping it over their backs. We ate the bread and talked to our hosts as best we could, trying to explain to the older woman that we'd come on motorbikes and they were parked down the hill. Another younger man with fine features came in. He took some bread, dipped it and sat down. He was pretty cool, nonchalant in our presence, a woollen Rasta-style hat on his head.

The tea was superb, the old lady served us in tall glasses and with the bread and spicy paste it was a good breakfast. A family in Ethiopia: this was why we were here, to meet the people, see how they lived and share a meal with them.

CHARLEY: The paste blew my mouth off and I almost spilled the basin of water. The people were lovely, though, and their home beautiful. They had newspaper cuttings on the walls and religious pictures, icons: this was predominantly a Christian country with only about 30 per cent of the people Muslim, and they tended to live more to the east, nearer Eritrea and the Afar Depression.

The little walkways between the huts and the enclosures for animals were puddle-strewn and daubed with animal dung. The kids were barefoot, their feet and legs streaked with filth and one or two had gummy eyes, like conjunctivitis, only it looked much worse. These were very poor but very proud, very hospitable people. We could hear the boy cracking his whip again, it really did snap at the air like a gunshot. We said goodbye, slipped the father some money for our food and went back to the bikes.

When we got there we found Claudio's jacket was gone. Ewan and I had been wearing ours but he'd left his draped over the tank bag and someone had stolen it. It put a bit of a damper on what had been a special morning.

We rode on, climbing higher and closing on the Simien National Park. I passed an old man driving a really skinny horse and a little further on I was behind Ewan when we came to a bunch of kids. They waved at first as they always do, but then they bent for stones.

'Oi!' I yelled. 'Oi!' I lifted a finger, looking back sharply. We weren't hit but we had been warned, our first stone throwing moment, the little bastards. We rode ever higher and the air was getting thinner. We were in open upland, the clouds so low we rode right into them.

We came to a herd of cattle and slowed to almost a stop. A kid on a pushbike zipped by us and ploughed on, parting the cattle before him. We rode through another town and saw what looked like a bunch of prisoners; men dressed the same and breaking a pile of massive rocks: I could hear the zing of sledgehammers on stone. There were a number of other guys standing there with these great lengths of wood, like huge rough poles. They looked weird, as if they were on parade or something; three abreast, the poles upright like lances.

We were heading into the Simien Mountains to see the Gelada baboons. We'd both seen them on David Attenborough's programme *Planet Earth*, and were looking forward to seeing them for real. We set off again, climbing gently until we came to the entrance of the park. This really was the highlands and some of the most spectacular scenery I've ever seen; gently rolling hills and slopes, only you were twelve thousand feet up. The roads got narrower, tighter and twistier – too much on the throttle and the back wheel would slither. You needed a bit of back brake to get round some corners where the mountains shouldered one side and the drop would kill you the other.

Rounding one final bend the baboons crossed the road in front of us. There were tons of them; long haired and totally unafraid of people, they were all across the mountain. Parking up we sat down and watched them.

'I can't believe it,' Ewan said. 'I mean, you see them on *Planet Earth* and there they are.'

'And the view,' I said. 'What do you think of the view?'

'Amazing: the clouds, like smoke over the mountains.'

'Yeah, bloody smoke machine . . .'

The view was staggering: mountains that stretched for mile after mile, valleys between them, canyons and gorges green with trees and grey with rock, thousands of feet below. We wandered right to the edge of one drop, the land falling away at our feet.

'How about camping down there?' I said. 'A ledge or a tree, maybe; you know, strap yourself in and watch the sunset.'

'Fine,' Ewan stated. 'I'll watch you from up here.'

EWAN: I kept thinking about the children, no shoes, scabs everywhere, running eyes and shit all over their feet. People and animals living all together and no sanitation, no hygiene, God knows what kind of infections they carried.

Claudio's jacket had been a bummer. I suppose the people here have nothing but even so it's a riding jacket and he needed it. I tried to focus on the positive – the family's hospitality, and the national park had been amazing. Some of the roads were pretty terrifying, though, especially on the way down. They were serious hairpins with a drop to nowhere and no barrier: it made the hairs on your arse curl up. We stopped at one place where the fall was just ridiculous and Habtamu, our fixer, told us that when Ethiopia was under communist rule, the governor of the Gonder region used to bring dissidents up here and chuck them over the cliffs.

Gradually we descended, crossing bridges and taking the corners gently. We passed an old tank half buried in red soil, and then we passed what looked like some old military outpost, yellowed stonework and rounded corners; an old fort perhaps.

It was raining now, the cloud so low that visibility was hampered. We made camp and the ground was soaked, our tents still wet from last night. Charley and I mooched around in our waterproofs. Jimmy Simak was filming and he asked me what I thought so far.

'Ethiopia? Brilliant,' I said. 'But rain. The word of the day is rain.'

'What do you think, Charley?' Jimmy called.

'What?' Charley peeked from under both his hat and his waterproof hood.

'What do you think of Ethiopia so far?'

He hunched his shoulders as water dripped on his head. 'Yeah, whatever he said,' he muttered.

18
The Road at the End of the World

CHARLEY: Axum is in Tigray region and had been the centre of the ancient Axumite Kingdom. It goes way back to the time when the Queen of Sheba was seducing Solomon, or he was seducing her maybe. Either way, it's said she came from that area. There's a ruined palace on the outskirts of town that local people believe to be hers though archaeologists claim it was built fifteen hundred years too late. Her bathtub is there, though; a massive square pool with twenty-foot sides where people, kids mostly, go to collect water. You see them on the road all the time, tiny little things carrying huge jerricans, usually tied by a length of rope on their backs. Sometimes the nearest fresh water to where they live is a few miles walk and carrying water is a chore the children help with. It's one of the reasons some kids never make it to school. That and the firewood – we saw people gathering it all the time, old women bent double under huge bundles wrapped in calico cloth.

I was following Ewan. We'd camped with the others last night and it had finally stopped raining; so far today was dry but the cloud was low and the world looked pretty misty. The road wasn't too bad. We were coming through the mountains and it was twisty enough to begin with but not severe; baked dirt with a covering of gravel. Apparently the road had been built by the Italians and in places we could see stones almost like cobbles that reminded us of the Appian Way.

We hit a series of tighter bends and Ewan took a corner with the bike pretty keeled over. He asked for the power and the back end stepped out, the wheel sliding sideways. Suddenly it gripped and he was pitched out of the saddle.

He saved it, kept upright and nosed the bike into the grippier stuff, and I think watching gave me more of a fright than it did him. He didn't say anything; didn't stop and he didn't look back. A muttered curse over the radio was all I heard about it.

The villages were much the same here, buildings made of wooden uprights and wattle and daub which I guess was part mud and part animal excrement. The further north we got, however, they started to look a little more affluent (though that's a relative term in this country). We saw more vehicles, the blue and white buses particularly, crammed to the nines. The drivers kept flashing us, as they'd done throughout Africa; the BMW headlights were permanently on and that seemed to bother them.

Ewan pointed out that although we weren't the only bikers these people had seen, we were far from a regular occurrence. We'd rumble into villages all suited and booted and some people would look round as if they'd seen a ghost. Kids popped up from all over; not just the villages, but the hillside, from great drops where the road bordered the gorges, they'd be on bridges, along the river beds ... everywhere. Ninety per cent of them were terrific, all waves and smiles with just a handful who liked to wave sticks or bend to pick up rocks.

We passed through a town where some of the buildings had glass in the windows, built of stone with tin roofs, and some with electricity. Beyond that we were descending again, the same kind of uncertain gravel, and taking a left hander Ewan lost the front. It just washed away; no warning, no reason other than the transfer of weight and subsequent loss of traction: just as my bike had done that day on the Dakar. He was off before he knew it and my heart was in my mouth. By the time I pulled up he was already hefting the bike from the dirt. He didn't say anything, just took a cursory look for damage and refixed the tank bag. I can't stress how tough it is for a guy who so rarely rides off-road to spend day after day on this kind of surface. Twice this morning he'd had serious moments and had ridden on without complaint.

EWAN: I was used to the spills by now and what choice did I have anyway? What was I going to do, leave the bike and hitch a lift? Riding along I could smell eucalyptus, a scent that will always remind me of this country. I watched the different colours of the earth, thinking about how it changes so much and how you can see it, the yellow and black of Sudan to the green and brown of

Ethiopia. On a motorcycle you really feel it, smell it, you're part of it. Every now and then you come into contact with it and it hurts. Make a mistake and the bike spits you off. That's just the way it is.

We climbed and descended, crossed rivers on bridges built by the Italian army back in the 1930s, passing cattle and sheep that were often just lying in the road. We were seeing a few camels now and hundreds of donkeys; poor put-upon little creatures carrying everything you can imagine in metal panniers slung across their backs. I was thinking how I'd like to come back and rescue the donkeys, take them back to England – them and some of the people. Maybe we ought to have some kind of people sanctuary, what do you think?

As it turned out all we were able to do was grab some lunch in Axum. We paid for a hotel room and took a quick a shower: it was almost a week since the last one. We had no choice but to press on as the UNICEF team were waiting for us in Adigrat. Allegedly it was four hours further, three and a half maybe, and about a third of the road was tarmac. I was hoping we could do a three-and-a-half-hour ride in three and a half hours for once, but I suppose that was optimistic. So it was a bite to eat, a quick douche and five minutes crashed out by the bike.

The route looked pretty gnarly in places and it was being worked on. I'd been down the road once already today, not to mention losing the back end, but I was in good spirits. I actually thought the riding was fantastic and I'd fallen in love with Africa all over again. The very fact that the roads were so tough meant we could stop and talk to people, laugh and joke with them, see how they lived – and that was why we were here. It was a pity about Axum, though; I really would've liked to have spent more time there. I'd heard a lot about it and the history really appealed because our view of Ethiopia is nothing like the reality. Historically it had been such a diverse and powerful nation – up until fairly recently the currency was salt bars, and to this day camel trains bring salt from the Afar region to the market at Mkele.

There are huge standing stones in Axum, it's a UNESCO world heritage site; massive obelisks erected by the kings as tombstones. The largest is twenty-four metres high and was put up by King Ezana something like sixteen hundred years ago. There's another even bigger one that fell during construction and it's said to be about thirty metres.

According to the people the Ark of the Covenant is in Axum, guarded night and day by a priest in the Church of St Mary of Zion. It's also where Ethiopian Emperors were crowned or inaugurated or whatever happens to a new Emperor when he takes over.

We were heading towards the Eritrean border now which in itself was amazing. Travellers just don't go there. For thirty years Eritrea and Ethiopia were at war with each other; Eritrea finally gaining independence in 1991. But between 1998 and 2000 the fighting flared up again. It was all to do with territorial demarcation lines. A lot of lives have been ruined, families split; people who've lived side by side for hundreds of years. It was tragic, especially when you consider the countries share pretty much the same traditions and religious beliefs.

Anyway, that's where we were headed and the road was part dirt, part pothole and part sand (I was starting to take this personally). When it rained the tarmac part looked like a sheet of glass.

And boy did it rain. I've never ridden in anything like it – far worse than the rain in France at the beginning of our trip. Charley had a dark visor on his helmet and had to partially open it to see, which meant the rain got in. That's a nightmare in the wet because droplets form on the inside, mist up with your breath and there's no way you can demist it.

In some ways the landscape was even more spectacular in the rain. We were climbing to these rugged, open plateaus with the most fantastic cloud soaked mountains all around us. I could see bolts of lightning, and the thunder that followed was crashing right overhead. The raindrops were fucking monstrous, falling hard as hail, and in no time the world was running with water. The whole earth seemed to steam, a thin fog rising from the ground, and to make matters worse there were men working on the road. Lorries were hauling gravel, turning round and dumping it. There were massive wheelbarrows all over the place and with the visibility as bad as it was I almost clattered into one. I was soaking, riding without the inners to my trousers because I'd not had time to put them on.

CHARLEY: The ride was fantastic except for the dark visor. The rain was so fierce I ended up with the visor fully open and my left hand shielding the side of my face because it was the only way I could see. A mountain road in a thunderstorm and riding one-handed. Fucking amazing! I could hear Ewan whooping it up over the radio; his being the only one that was transmitting now and as it turned out that was about to pack up. Not before I heard his latest song, though; he makes them up as he's riding and this one went something like: 'Riding along in the pouring rain, think I might be quite insane'.

I'd managed to get my waterproof trousers on so by the time we got to Adigrat all that was really wet was the bottom half of my T-shirt. I loved this country, though it was a tough life for the people, it really was. But to ride through it was just incredible; it had sand, mud, gravel, rain . . . everything you could possibly want. It was just beautiful.

It was already dark when we finally arrived, but UNICEF had organised a small hotel in a gated compound where the bikes would be safe. The town was buzzing, a real border place full of soldiers, bomb disposal experts, truck drivers and the kind of professions that followed them.

Sarah and Wendy were waiting for us and it was great to see them. They introduced us to Indrias, the UNICEF communications officer who was to be our guide. He was Ethiopian but had been to school in Massachusetts and university in Philadelphia. He was based in Addis Ababa but worked a lot in Tigray region. Previously a journalist, he'd covered the Eritrean War.

Ewan was soaked and all he wanted to do was get dry so he could concentrate on the briefing for tomorrow's visit. First things first, though, the girls had been in touch with our families and brought out some food parcels, namely chocolate and sweeties. For Ewan there was also a photo of all of his girls, and for me pictures of Doone and Kinvara on holiday in France where they'd made 'still life' tableaux of Long Way Down.

The following morning we were up early and in the back of a UNICEF 4x4 heading for the border. The UNICEF drivers are locals with years of experience. They know every inch of the road and for once it was nice to be off the bike with someone else responsible for getting us to where we were going.

Indrias sat between us and we talked about the country generally. He cited the successes UNICEF was having with education: these days 70 per cent of Ethiopian children are receiving at least primary education whereas just a few years ago the figure was only about 15 per cent. Although AIDS is a huge issue (as it is in most of Africa), with one and a half million people infected, preventable diseases had been greatly reduced. Basic sanitation such as we'd seen in Kenya had brought the mortality rate among under-fives down significantly. Indrias told us that as recently as 2005 almost half a million under-fives were dying of things that could easily be prevented. In malaria-affected areas, twenty million nets were being distributed, although along some of the rivers the men used them for fishing. Dug latrines, wash basins and soap were preventing diarrhoea and therefore dysentery, another big killer. UNICEF was also drilling thousands of wells fitted with handpumps, just one of which could serve five hundred families.

We were about forty to fifty kilometres from where the serious fighting had been and many of those displaced had fled to Adigrat. Technically there was no war any more but then there was no peace either. Indrias explained that the level of rhetoric had risen again recently and the people lived in a constant state of fear.

Most of the fighting had been from trenches, lines and lines of which were dug along the one thousand kilometre border. The casualty figures were staggering and the conflict had been compared to World War I.

Three hundred thousand people had been displaced, many of them Ethiopians deported from Eritrea who, when the ceasefire was declared, had no homes to go back to. The ones that did go home found their houses and watering holes were now in the middle of minefields. Both sides used mines but at least the Ethiopian government was able to furnish the UN with maps. The Eritrean mines hadn't been mapped and subsequently the casualties mounted. Over five hundred people have been injured in Tigray since 1998 – three hundred of them children – and a quarter of those died. There are more than a million mines along the border and Ethiopia is one of the worst affected countries in the world. It costs three dollars to lay a landmine and $1,000 to destroy it. UNICEF estimates that more than two million Ethiopian children live in mine-affected areas.

EWAN: Indrias explained what steps UNICEF was taking to try to combat the risk. They'd initiated a Mine Risk Education Programme. Education (particularly for children) is the key and so far they had reached over two hundred thousand youngsters through school clubs and out-of-school peer education. As a result, 69 per cent of kids had altered their behaviour. Tigray had been really successful but nevertheless huge numbers had sustained hideous injuries. UNICEF hopes to provide at least three thousand of the most badly injured with a new Mobility Cycle, one of which was on the roof of the truck ahead of us. Specifically designed with mine injuries and the tough terrain in mind, they're powered by hand pedals which work independently of one another. They can climb and descend, they have three gears and the difference they make to a child's independence is incalculable.

Indrias went on to explain that as part of its Mine Action advocacy work, UNICEF was calling on all countries not only to sign but also to ratify the Ottawa Treaty banning anti-personnel land mines. Ethiopia signed the treaty more than ten years ago but only ratified it in 2004. Countries such as the United States and China have yet to sign it.

It isn't easy to get countries to give them up, however, because landmines make the perfect guard. An army can occupy an area, scatter the mines and clear off again knowing they don't have to feed or pay anyone, plus they have an early warning system in place. Trouble is, when the war is over the troops leave and the real victims start appearing. One wrong step and lives are either over completely or ruined for ever. In this particular conflict mines were deliberately placed where civilians would come into contact with them: along river banks, for example, where water carriers or goat herders would get blown up; around the cactus plant that bears the prickly pear, a fruit often picked by children. Worst of all, though, were the ones deliberately planted on somebody's doorstep.

We were in high desert now having climbed beyond rivers where we saw women washing clothes, people taking baths, other people washing buses. The country was no longer green, the terrain barren and sand coloured, though the fields were cultivated; we watched men with oxen and hand ploughs tilling the soil in the same way they'd been doing for a thousand years. Off-road we headed for Addis Tesfa, a small sandstone village of low walls and cacti. There was a desolate beauty to it – kids running around barefoot, donkeys wandering here and there, and of course the skinny but beautiful cattle. With their huge horns and soft eyes they reminded me of drawings we'd seen on tombs in the Valley of the Kings.

We had come to see a guy called Tesfu. He was twenty years old, slightly built with cropped hair and a pencil-line moustache. Six years ago he lost his right leg to a mine.

Shaking hands he showed me and Charley to a bench that ran along the wall outside his house. He spoke little English and Indrias interpreted.

Tesfu had been a bright student and had got as far as the equivalent American eighth grade, but because of his injuries he'd had to drop out of school. Even now, almost 85 per cent of Ethiopians are illiterate and Tesfu is acutely aware that education is the key to his future.

His voice had a gentle timbre and he was a guy who used to love running and playing football. When war came he and his family fled to Adigrat where they stayed for two years. When it was deemed safe to go home they found their house all but ruined and that same day started building a new one. The old house had been on the other side of the courtyard from where we were sitting. They'd been back a couple of days perhaps, trotting in and out without incident, when one afternoon Tesfu was by himself and went inside to get something. The mine had been laid right outside the door.

He remembers the time – four o'clock. He was fourteen years old. Fortunately there was a soldier in the area who heard the blast, but it took two hours to get him to Adigrat and medical attention. Four days later he regained consciousness with one leg missing below the knee and the other a mass of shrapnel slivers.

He told us the mine had been waiting for him.

He has a prosthetic leg now but to be honest it was a bit knackered. It was held above his knee with a strap and the foot part was actually broken. But it was better than nothing and he didn't want to use one of the new cycles even though once trained he could then train others and UNICEF would pay him. He needs an income and with the sort of daily challenges he faces, it might be an idea. But emotionally he says the last thing he can deal with is a wheelchair: not even when he's an old man. He's young, male and proud, and who can blame him.

He really wants to be a doctor, because doctors saved his life and he wants to save other lives. The problem is school, though, because the nearest one is a three kilometre walk and he can't make it. The wound where they tidied up his leg wasn't brilliant, apparently, and it gave him a lot of pain. A better prosthesis is what he needs, but the real pain actually came from the shrapnel still embedded in his other leg. He showed us a hole in his kneecap where the skin is stretched and white from scarring. His body is apparently repelling the shrapnel and they can't operate right away. Tesfu told us that the leg was examined recently and perhaps something can be done but he has no idea when. In the meantime he's doing all he can with massage and a traditional healer.

CHARLEY: He was a brave kid, and who could blame him for not wanting the stigma of any kind of wheelchair? As far as he was concerned he could still walk, he just needed a little help, that's all. He had a few tears in his eyes when he showed us where the entrance of the old house had been, and relived the ordeal. He was brave to roll up his trouser leg and show us the false leg. He was brave to show us his other wounds; like some old warrior seated on a chair outside his mother's house. He desperately wanted to finish his education to the point where he was trying to figure out how he could get the money to rent a room in a town with a school. He told us he was unlucky and yet lucky, God had saved his life. He wanted his independence and he was active in helping educate other children about the dangers of mines. I really admired him and at the same time I was disgusted by the cruelty he'd been subjected to. I couldn't get my head round a person who'd place a landmine on a doorstep, a deliberate act to fuck someone up. What we were seeing was the reality, the pain and suffering, young lives ruined and we'd heard it from the horse's mouth. I really felt for the poor guy, he was so clearly struggling to find his niche and get educated so he could do something with his life.

Tesfu went with us to Addis Alem, where we were greeted by

a procession of school children. The flags were flying and a banner had been put up proclaiming a welcome to Ewan and Charley. Talk about humbling: there were hundreds of kids – boys on one side and girls the other – all clapping their hands and singing a song of welcome.

The first of the mobility cycles had been delivered to a fifteen-year-old girl called Abrehet. Three years ago she was walking home from school when she stepped on a mine. The blast blew off one leg and ripped the flesh from the other leaving just the bone. It meant she couldn't walk with any kind of crutch. She could handle the bike, though, and seemed pretty proud of the fact.

She led the procession down to the school buildings where the children were going to show us one of the plays they'd devised specifically to educate other children about mines. Abrehet was one of the first people in Ethiopia to receive the mobility cycle and after only three days she was using the controls to go forwards, back up, brake and turn circles; she gave us quite a performance. And if she suffered from the same feelings of stigma as Tesfu, she didn't show it: I reckon we were there for an hour or so and the smile never left her face. Ironically it was watching her that changed Tesfu's mind; having seen the bike in action he realised that far from being embarrassing it was actually quite cool, and by the time we left he'd told Indrias and Ewan that he'd like one. It was brilliant: now he had a way of getting to school, and with school he had a future.

We were told that Abrehet received nine hundred *birr* – around $100 – as compensation from the government, and she'd used it to buy eleven goats. Her favourite subject at school was social studies and she wanted to become a businesswoman. By my reckoning she was well on her way – a year after she bought the goats the eleven had become nineteen.

Welcoming us, the head teacher told us a little bit about the area and Ewan and I were appalled when he explained that forty-eight people had been killed by mines and another 127 injured. He spoke about the challenges the community had overcome and those they were still facing. He told us that the immediate area had been cleared and they had found a staggering 3576 mines.

We were then introduced to Daniel, a young guy who cleared mines for the UN. He showed us how he located them and just how long it took.

First, however, he showed us the mines themselves. There was one in particular, Jesus Christ; it looked like a bit of wood some kid would pick up for the fire. Daniel told us it was an RGD6 and came from the old USSR; the cover was wooden and it contained four hundred grammes of TNT. We saw various other mines and metal fuses that could blow off a child's fingers. Three dollars to lay a mine, remember, and $1,000 (not to mention the decades it takes) to get rid of them.

That's what Daniel does. Dressed in a chest plate, protective helmet and knee pads, he uses a piece of wood that's about a metre in length. It's painted red and coiled with string at both ends. The other end of the string is tied to a couple of rocks and with this contraption he forms a pathway through a minefield.

He uses a mine detector (like a long handled metal detector) and if it throws up a sound he marks the spot with a stone which later he sprays with yellow or red paint. Then he's on his knees and using his prodder, a metal spike on a plastic handle. He curls one finger over the spike like a pool cue and very slowly digs around the area. It's painstaking work, not to mention incredibly stressful. If it is a mine he will either render it safe or – if he thinks it's booby trapped – blow it up in situ, using a shaped charge or a hook and line. This is tough manual work and takes amazing patience. If Daniel is lucky he can clear a metre of ground in a day.

EWAN: The children acted out a scene from a hillside where two young lads were herding some cattle. It was very funny at first, the boys beating the cattle (two other kids wearing animal skins) with sticks, when along came a bloke carrying a sack and yelling out like a rag and bone man. Apparently there were peddlers who travelled around the area buying up old bits of metal, which they sold on to blacksmiths in the bigger towns.

The children know they can get money for any metal they find, the trouble is most of the fragments are left over from the war. Anyway, the metal-peddler was chatting to the kids when one hurried off to find something he'd spotted earlier.

It was a fuse and the mine went up. It was very dramatic. The boy made it look as though his arm had been blown off and was rolling around, screaming. The other kids backed off immediately. The extent of his plight was really brought home when I realised no one could get to him. An injured child in agony, perhaps bleeding to death and no one could get to him. The whole area could be mined and there was nothing anyone could do except get hold of someone like Daniel.

The children read poetry then acted out another scenario, this time a classroom scene where the dangers of what they might find lying around were spelled out. Peer education. It's worth repeating that since UNICEF began the programme 69 per cent of children have taken it on board.

After that we danced, the kids with drums and a man playing the krar – a traditional Ethiopian instrument with five strings on a frame, his carrying a sign that said: 'BAN LAND MINES'. Charley and I were each given a calico sarong to wear and someone handed me a banner: 'A MINE DESTROYED IS A LIFE SAVED'.

We danced with the kids, clapping and singing. The whole experience was really moving. I told you I'd always thought Ethiopia might be the nirvana that Mongolia became on Long Way Round and it certainly is an amazing place; a country that for a while forgot the world and was for a while forgotten by it.

We were due to go on to Zelambassa, but still had one last privilege to perform in Addis Alem. The name translates as New World and that is fitting because in Ethiopia the year is 1999. They use the Julian calendar and their millennium is ushered in on 12

September. Indrias told us that as part of their millennium celebrations the country is planting sixty million trees, twenty million by school children. A hundred years ago, 40 per cent of the country was covered with trees, today it's less than 3 per cent and they're cutting down more trees than they're planting. On top of that the most prevalent tree is the eucalyptus; it's not indigenous, its roots spread disproportionately, and it sucks up all the nutrients in the ground. When the kids were asked what they wanted to do to mark the millennium they came up with the idea of trees to make sure their country had a viable environment for the future.

We were each given a native cedar sapling. There was a mantra: 'Plant a tree, protect yourself, and protect Ethiopia's future.'

CHARLEY: This was the third such visit we'd made since we left John O'Groats and it was hugely inspiring to see what one human being can do for another, especially when set against the backdrop of what one human being can do *to* another. We both felt very emotional, we were exhausted from the riding and Ewan was especially thoughtful. He's not mentioned it but only yesterday we'd heard about William. We'd met him at Robin House, the children's hospice in Scotland, just over a month ago, and his ambition had always been to meet Ewan. A few days after he achieved that ambition he passed away. We'd only just heard however. It was very sad news and our hearts went out to his family. His mother said that William loved meeting Ewan. He told all his friends that he was meeting him and loved making everyone jealous. He was so happy he got his DVDs signed and couldn't wait to show everyone. It was a great moment; a memory the family could share forever.

The news reminded us that much of what we're doing is about awareness; it's about raising the profile of these places so UNICEF can go on with its mine education programme, Riders for Health can make sure AIDS victims survive and CHAS can continue creating memories.

Leaving Addis Alem we headed for the border town of Zelambassa, the last stop on the road from Adigrat. The reception blew me away. It seemed as if the whole town had turned out. Seven years ago Zelambassa had been at the forefront of the fighting and had been evacuated. The Eritrean forces razed it to the ground. It has only been partially rebuilt, bomb-blasted buildings line the streets and the only roofs are made of tin and have been provided by UNICEF.

The noise was incredible; women creating a high pitched, shrill sort of shrieking led by one woman with a microphone plugged into a bullhorn. She took us through the battered streets; a war zone still and the only one I'd witnessed first hand. We were surrounded by crowds of men and women wearing their traditional shawls, the gabbi and the netella. Most people carried umbrellas, all different shapes and sizes, to protect them from the sun, and they congregated in two shattered buildings – the remants of what had once been the commercial centre. They perched everywhere: on piles of rubble, concrete blocks, the upper floors where the roofs had been blown off; they sat on steps, bricks, half ruined walls . . . everywhere we looked, there were people gathering round us.

The district officer spoke for a few moments then Ewan and I thanked the town for such amazing hospitality, people with so little giving so much. An elder got to his feet, a gentle and intelligent looking man. He explained that Zelambassa had been a bustling place, a centre of commerce and trade and yet after seven years it still looked like this. He said the people had a strong bond with UNICEF, who had provided essential services and were still doing so. He said visitors were always welcome and the people appreciated those groups who were helping them. He was proud of his town; it had been a big town, a well known town before it had been destroyed. He said that people were still suffering. Countless had been injured by mines.

He told us that Eritrea had agreed to pay compensation but no monies had as yet been forthcoming. There was support from the

Ethiopian government but so far only those who owned their own homes had received help. Not all the schools had been rebuilt and not all the health facilities; there was a shortage of basic essentials. He thanked us for coming and thanked UNICEF in particular and all the agencies who'd remembered Zelambassa. But he asked us not to forget that the problems still went on.

He sat down and we were about to walk up to the border when another old man spoke up.

'Don't rush off,' he said. 'We have lots of problems we want to tell you.'

A UNICEF official explained that Ewan and I weren't from an agency and though we could raise awareness there was little we could do personally about specific situations.

As we walked to the front line a young policeman who'd previously been in the army, told me this was the road at the end of the world. The road no longer went anywhere and so many people still lacked the most fundamental things like shelter, food and clean water. He said the people didn't understand who we were but knew we were from the west and they hoped we could help. He doubted many westerners had even heard of Zelambassa. Maybe we could tell them.

EWAN: We ate *injera*, the traditional Ethiopian dish that's made from a millet pancake, with goat's meat and lamb curry, or the vegetables people eat on official Fast days. A woman made coffee with a charcoal stove on the floor, grinding the beans in front of us whilst seated on a carpet of grass. This is long-established Ethiopian hospitality and riding through some of the river deltas we'd seen women gathering grass for just such occasions. The fire is laced with frankincense bark and the smell is amazing.

Charley and I sat with Tesfu and Luam, another amputee, a beautiful young girl wearing a red netella and a flip-flop as part of her prosthetic foot. While we do have an opportunity to tell the world about the plight of Zelambassa, we had come specifically to meet young people who had fallen victim to landmines. Mines ensure there's never any peace. They devastate lives. Both Charley and I are absolutely convinced that there should be a blanket ban on their use. So on behalf of Tesfu, Abrehet and Luam; on behalf of every child who has lost a limb or lost their life to these grisliest of weapons, we're calling on every country that makes, sells or uses land mines to stop.

Simple humanity isn't it?

19
Stewed & Brewed

CHARLEY: I had three nails in my back tyre, one so seriously embedded I thought I'd leave it, another had just the top poking out, and a third was bent over. I'd have to do something about those two. Pulling them out I plugged the holes with rubber and cement, the same kind of kit I'd used on Claudio's bike when we made Long Way Round and he'd got all the way across Russia without incident.

After the day with UNICEF I was looking forward to riding again; we had time on our side for once, tarmac ahead of us and we planned to look at a monolithic church, the oldest in the country.

Ewan was all ready to go. Dragging his helmet over his head he told me it felt like sandpaper: seven thousand miles of sweat, dust and rain.

Today was Saturday and people were on the road in their hundreds, driving animals and carrying goods to market. I saw one woman weighed under by what looked like a stack of straw hats; she had them hanging off her everywhere. After a moment I realised they weren't hats at all but pots for *injera* pancakes.

We passed a procession of school children carrying 'World Vision' banners – some kind of outing or rally, I wasn't sure – but they were waving and smiling, calling out to us. Coming down from Adigrat we were into scrub desert, with sand edging the road. I noticed the towns looked more prosperous and urban. They were built of bricks or stones and painted in bright colours and we began noticing that some of them had health centres.

Mkele was not far down the road, the capital of Tigray region, and beyond that Maychew and eventually Addis.

In case you're wondering how my knowledge of these countries has become so good it's all down to my teeth. I've realised I hear voices in my teeth and strangely enough they sound sort of like our fixers: Tunisian, Libyan, Egyptian; the latest voice sounded just like Habtamu.

EWAN: I'm beginning to think Charley and I need to talk. He's right, though, it was wonderful to be on tarmac and I was feeling good. Yesterday had been great. I'd really enjoyed it and had been touched by all we'd seen on the road to Zelambassa; particularly the procession when the children led us into Addis Alem, waving branches and singing that marvellous song of welcome, it was a special moment and one I won't forget.

I was looking forward now to seeing this church and, checking the map, we found the dirt road and headed into the hills. The road wasn't bad, though there was the odd hairpin and loads of children, of course. One boy started after us.

'Give me pen,' he was yelling. 'Escrito, escrito.' There's still quite an Italian influence here left over from the days of occupation. The boy just wouldn't quit and pretty soon he was joined by another child and another until a whole tribe was tearing after the bikes. There were more on the hillside, a couple on the roof of a house. Claudio was filming from the back of Charley's bike and as we sped off he felt a stone thwack his helmet.

We came to a little village hunkered down on the valley floor, the tin-roofed houses shaded by trees. I could see the church carved into the mountain and a flight of stone steps climbing to the gates.

'Did I tell you this was one of the oldest churches in Ethiopia?' Charley said. 'It's seventh-century . . . no, wait . . .' The voices were talking to his teeth again. 'I'm sorry, it's actually fourth-century. That's really ancient, older than Lalibela; the rock churches there only go back to the eleventh century.'

We'd decided not to go Lalibela; it was 180 miles of mountain hairpins and we were just too exhausted to make such a detour. The churches there are monolithic, cut from the hill in their entirety. This church was only partially monolithic with a new façade added in the nineteenth century.

'In the really early days monks used to come here to pray,' Charley was saying as we headed for the steps. 'And there are some churches where the only way to get to them is by climbing a rope.'

'You know,' I said, indicating the building, 'I think the front looks more fourteenth-century than nineteenth.'

'Fourteenth? No, Ewan, it's nineteenth.'

I looked quizzically at him, my best intellectual expression. 'Are you sure?'

He shrugged. 'Maybe it's Roman. I don't know. Did the Romans come here?'

CHARLEY: A couple of elderly beggars greeted us as we went into the churchyard accompanied by Habtamu.

The church door was massive and looked so old and so worn it was hard to believe it was only nineteenth-century. We were asked to remove our shoes, a tradition in this country.

'Oh well,' Ewan sighed, 'apologies to everyone within a two mile radius.'

Habtamu indicated a series of crosses, explaining that there were three types of cross in Ethiopia: the processional cross, the hand cross, and those like the one on his necklace, with twelve arms coming off it to indicate the twelve disciples.

The interior was only dimly lit, the history seeping from walls painted with stories from the bible that were sixteen hundred years old. Habtamu told us the construction had been completed inside a year.

Ewan couldn't believe it. 'A year!' he said. 'How did they do that?'

Habtamu smiled. 'The people had angels to help them.'

The church was quite small but the ceiling was high and dark and supported by massive pillars. Electricity had only been installed recently and before that the church had been lit with long tapers donated by the villagers. The ceilings were painted with gold and silver lines, like elongated interwoven crosses. They once used to reflect the gold and silver icons, but a pagan queen had stolen those in the ninth century. Every church in Ethiopia has three chambers; a curtained area where a replica of the Ark of the Covenant resides (we would have liked to have sneaked a glimpse, but weren't allowed to), the second chamber for priests and deacons, and the third for the congregation.

The congregation stands throughout, so the elderly are provided with sticks to lean on. The music comes from huge drums and a hand-held percussion instrument, a sort of cross between a cymbal and a rattle.

Habtamu showed us a pillar with a scar in the stone. He explained that the church was completed on 4 October and annually ever since water has seeped from that scar. To this day the villagers anoint themselves with it as holy water. Apparently part of Christ's actual cross is in Ethiopia. It was found by Queen Helena, the mother of the Roman Emperor Constantine. According to legend, she lit a bonfire and the whereabouts of the cross was revealed to her in the smoke. The event is commemorated every 27 September when bonfires are lit in every town and village throughout the country. Habtamu told us that Christian faith is inextricably linked with Ethiopian culture: 'It's like blood for us,' he told us.

EWAN: It really was a privilege to be there and the view from the church was absolutely stunning in the heat haze; the valley floor seemed to stretch forever, the sun glinting off tin roofs that peeked between the trees. It was an idyllic yet thirsty-looking landscape; there was a barren beauty to it.

Back on tarmac we headed south once more. My bike was feeling a little bouncy, the suspension perhaps a bit soft. I noticed how slowly the landscape changed; it was subtle, not like at a border where the change always seemed to be so dramatic. Riding a bike through a country you don't feel like a tourist, you're exposed to the elements and because you're seeing everything up close you really feel as though you belong.

Coming down, we were into the twisty stuff, hairpin city, and my bike didn't feel good, what with knobbly tyres and yawing suspension. The set-up felt loose and seemed to load up, almost weave, as I took the corners. I was saying as much on the video diary. Avoiding a lorry and sand on the road, I peeled into a left hand hairpin.

Shit, I'm down.

The front died; I was on my side, the bike sliding away and pirouetting on the tarmac. Kind of cool, actually, my helmet cam kept filming and, watching the footage later, it was like something off Moto GP.

Charley was a few bends further on and initially he had no idea I was down. The bike weighed a ton and the horn was blaring. I managed to wheel it to the side of the road and a few minutes later Charley was back. We checked for damage: the pannier was scraped and one of the bags on the crash bars but that was about it.

'There's oil on the front tyre.' He bent to show me. 'You

picked up some oil, Ewan; it's why the front washed out. Classic low side, loading the front and it just washed out. Are you all right?'

'I'm fine.'

'You've got oil on your arse.'

I looked down at my jacket and he was right, the bottom of my rally suit was stained with oily dust.

'This tarmac's like glass,' Charley went on. 'I felt the back slide myself, coming out of a couple of corners.'

Moving to the wall we took a look at the view across the valley.

'What's that big town down there?' Charley pointed.

'Birmingham.'

We laughed.

'Christ, I feel like Dickie Attenborough. Here we are in the middle of Ethiopia.'

'Did you see that truck back there?' I asked him.

'You mean the one that missed the bend?'

We'd seen it earlier. A lorry had completely missed a bend and dived over the edge. It was in two pieces, one still above and the cab smashed to bits on the section of road below. Debris was littered all across the carriageway. God knows how long it had been there.

A reminder, if we needed it, that tarmac could be even more dangerous than going off-road.

CHARLEY: In Maychew we stopped for petrol and a cup of coffee. Ewan went to buy some food for dinner and I videoed a few kids then showed them the footage on my handlebar screen. I grabbed a coffee in the cafe, sitting on the veranda where the kids who hung around me were ushered away by the older men.

When Ewan got back I gave the waiter ten *birr* and he gave me seven back. I looked surprised.

'No, no, it was only three,' he said.

I hadn't got a clue how much the coffee was but was really

impressed by such honesty, particularly when you consider these people have so little.

Ewan managed to buy some potatoes, a few tomatoes and what he called 'these oniony things'. It was getting late; the sky threatening and we started thinking about camping.

We found a great spot in the eucalyptus and were putting the tents up when the kids arrived as they always do. One teenager wearing a safari jacket told us this was forestry land and we weren't allowed to camp. We persuaded him that it was all right, and I'm sure he had no jurisdiction anyway. We made a deal that in the morning we'd go to his village for breakfast. Fair enough, he said, and after asking for our empty water bottles, they left us.

As we were putting the tents up it started raining, but stopped again pretty quickly. There was a good breeze and with both ends open the ground sheet dried completely. I made Bovril and organised some boil-in-the-bag chilli while Ewan set about making his stew.

EWAN: It's a speciality that requires very old Ethiopian ingredients: eight-year-old tatties for example, tomatoes and ancient Ethiopian onions. This was the vegetarian version, though of course you can use meat, chicken maybe, or lamb. Or bacon even. Slice the vegetables using a Leatherman or Swiss army knife; place them carefully in a billycan and add lots of water. Sprinkle liberally with garlic salt and place on the primus.

Bring it to the boil then let it simmer.

Have a little taste.

Christ, that's fucking hot.

Continue to simmer until the potatoes are not too soft but not too crunchy either. Serve immediately in a plastic mug with the plastic fork/spoon combination. For non-vegetarians the dish can be supplemented with a bag of chilli con carne.

'What do you reckon, Charley?' I asked him.

'Bloody great. Well done. What's it called?'

'McGregor stew, the Ethiopian branch of the family.'

I slept for eleven hours. We'd been so tired we were in bed by 8.30 and the next thing I knew it was light again and I could hear movement outside the tent.

Poking my head out, I saw our friends from last night helping Charley roll up his fly sheet: half a dozen teenagers swarming all over it.

Charley indicated the lad in the safari jacket. 'He knocked on my tent at 6.30. I'd been up to have a pooh and I think he spotted me.'

He told us his name was Kasai and he was eighteen. He went to school in Maychew and wanted to be a dentist or an eye doctor, maybe. He wanted to go to university and there was a new one opening in Axum; first, though, he wanted us to come to his house for breakfast. Cleaning my teeth, I packed my tent and got the bike back to the road. There were about eight kids now and Kasai jumped on the back of Charley's bike while I took his brother.

I'd had the weirdest dream; I was at the bottom of a sand dune in bare feet, trying to get to the top where there was an airport terminal. But I'd lost my ticket and as I climbed I realised there were broken bottles sticking out of the sand. My bike was lost and I found a bicycle and was frantically trying to get to the top. Almost there, the pedals broke and I crashed backwards falling all the way to the bottom.

Kasai's village was quite large; a dirt road led from the tarmac beyond rows of houses to a square surrounded by what looked like communal buildings. There were donkeys wandering about, and cattle, of course.

Within seconds of parking the bikes half the village turned up, and within minutes the other half joined them. Kasai was the eldest of five children. His mother had tea boiling in the back room of the two roomed house and we sat down on a wide bench covered in animal skins. Later I discovered it also served as the bed Kasai shared with his brothers and sisters. Out the back the garden was piled with firewood and a haystack for the animals; the land that stretched beyond was tilled by his father. He arrived soon afterwards, a proud-looking man of seventy-five; Kasai said it was old for an Ethiopian and to have a father that age was good luck. The kitchen was also outside – a roughly built shelter with pieces of tin for the roof, the walls the same pole construction as the house. It was about kneeling height and there was a charcoal burner for coffee and a large circular pot for making *injera*.

Back inside the house was dark, both the door and window were open but children lined the wall leading out the front door. Another great crowd filled the window space. In the back room a series of pigeonholes like open cupboards had been fashioned from wattle and daub. Kasai's brother showed me pots and pans and a basket of something. On the top shelf he pointed to a bottle. 'Hair food,' he said.

I had to think about that. 'Ah, shampoo.'

They brought bread for us and we were waiting for the tea. It didn't come, however, and we couldn't work out why given that Kasai kept telling us how good it was and that tea and bread was what Ethiopians had for breakfast. Finally we realised they always served tea with sugar and clearly they didn't have any.

CHARLEY: It was my fault, I was sitting there and Kasai was sort of hovering. He spoke about buying sugar because it was so cheap and it took me ages to figure out they didn't have any money. Cottoning on at last I gave him fifty *birr* and off he went to the shop.

We're not exaggerating when we say the whole village turned out. The square was heaving: men and women, boys in football shirts, girls with their hair pressed to their heads and fanning at the shoulders in the traditional way they wear it. There were hundreds of young kids surrounding the bikes and I was getting a little nervous: it wouldn't take much for one to topple over and I had horrendous visions of a child being crushed.

Breakfast over we said our goodbyes, shook hands with Kasai's father before heading off. The younger children followed us across the square and halfway to the tarmac. No one threw any stones.

We saw more baboons; nonchalantly they appeared on the mountain one side of us, ambled across the road and disappeared into the trees. Last night there had been hyenas in the hills. Kasai said they were all over this area but fortunately he didn't tell us until this morning. It's a good job too, because if we'd known last night every sound would have had us jumping. Hyenas are not to be messed with – a bite that helps rot their food and more jaw pressure per square inch than any other land mammal.

We crossed a huge valley with mountains rising in the distance. We passed one town where we were sure we saw a dead guy. He lay awkwardly on the ground and he wasn't moving. He had a rope tied round his neck and a whole group of men were gathered around him. Ewan thought it looked like some kind of lynching. We can't be sure: we didn't stop and only glimpsed it as we were riding by.

By midday I was ragged; I'd noticed recently that with all the riding, by eleven or twelve I was exhausted. We really needed the few days we were taking at Addis Ababa. Little things were niggling again – something I'd say, something Ewan would say – it was just because we'd had no time out. Pulling over at a cafe we started chatting to a bloke who told us his name was Musay. He was an interpreter and spoke really good English. Ewan asked him why some of the children threw stones.

He said they just thought it was fun; no one told them not to do it so they didn't know any better. He told us it had been the same when he was a kid; he remembered lobbing a stone at a woman in a car and smashing her mirror. He thought it was great fun.

EWAN: I was trying not to say the 'tired' word because it's boring. But I was knackered and my concentration was slipping. We were on a much more gnarly stretch of road now, heading into the mountains and the town of Kembolcha. Tomorrow we were going to the market in Bati, where people came from Afar to sell animals. I was looking forward to it, but right now I was exhausted and there were geep all over the road. That's what I christened them anyway – the sort of sheep/goat or goat/sheep animals we kept seeing. They wandered along as if they were permanently in the rain: heads down, jaw dragging, their fatty, liquidy tails just hanging. They had this habit of drifting across the road, finding their mates, then all of them would lie down together for a kip.

The road was awful, blind hairpins with no run off and crazy drops down the mountain. Stones and gravel, dust, rock slides – the works.

I came off again and I have to tell you it was really pissing me off. Going too fast, too confident, I don't know, but the next thing I knew I was slammed on my side and I could feel a knock on the leg I broke back in March.

My pride isn't bomb proof and I could see with this trip it would take another battering. It's a shame because I get sick of off-road riders coming up to me in restaurants, looking smug and telling me I fall off all the time. Maybe I do, I don't know; maybe I'm just not very good at this. It's true that at the moment I'm not getting any pleasure from riding in the dirt. But I reckon I've been riding for fifty days now, half of them off-road, and I imagine even the most ardent dirt bikers would fall off a few times if they rode solidly for twenty-five days.

Anyway, this time the crash bars had bent and a bracket holding one of the lights was buckled. With Kembolcha finally ahead I started fantasising about the Vintage California I'd seen at the Moto Guzzi factory. What I wouldn't give to be on one of those right now, in a pair of jeans and leather jacket, an open face helmet cruising some highway in America.

20
Lola

EWAN: We were approaching the Kenyan border and the Africa most people are familiar with.

Our last few days in Ethiopia had been pretty eventful. In Addis Ababa Charley and I had a big heart-to-heart about all the petty niggles that had gone on during the first part of the trip. With the tiredness created by the miles maybe we hadn't been communicating but with three days R&R we cleared the air.

Before we got to Addis we'd visited the market at Bati, a bustling town close to the Afar region and been absolutely mobbed. There were hundreds of little kids all over us as soon as we pulled up. They were chased off by bigger kids who were in turn chased off by even bigger kids with long sticks and no compunction about using them. Finally surrounded by some self-appointed bodyguards, Charley and I wandered among stalls selling everything from cloth to spice to live chickens and chewable roots with hallucinogenic properties. We saw tall, thin men with afro hair that had been lacquered until it looked wet. Women keeping the sun off with umbrellas sold millet and maize, donkeys, geep and camels. Legs tied together, the geep were tossed on top of buses to be transported. Across the way from the livestock, black-winged vultures sat watchfully in trees, waiting for the carcasses of the weakest to be tossed over the fence.

South of Addis we stopped at Shashmene, the home of Rastafarianism. I'd been in Jamaica earlier in the year and wanted to find out more about the link. We met an old guy with long dreads and grey beard called Gladstone Robinson, and he told us he was the oldest settler in the town. He had a young wife and a six-year-old daughter. He didn't look well, a little green around the gills, and he didn't really answer my questions. I'm not sure I left any the wiser. He had a picture of the Emperor Haile Selassie on his wall and said that Rastas believed him to be the reincarnation of Jesus Christ and hence they worshipped him as their saviour.

No sooner had we left than he collapsed. We heard his wife start wailing and, grabbing the medical bag, Dai and Jim rushed in. Dai felt for a pulse at his wrist but found none and the old guy was very cold. His wife told them he'd had serious diarrhoea over the past few days and had been very weak. Dai located a faint pulse in his neck. The oxygen level in his blood was very low and they got a mask on him. He was dehydrated and they gave him some rehydrate fluid and gradually he came to. He went to the toilet, though, fainted again and they had to resuscitate him.

It was very scary for his wife, poor soul. All she could do was stand by and watch. The life returned to his eyes, however, and taking off the oxygen mask, he thanked Dai and Jim and told them he was ready to run a race.

Beyond the Kenya border we had armed guards with us – four soldiers appointed by the government. This was a dangerous area, with clan warfare, poaching and general banditry. 'Shiftas' operated here, and they liked to target anyone who looked like a tourist. They were particularly busy around the border and our fixer suggested we crack on to a lodge five hours drive away. Five hours: that meant seven or eight in reality. It would be well past dark before we got there. This was gravel road and the last thing I wanted to be doing was riding it in the darkness.

We'd been travelling maybe forty-five minutes when Claudio's suspension exploded. We couldn't believe it; the shock absorber was new and had only just been fitted in Sudan. The seal went, spraying oil everywhere and reducing rideability to zilch. Fortunately we had spares we'd picked up in Addis, so grabbing tools Charley and I set about replacing it. We got the old one out and the new one fitted inside fifty minutes. Not bad for the side of a dirt road with shiftas looking on from the hills.

And talking of shiftas it was getting late and there was no way we'd make the lodge before dark. The fixer knew a place, though he didn't seem delighted about it – but we did have four Kalashnikovs to fall back on.

We camped in the lee of a rocky outcrop, scattered with thorn brush. By now we were used to being told how dangerous Africa was and we'd come to the conclusion that 90 per cent of what was said was bullshit. But everyone we'd met on the road had told us this area was pretty dodgy. Funny as it was to see a soldier carrying a Kalashnikov, I was glad he was there. Charley and I got the tents up and were thinking about our stash of boil-in-the-bags when the fixer said he was cooking goat for dinner.

Fair enough, we thought, we'll join you for goat then: what time shall we say – half-past?

I had a quick wash and got changed and wandered over to where the soldiers were making a fire. Then we heard it: 'Baaa, baaa, baaa.'

The goat was alive and in the back of the truck, not pre-packed in cellophane from some supermarket.

I decided I would have to watch them slaughter it. I'd never seen an animal killed before but given I eat meat I didn't think I should turn my back. They took it to a flat stone, held its mouth and quickly slit its throat. Less than a minute and it was gone; I didn't enjoy the sight, but as I said I felt I ought to watch. It was skinned and butchered expertly, the innards tossed far into the bush so the hyenas would feast tonight. The meat itself was grilled over the fire and we ate it with pancakes. It was fine, I suppose: though I have to admit I didn't really enjoy it, not after seeing it killed. And, I suppose, given that, I'd have to consider the whole meat eating thing.

CHARLEY: It's hard to watch an animal being killed, but I grew up with livestock around all the time. It occurred to me that the almost gentle way our fixer took this little fellow's life was far more humane than some slaughterhouse where dozens are killed in fear. It was quick and simple and it was African. Families bred their goats to slaughter them: it was the way of life out here and we were following a pattern passed down for generations. We arrived, put up the tents and killed the food we'd eat.

The campsite was pretty spectacular, with birds and monkeys shrieking from among the rocks. I imagined the kind of silence that would descend if they were disturbed suddenly and it was comforting to have the soldiers with us. The food was good, beautifully butchered, and we wrapped the meat in pancakes and ate it as a goat sandwich.

In the morning we were off early and heading south-west on decent gravel that shifted from grey to red depending on the amount of clay in the ground. Ewan did really well, riding with his elbows out, soft hands and leaning back as I'd told him. He'd had a hard time in Ethiopia and coped brilliantly, now I got the feeling things would click. Do this for long enough and that's what happens. Your confidence is up and the whole experience becomes more enjoyable.

This morning the road was wide red gravel; it blended into the landscape, which was low and stubby, lots of bushes and very few trees. This was the African prairie and it seemed to go on forever.

We came to the Gabran people's village of Turbi. We'd read about it, seen it on BBC news and our mood sobered considerably. A clutch of buildings surrounding a sun-baked yard, we parked the bikes in the shade of acacia and took off our helmets. Immediately we were mobbed by children of all ages in pale blue shirts and green shorts. This was the school where two years previously twenty-two children had been massacred. Their head teacher Gabriel came over and we shook hands, told him who we were and that we'd heard about the atrocity.

He was in his forties, well spoken, and it was obvious he was the pillar around which the community had rebuilt itself. He told us he had no real idea why such things happened, but the disputes over land, pasture and water for animals went back generations.

It had been six o'clock in the morning, the children in school, when men from the neighbouring Borona clan opened fire.

'I saw men in uniform,' Gabriel told us. 'They just started shooting and they were still far away. I shouted to the children. Run. Run. Run.' He shook his head. 'The older ones, most of them were nine or ten, they understood the danger. But the young ones, they just stood there.' He pointed to the square, the open ground between the buildings where the children were playing. 'They were cut down, slaughtered; the young ones, the babies. Not with guns, with knives, machetes.'

EWAN: It was horrific, incomprehensible. But I could imagine the scene; bullets flying, the older kids knowing what was happening, but the little totty ones just standing there in bewilderment. Moments later, they were hacked to pieces.

'There was nothing we could do. They just died,' Gabriel said. 'They just died while we were watching.'

I remembered the BBC news reports when it had happened. Incredibly distressing, yet the place seemed to have recovered: clearly this man held the community together. Over eighty people had been killed in total and many of the children were orphans: some of them lived in the school. Gabriel told us that he had a problem getting the money together to feed them but they didn't want to be farmed out to relatives because they loved school so much. Right then I determined I'd find a way to make sure this man had the money to feed them. It was a promise I made to myself and I wouldn't forget it when I got back to London.

We spoke to a boy of about fourteen who'd been working when the gunmen burst in and started firing indiscriminately. Dropping behind the desk he hid for three terrifying hours.

Another lad rolled up his trouser leg to reveal a hideous scar on his shin. Flesh was missing to the bone, the scarring white and puckered so that it looked as if the leg had exploded from within. In a way it had: this was the exit wound for a bullet that hit behind his knee. After he was downed one of the raiders speared him. We saw a tiny girl with machete scars on her forearms; she couldn't have been more than three when it happened, her brother cut down right in front of her.

Gabriel took us to the mass graves; eighty-two villagers dead and twenty-two of them children. The marauders stole cattle, goats and donkeys, leaving the survivors with nothing. The graves were marked with beds of dry reeds and on the beds were personal belongings of those who'd been slaughtered. A small wooden barrel, a tin mug painted with flowers. Little children killed with machetes; I found it very, very difficult.

We headed towards the lodge now, the road pretty fucking gnarly. I'd been trying not to swear so much, for my dad mostly as he really hates swearing. Sorry, Dad: but this was a nightmare, the bikes so heavy it was like driving a bus on two wheels down a gravel track. It was awful, as if I was systematically trying to destroy my motorcycle: fucking washboard shit, shaking the bike to bits. My hands were numb, my feet. I couldn't even look sideways for fear of hitting something and losing the front completely.

'Charley,' I said over the radio. 'Let's stop for a moment.'

We took a breather so the blood could find its way back to our hands and feet. 'Such incredible scenery.' Charley waved a hand at the vista, 'but you daren't look at it in case something goes bang.' He grinned. He was in his element. 'Mind you I really like this kind of road, you have to concentrate so hard yet stay loose at the same time: it's really challenging.'

'Yeah, challenging, right. I like it about as much as I like sticking a needle in my eye.' I looked up then, scanning the horizon where I could glimpse wildlife far in the distance.

'Look over there, Charley. That's either giraffe very far away or goats very near.'

We came to the turning finally; the track that led to the Marsabit Lodge, and it was probably as bad as anything we'd ridden so far, bumpy as hell and thick with sand. I was all over the place.

But oh boy, was it worth it. A 1950s-style lodge with log walls and a tin roof, a wide porch, tyres painted white and embedded into the ground. Beyond the buildings against the trees was the most magnificent waterhole. Clouds massed overhead, great wreaths of them reflected in the water. Banks of grasslands carried the slope, and beyond the lake these great swathes of trees. I stopped the bike and the smile just got wider. They were wandering amid the shallows. Oh my god. I'd ridden my bike to the elephants.

There was a family of them in the shallows on the far side of the waterhole. A squabble broke out among the youngsters and the adults came in, mum and dad, we could hear their bellows echo across the landscape.

When it got dark the elephants wandered around the lake and came right up to the restaurant. We crawled on our stomachs to get closer without spooking them. That hundred and fifty miles of shit road had been worth every jar of the teeth, every curse for which I'd apologised. This was Africa, and I was lying in the grass with wild elephants a couple of yards away.

I could have stayed for days. There wasn't time, of course, and first thing in the morning we were on the road again, the really grim stuff now; big rocks and heavy dirt that kept the front wheel wobbling. I ignored it and carried on, standing tall and keeping relaxed, thinking about the village ahead where we hoped to meet the Samburu people.

CHARLEY: We were into the red dirt again; heading south towards the Losai National Park. Sudan and Ethiopia had been vast countries where we'd taken protracted routes. We were cutting across the north-western corner of Kenya, though, and taking less time. We passed old and bent women carrying huge bundles of wood. The sights were different and yet similar to what we'd seen in Ethiopia and it amazed me to see what these people had to do every day of their lives.

I could hear Ewan muttering into the radio. 'The red dust. Oh well, soft hands, lean back and power on through.'

Claudio came off right in front of me, he was there one minute, down the next and I almost hit him. As it was I had to lay my bike down. Classic case of riding too close when I spent my life reminding the other guys that we mustn't do that: a case of do as I say, not as I do. Clouds was really pissed off: 'Really,' he said. 'I don't like this sand. I hate it. Fucking hell, I never know what to do.'

'Just keep the power on,' I told him.

'I did that.' He gesticulated at the massive rut where he'd fallen.

'The wheel got caught in there, Clouds,' I told him. 'Locked the front and when you tried to power on it flipped you off.'

He went down again shortly afterwards. The sand was deep now: Fesh fesh, like red talcum powder, so loose it was almost like riding on liquid.

We hit better roads finally and stopped for a breather. Ewan considered the open savannah, rolling hills in the distance and acacia trees spreading their bows to offer a little shade. 'I'm riding along wondering what I'd do if a lion came after me,' he said. 'I mean, they hunt like that, don't they. Stalk a gazelle, sweep round then come charging up from behind. How do we know they're not doing that with us – a massive great lioness bearing down on the bikes?' He made a face. 'Still, I suppose that would be the way to go, from behind so you wouldn't know much about it.'

The Samburu village was temporary. We met the chief, a man wearing the traditional red robes of his people, a sash over one shoulder similar in style to the Masai. It was hard to age him, late forties, early fifties perhaps; people out here have a hard life so he could have been a lot younger. He wore a woollen hat and told us that the tribe had come together from various villages for a special ceremony; they were in the process of putting up their huts, made from a dome-shaped framework of poles covered by animal skins.

We asked the chief what the ceremony was and he told us that seventy young men were going to be circumcised. There was no anaesthetic and the boys must show no emotion, no twitch of an eye or curl of a toe whatsoever. The chief explained how the foreskin is cut in four places then peeled . . . well anyway, it sounded about as painful as it gets. He told us, with no hint of amusement, that his son was in the ceremony and if he so much as made a sound he'd kill him. Even now we don't know if he was joking.

We asked him if it would be possible to camp with them. He seemed to think about that for a while, then left us and, gathering the elders, wandered over to the animal corral and discussed it. It was the tribe at work, a real community and after a while the chief came back and said we could camp, only not in the village. He indicated an area about a hundred yards off. He asked us if we had a doctor with us. As part of the deal he wanted Dai to take a look at his wife: she'd given birth yesterday and wasn't doing so well.

The village was buzzing with children, camels, donkeys: all you could hear was the bleating of young goats – they were kept in a covered pen separate from their mothers because that kept the mothers from wandering off.

Naked children were running around; little tots with shaved heads. The women wore the same red shawls as the men and many of them had weighted earrings that stretched the skin of their ear lobes. Both the men and women wore masses of brightly coloured necklaces and looked much like the Masai we'd seen near Kilimanjaro. We found out the two peoples were related and, as with the Masai, livestock was the Samburu livelihood. They were semi-nomadic and they kept cattle, donkeys, camels and goats. Their main food was milk: sometimes they mixed it with blood. Thank God for those voices in my teeth. Eh?

EWAN: Dai came out of the chief's tent and told us his wife would be fine. She was quite young, had bled heavily during the birth and had been suffering some stomach pains because of it. But he'd asked the other women if this was normal for her and having watched her give birth to three other children, they said it was. The placenta was out and the uterus retracted so nothing major was wrong. Dai gave her multi-vitamins, some iron tablets and paracetamol for the pain. She was the chief's second wife, and he had six other children with his first one. Sitting in his other tent he told us he was thinking of getting a third wife and Charley piped up that Ollie would beat him if he asked her even for a second wife.

The dome-shaped hut wasn't quite completed yet and the chief's first wife told us that it took about four days from start to finish. We sat on mats made from interwoven reeds and there were all sorts of things hanging in there – halters for donkeys, leather panniers; there was nothing man-made at all.

Now that Dai had been seen with his bag and stethoscope he was much in demand. Amongst his patients one young guy was coughing white sputum created by wood smoke and it gave him breathing problems. Dai listened to his chest and gave him an inhaler he had in the pack.

I was in my element; elephants last night and now these people. This was the Africa I'd dreamt we'd get to see. Goats bleating, donkeys, camels, young warriors, very cool, carrying sticks and spears. Hundreds of kids running around, everyone wanting to talk to us: it was marvellous. I wandered among the livestock; donkeys who were tethered by their nostrils. At night all the animals were secured inside thorn bush corrals to stop hyenas or lions getting at them. The people seemed pretty well fed considering their diet of milk and blood; apparently they only ate meat on special occasions such as rites of passage ceremonies like circumcision. It made my eyes water just to think about it.

We spent the night just a little way off and I sat outside my tent listening to the animal noises; donkeys and camels, the little fatty bloaty sheep we'd seen – sheep with fatty tails like the geep in Ethiopia only these ones had goitres to go with it. I watched the sun go down and exchanged a glance with Charley.

'Just another fucking perfect African sunset, Charley.'

That was our line, like Sarah Miles all bitter and twisted in *White Mischief*.

We'd had a few such sunsets and since we'd had our chat in Addis everything seemed to have clicked on a gear. I even felt better about the dirt, I was following Charley's advice and it was easier: parts of today I'd actually enjoyed the riding.

In the morning we said our goodbyes and one old man in traditional robes and a chewed looking baseball cap kept hugging us. He waved us off and we hit the road once more.

Heading towards the equator the road was very dusty, and just when I thought I really was enjoying myself we hit more deep sand. This was worse than anything we'd seen: we'd been warned about gravel but not this; you could stir it, it was that soft. The bikes were all over the place; even Charley was finding it hard to cope. Great red clouds kicked up and in three miles we had ten separate incidents. I saw Claudio go down and my front end shook, the handlebars almost wrenched from my grasp. A couple of tribesman wandered across the road in front of us, carrying a stick apiece and a spear. They looked on vaguely as we struggled to get the bikes upright.

'I don't like sand, Ewan,' Clouds was saying. 'No matter what Charley says nothing works. Nothing works when you're riding in sand.'

Tell me about it, I thought.

A few yards further and he was off again. I was off. Then Claudio fell again. Jesus, I thought, how many fucking miles have we got of this stuff?

Finally we hit the scrub and it was a joy to see hard gravel, big stones; feel the sudden jarring of washboard. I thought I hated the gravel, but that fesh fesh: it was worse than anything we'd encountered in Sudan.

We rode for a few miles on washboard and then the real drama began. Mud, no, not mud. A river crossing: actually it wasn't a river so much as a swamp. The road petered into nothing but brush and bushes, thorns that would impale you. I could smell the water first and then I saw it. There was a river of sorts blocking our path ahead. Not deep, but blood red and cushioned by great banks of mud that had water courses of their own, ponds, puddles, mush, swampy little lakes. It was hard to see where the narrowest point was.

This was really challenging. At first I couldn't see a way through and thought we'd have to go back through the deep red sand the way we'd come. It wasn't happening, there was no way; not after making it this far. Charley and I wandered indistinguishable paths trying to figure out a way across.

The trucks arrived and even our fixer seemed perturbed. Scratching his head he considered the landscape. 'I think we can get the cars over,' he said, 'but the motorbikes?'

We took a walk, leaving the four-wheelers to consider their options while we tried to find a simpler way. We found a handsome young kid with a spear over his shoulder, chewing a stick; bare-chested he was tending his cattle. We asked him about suitable spots and he pointed us off to the right.

On investigation it was about as good as we'd seen: a potential crossing that came at the water along ruts there were quite solid; little mosaic squares of mud with ridges where the sun had cracked them. The water was very shallow; the mud not too deep. Prodding around with sticks we figured that with help, we could get the bikes over.

'We should move one of the trucks first,' Russ suggested, 'and that way we can thread the winch round the forks and drag the bikes over.'

Charley disagreed. 'Let the bikes go first,' he said. 'We'll walk them over. If the trucks go they'll churn up the bottom and we'll never get across.'

It was agreed. Charley and I played stone, paper, scissors and he won. With him guiding the throttle and clutch; me and two of the soldiers assisting, we wheeled his bike across the ruts into the soft stuff. In gear with the engine running we half drove, half pushed it through the water and up the far bank. Dry land, we'd made it and celebrated in the traditional style with much yelling and whooping and throwing of imaginary hats in the air. With Charley's bike safely on her side stand with the savannah stretching ahead, we went back for my bike and finally Claudio's. This was boys' own stuff now and with the first job done I had time to do a few things to my bike while the others set about thinking what to do with the trucks. The fixer tried to get his across first and it got well and truly stuck, listing badly in the mud, dirty brown water up to the door.

They decided to get our two trucks across and worry about the fixer's afterwards: drive hard and fast and get as far as they could, then fix the winch line to a fairly inadequate looking tree and haul the last bit. Once they were both safely on the other side we could attach the fixer's truck to both winches and haul him out.

Russ went first, really gunning the engine with Jim Foster knee deep in water alongside. He got a good distance but grounded in the mushy stuff and Jim attached the winch to the tree. I looked on from behind the big camera, thoroughly professional yet somehow never managed to capture a single frame.

We hauled the truck out then it was David's turn. He took a massive run up and steamed into the water. He almost made it, got to the far bank and half up it before the wheels dug in. Winch attached he was out and half an hour later so was the fixer. We were covered in mud and grime, water and slime, but it was high fives and lots of whooping as we realised we'd overcome the most difficult natural challenge on the trip thus far.

CHARLEY: We were still full of it fourteen miles later when Claudio's shock absorber went again. I couldn't believe it – two BMW shocks and both had blown their oil seals. Professionals now, Ewan and I had it changed in ten minutes: even Claudio was impressed.

A few miles later the shock went again. Two in one day, three in two days: it was uncanny.

We fixed it again; alas we didn't break the ten minute record but I was thanking God for Addis and the chance we'd had to regroup. We hadn't had to replace a single shock absorber on Long Way Round and here we were with three in two days: five so far in total.

I loved it all, though: perhaps the hardest day, certainly the most challenging, and yet for me maybe the most rewarding. No matter what the road had thrown at us – sand and shit, gravel and rock – we'd dealt with it. And just when we thought it was getting easier, a swamp that masqueraded as a river.

Ewan pulled over, yelling at me across the radio. They'd been fixed when we took those three days off in Addis Ababa. 'Charley, zebras; wild zebras.' He slapped his tank. 'My brothers and sisters. Look.'

There was a small herd by the side of the road that paused to take a look at us.

'I had no idea they were so big,' Ewan said.

'I don't remember their ears being that long, either.'

He laughed. 'Maybe they're the long eared kind.'

The following morning we finally met Lola. You've been wondering, I know you have. Some Kenyan goddess, olive skinned and . . .

We took time out at a wildlife park and from the back of a jeep saw eland, impala, giraffe and white rhino. This was open country covered in green thorn bushes and yellow grass where I imagined lion or leopard lurking. Acacia trees offered a hint of shade and rocks jutted in piles of stones and massive distant cliffs. There was one enormous rhino, I mean huge, about thirty feet from the truck and Ewan was gobsmacked. 'I can't believe how long his horn is,' he said. 'I've only seen those stumpy little nubs but that's a huge long one.'

'Massive,' I echoed.

And there she was, square-faced with not even so much as a little nub of a horn. Lola the baby black rhinoceros being fed by a ranger from a two litre bottle. She was the sweetest thing you've ever seen, sucking away, long lashes across her eyes, skin all wrinkly and tough like an elephant. She looked old already.

She was actually only fifty-six days old and her mother was blind and couldn't look after her. The same mother had had five other calves and hadn't been able to look after any of them either. It didn't seem to stop her hanging out with the guy rhinos, though.

There were two rangers taking care of Lola twenty-four hours a day. They fed her a bottle of milk every three hours. The guy we spoke to rolled out a blanket at night and slept with her. He would be by her side every day for the next three to seven years until she decided she didn't need him any more and wandered into the bush. Ewan and I took turns to feed her and she sucked noisily until all the milk was gone. After that she'd get really frisky and even though she was little she could knock you down. I took the odd whack and I tried to imagine being charged by an adult – you'd be in pieces. The guide told us that the rhino population was increasing. There had been some really bad poaching about ten years ago, but the park held a hundred rhinos now and forty-eight of those were the endangered black variety. After her food and a bit of a play Lola crashed out – she lay on her side flicking her tail in the dust while Ewan stroked her chin.

'No, mate,' I said, catching the look in his eye. 'We've already earmarked a donkey sanctuary. I don't think even Eve would stand for a rhino.'

We were on tarmac when we made it to the equator. With everything that had happened I'd forgotten it was in Kenya that we'd cross to the southern hemisphere. We were two thousand metres above sea level and twenty metres north of the line we tested the theory. Yep, water went down the plughole clockwise. Striding south we tried the experiment again. No question it was anticlockwise. At the very point of the equator it went straight down. So now I knew for certain, it's exactly how they say it is so don't let anyone tell you otherwise.

Staying the night at a small hotel in Nkuru I realised we were only half an hour from some friends I've known for years. Rod and Claire Jones; they own a beautiful place on the shores of Lake Naivasha: I couldn't ride past their door without popping in for a cup of tea.

EWAN: It was an amazing place and gave us a taste of another kind of Africa – one perhaps we might not have experienced. Claire's family had been in Kenya for generations and their lodge

Searching for – and finding – a family of gorillas in the Rwandan jungle.

Charley monkeying around.

The gorillas seemed to tolerate our presence quite happily.

We loved visiting the more remote villages, and joined in the dancing whenever we were allowed!

The tracks were holding up well even at this late stage in the journey.

Exhausted but happy in Tanzania.

At a game lodge in Tanzania –
allowing ourselves a short rest
before the final leg of the journey.

Ewan's wife Eve joined us at Malawi. Ewan was very happy to see her!

Ewan checks the route
ahead in Malawi.

Our final UNICEF trip – here
we are talking with a family
living with HIV.

Yes, it's all my own.

Ewan at the Victoria Falls in Zambia.

Charley prepares to bungee jump over the Falls. As if riding all the way through Africa wasn't enough of a challenge!

Some little kids dance for us in Zambia.

With Eve in Zambia. We were both amazed how good she was. She had only been riding for six months!

At the crocodile farm, with owner Ian McGregor Bruce – a fantastic character, with some interesting scars!

With Eve, taking a well-earned break in Zambia.

Eve back on the road again.

Just the two of us. Namibia was our last country before South Africa and the end of the journey – and we made the most of our last nights by camping out whenever we could.

African wild dogs.

The roads were getting easier by this point. Still had to watch out for the wildlife, though!

The infamous Skeleton Coast, Namibia.

Ewan offroad in Namibia.

We made it!

From John O'Groats to Cape Agulhas on the southernmost tip of South Africa – the Long Way Down.

Over a hundred bikers joined us on our last journey – from Cape Agulhas into Cape Town.

Time to celebrate – on the beach in Cape Town.

Charley and his daughters, Doone and Kinvara.

(Over the page) Sunset in Namibia – one of so many moments to treasure.

was exquisite. This was a hint of colonial Africa; a wide veranda and savage skies, the lake at the bottom of the garden. Claire keeps a small plane and she treated us to the most spectacular fly-past. We were in the air more than an hour and didn't once climb above seventy feet. Skimming across the wave tops, we saw hippo sleeping in the shallows, water buffalo, white-headed eagles skating the surface for fish. Everywhere the world was green, water plentiful – very different from the drier region we had just passed through.

The adventure was alive; the days slipping by too quickly: we'd only meant to stop for breakfast, but after the plane ride Rod and Claire persuaded us to stay the night. We took drinks and some food down to the shore for what they call a 'sundowner'. I could see a hippo in silhouette, the most dangerous animal in Africa. The sun was sinking, the night was cool, and the hippo slipped beneath the surface of the water.

It was our last night – the Kenyan adventure was over and we'd barely a month left on the road. At five the following morning we left for the Ugandan border.

21
Size Does Matter

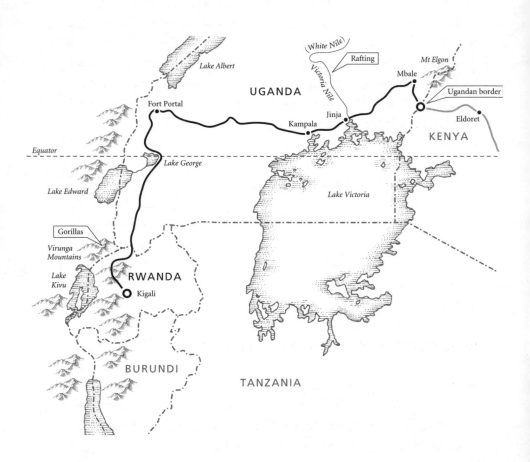

EWAN: In a way, Uganda reminded me of Britain. It was very green, with rolling hills and grassy verges, and trees that somehow didn't look African. I was almost homesick. The people at the border were particularly friendly, going out of their way to wish us luck on the road. It was a wonderful introduction. The country felt pretty laid back and gentle, we were gliding along on good tarmac and I was really enjoying the riding.

We stopped at a coffee-sorting house owned by a consortium of over three thousand farmers who supplied Cafédirect with organic beans. I love coffee, and it had been one of the little unexpected pleasures on this trip. In Ethiopia they crush the beans then boil them over a charcoal burner, gradually thinning the consistency. Then they pour it out and pour it back over and over again. By the time it's served black with a little sugar, it's wonderfully rich in flavour.

At the coffee-sorting house, wc were greeted with the same enthusiasm and affection we'd experienced everywhere on this trip. The women wore bright clothes and head scarves, orange and purple, lime green. The manager greeted us; a tall man, well-built; he introduced us to the head of security who was even taller and more well-built than he was.

Three thousand independent coffee growers – some of whom had five hundred plants, some maybe three hundred, some as few as fifty or even twenty; it didn't matter. They grew their coffee organically and brought the beans here. As a consortium they had the power to sell in quantity and cut out the middlemen. Good beans fetch a good price and this way the growers didn't lose out.

Part of the consortium's role was to persuade the farmers still using pesticides to switch to the organic method. There was a strong incentive because those outside the consortium were still subject to the vagaries of a market over which they had no power. Of course it took time to make the transition – if a grower had been using pesticides for three years it took three years for the soil to be clean enough to be considered organic.

We were taken to the main building, a vast open warehouse where dozens of women and children were sorting coffee beans. Charley and I got stuck in. As the beans passed by on a conveyor belt we had to try to spot the dodgy ones. Each bean had two husks, the outer skin, an inner silver skin and then the bean itself. The good ones were perfect ovals, sandy grey in colour before they were roasted: the poorer quality ones were easy to pick up because they were chipped and flaked, and discoloured where insects had got at them.

A beautiful young woman was in charge of quality control and she led us through the sorting process. Beans were rated according to quality, the highest being AA. These were generally the biggest. So it is true what they say then: size does matter.

CHARLEY: There was a bunch of testers, men and women, who took a little of each coffee on a teaspoon. We didn't need to be asked twice and, following their lead, supped it up with as much speed and noise as we could manage; the kind of thing your mum tells you off for when you're a kid. The manager told us the hard suck was important because it spread the coffee around the mouth, hitting all the different taste buds.

'Your whole mouth is a sensing organ,' he said. 'Sweet at the tip of your tongue and salt at the sides.'

Outside the workers gathered to sing some traditional songs. They held up a banner welcoming us to their country and once again I was overwhelmed by the hospitality. The women started up with their wailing; that amazing, vibrating shriek we'd heard so often. They were accompanied by drums and the beat really got to me. Half a dozen guys were hammering away at a massive wooden xylophone, all playing different sections of the keys and yet creating a perfect harmony. Then the dancing started, all hips and bums, and rather erotic; Ewan and I got right into it.

All in all, it had been a fantastic introduction to Uganda.

*

The following morning we were on the road to Kampala. I'd slept well and was looking forward to some R&R. We'd caught up with the rest of the team, and this was the first time we'd really had the opportunity to do something fun together on our long journey south. We were going rafting on the White Nile, a stretch of water that ranks in the top four worldwide for the quality of rapids. Rapids are graded – the highest they let a punter out on is grade five. The lowest we would see today would be a grade three. It ought to be an interesting day.

Kitted out with life jacket and tight-fitting pink helmet, I felt like a matchstick. All someone had to do was turn me upside down and I'd flare up.

The boat was rubber, of course, and we took up positions along the sides with our river guide at the back to steer. I'd heard there was only one rule in white water rafting: 'Paddle or die'.

Russ was far too interested in the next boat, which was full of girls hunched along the gunwales, to consider paddling. I watched as he went through the motions, his mind elsewhere and his blade barely touching the water.

The river was wide and flat and looked pretty calm, but as we drifted downstream I could see whitecaps. They weren't too big and we rode them easily enough, a little spray but nothing to worry about. Then we hit a couple of monsters and were almost tipped out of the boat. We spun round, our guide fighting hard to right us. The next rapid was a waterfall, almost. With water foaming over the prow, we spun broadside and the boat flipped. We were under the water, above the water, scrabbling for the ropes that hung off the boat.

Once we were upright again, Russ still wasn't paddling. He wasn't thinking about the girls now, he was just concentrating on staying in the boat. Claudio went overboard, there one minute, gone the next and nearly taking Dave off at the neck in the process. Typical Clouds, nothing less than spectacular. I was still thinking so when we hit a hole, the boat nosed and I was in the water.

*

We flew north from Kampala for our second UNICEF visit. Despite the ceasefire, it was too dangerous to ride because of banditry and the odd guerrilla incursion. There had been fighting in northern Uganda for twenty years between the Ugandan government forces (UPDF) and the Lords Resistance Army (LRA) led by Joseph Kony. Kony comes from the Gulu region and calls himself a spirit medium. When he was young he was a millennial fighter recruited by Alice Auma who led a rebellion in the mid-1980s after allegedly receiving visions from the Holy Spirit. Kony went his own way, however, and tried to fulfil his ambition of a state based on the Ten Commandments. His interpretation of the commandments seems a little vague, mind you; we were told that one of his edicts stated that you couldn't ride a bicycle and anyone who did had their legs chopped off. The United States has proclaimed the LRA a terrorist organisation and in 2005 the International Criminal Court indicted Kony in his absence for crimes against humanity. The ceasefire was brokered by the government of Southern Sudan in 2006 and signed by both the LRA and UPDF.

Politics aside, children are the first victims in any war, and in northern Uganda their fate was particularly grim. Over a twenty-year period twenty-five thousand children were snatched from their homes. Families, villages, whole communities were destroyed. Afraid of constant attack, those who weren't snatched or murdered fled their homes and now one million four hundred thousand live in Internally Displaced People's camps.

The camp at Amuru seems to go on forever – thousands of little round huts with thatched roofs eating into the grasslands, built so close together their roofs all but interlock, creating a labyrinth of passageways between them. Forty-five thousand people, living far too close to their neighbours with no privacy, little sanitation and inadequate healthcare.

EWAN: We'd come to see Sarah and were invited to the hut she shares with her uncle and nine-month-old son, who was carried in a pouch on her back. Sarah is seventeen and was abducted by the LRA ten years ago. Quietly she told us what had happened to her. She has virtually no memories of life before the war. All she can recall is that she had two sisters who died, and she has two brothers who also live in the camp. Her eldest brother was killed in the fighting.

The LRA came to the village and took Sarah, her brother and lots of other children to train as new recruits: child soldiers. Aged just seven, she had to walk all the way to the border with Sudan, which can take four days by car. It was a forced march, the children not allowed to slow down, and if they did they were punished. Sarah got an infection in her foot and by the time they got to Sudan she was crawling, traumatised, bewildered and forced along by her captors on hands and knees. After a brief period of rest she was forced into military training: guerrilla warfare, guns, mortars, machetes, hand-to-hand combat; unless they were pregnant or had a child the girls were treated exactly the same as the boys. Sarah was taught how to raid a village, how to maim, and how to kill. I repeat: she was seven years old.

The kids were brainwashed. Kony himself came to see new recruits, persuading them he'd rescued them from awful lives in remote villages where there was no hope of anything. He was a powerful and charismatic leader and lots of kids were sucked in. But not Sarah; she just wanted to go home. She didn't dare try to escape though – one girl who did was brought back and the new recruits were forced to beat her to death.

Watching her die, Sarah vowed she'd never try to escape. She'd take whatever was thrown at her and somehow she'd survive.

She was given to a local commander as a wife and maltreated by his other wives, older women, who starved and beat her. When she was twelve she heard her brother had been killed and she became very, very depressed. She cried for days, refused to eat; she became so desperate that she decided she'd try to flee.

She was shot during her escape attempt and brought back. Having been beaten, she became pregnant in 2005. Unable to keep up when the camp moved, Sarah was released by her commander and after walking for days she arrived at a UPDF camp. From there she was moved to a UNICEF-supported World Vision reception centre where she received counselling and her parents were traced.

At first she suffered terribly – flashbacks, nightmares about killing and combat; what she'd seen, what she'd been forced to do. Gradually, however, with the support around her and the counselling she received, the flashbacks dwindled and the nightmares became less frequent. When she was finally reunited with her parents she was so shocked she couldn't talk. She had to tell them her brother had been killed and discovered that they'd heard rumours and had already held a funeral for him; even though at that time, unknown to them, he was still alive.

These days Sarah lives with her uncle because although her family accepted her back, her father died shortly afterwards and her mother has only a little piece of ground to grow food and is also looking after orphans. Sarah has missed out on her schooling – she hasn't been in class since she was seven and with a baby at seventeen it's too late. She's learned to use a sewing machine and has a tiny tailoring business in the square. Her life is very tough but she's happier than she was, and she's part of a group supported by UNICEF called 'Empowering Hands'. Sarah helps other displaced and abducted children, 'come back home kids' as they're derogatorily called, to reintegrate into society. There's a lot of suspicion and fear amongst the people because many who weren't abducted believe the ones that were went to the LRA voluntarily. People like Sarah raided villages, killing, maiming and abducting other children. There's huge distrust. When she first arrived at Amuru she was too scared to go outside.

Listening to her appalling story, I was profoundly shocked. Of course I had heard there were child soldiers in Uganda but hearing the realities of Sarah's life was so hard. I had no idea these massive Internally Displaced People's camps existed, no idea that young girls like Sarah had been so physically and psychologically ravaged.

Charley and I left her hut in silence; neither of us quite knowing what to say, aware that we'd been in the presence of a dignified young woman who was desperately trying to come to terms with what had happened and to pick up the pieces of her life. But it wasn't going to be easy – her childhood had been stolen and she could never get it back.

We then went to St Martin's school in the neighbouring Copee camp where the children wore white shirts and maroon shorts and gave us a wonderful welcome. We'd come to deliver supplies from UNICEF – what they call 'school in a box' – which is one of the many really positive things happening in northern Uganda. When you hear horrific tales such as Sarah's, it's so important to remember that humanity has this amazing capacity to overcome adversity. For every self-delusional despot there are thousands of people determined to bring hope and stability to their communities.

One thing I see over and over again in Africa is the passion the kids have for school. They hunger for it, so conscious that education is the only way they can have any kind of future. That's why 'school in a box' is such a great idea: a box containing all the materials to set up a classroom for eighty children – pens, little blackboards, chalk and notebooks. Each box costs £120 and Charley and I delivered ten to St Martin's. We handed out the goodies to each child; a UNICEF bag containing two jotters, a couple of pencils, a ruler and a pencil sharpener. The kids were all scrumming round us, desperate not to miss out. I tried to explain that no one would, but when you've had so little it must be hard to believe you'll get anything. The box didn't just contain school books, but skipping ropes and footballs too; we watched the absolute delight a football gave them. No sooner was it out of the box than a game began that was about ninety-five a side.

CHARLEY: They called us 'Sir' which sounded strange but nice. We took the boxes into the classroom and were greeted with 'Morning, sir'. I could get used to that. They have a tough life, they really do, yet they're so hopeful; especially the young ones. It was a tragedy that Sarah and thousands like her had missed out. Daniel, however, still has a chance. He is being taught at the level of a twelve-year-old even though he is fifteen. But at least he is in school. We sat with him in his hut and he was wearing a football shirt, looking for all the world like any other teenager. Except for his eyes. His eyes were deep, very deep, and they looked way older than he did – his mannerisms, the considered way he spoke, echoed all that he'd been through.

His village had been right in the path of one of the LRA's raiding routes. They would pass through abducting people, cutting them down with machetes. They didn't kill everyone, some they just disfigured; cutting off lips, ears, eyelids . . . and leaving their victim alive. Daniel was abducted when he was seven and remained with the LRA until he was ten. He was one of hundreds in the camps and saw children born to commanders and young girls, children who would know nothing other than the brutality of guerrilla war. When the raiders came to Daniel's village he was given a choice: go with the LRA or be killed. He was terrified – it's so hard to imagine a child younger than both Doone and Kinvara being given that choice. Come with us or die, the soldiers told him. It was no choice at all.

And the parents, I couldn't begin to imagine what they must have gone through. Their sons and daughters abducted; never knowing if they were alive or dead, if they'd been raped, beaten, maimed.

Daniel saw people killed and their bodies dumped in streams he'd have to drink from. Bloodied streams; he was drinking the blood of his so-called enemies. He was taught to use a machine gun, a machete, mortars; he was taught to raid villages and strike fear into people – all-consuming, paralysing fear. He was taught how to kill. He saw people killed and he wasn't even ten years old.

He managed to escape during a firefight with the Ugandan government forces; his unit was scattered and together with an older boy he just ran and kept on running. They spent days walking together before finally splitting up. After being gone three years, somehow Daniel was able to find his way back to his home town.

Imagine how that must have been for his parents, three years of not knowing and then one day the son they lost forever walks into the village.

Daniel couldn't stay, however. Infected with the fear of re-abduction he went to Gulu town to stay with an aunt. Daniel's older brother had also been abducted and still he hasn't returned.

Daniel got involved with Empowering Hands and countered any stigma he felt about being a 'come back kid'. He's in school, even though three years behind, and it's a fair distance for him to get there. What amazed me is the fact that the school itself is displaced. Like so many schools St Martin's was moved from its original site because its pupils were gone. When the pupils were relocated to the camps, so was the school.

We were as touched by Daniel as we were by Sarah: the way he was dealing with his life, his desire for schooling so deep that he didn't care about being in a class with kids much younger than him. I kept thinking about bicycles and the commandment I'd heard about. Before we left we bought Daniel a bike so he could get about more easily. He had no idea and we left it for others to give to him. I hope you like it, Daniel.

The visit ended on a high: we helped UNICEF doctors with a programme of inoculation – little vials of polio vaccine for the children, jabs for their mothers, de-worming tablets. The camps are vast and poor; the sanitation and healthcare limited, and all the schools are overcrowded.

The people gathered for us yet again and we sang, played drums and danced. They love to dance in Africa. The drums were amazing, that heavy 'jungle beat' really gets into your soul. One poignant image will stick in my mind, though, of a tiny, malnourished kid, stomach distended under a raggedy green jumper. He was holding a toy pistol.

An amazing and humbling place; I go quiet when I'm doing these kinds of visits. I find it hard to know what to say – it's so desperate and yet so hopeful. Ewan always says it takes a couple of days to sink in, and I remember how I was at Robin House, how I was when we met those kids in Ethiopia. Sarah and Daniel, just two of twenty-five thousand stolen children. It had been a privilege to hear their stories. Leaving the camps I had one thought in my mind. The two things that will free these children are health and education.

We headed on towards the border with Rwanda. The tarmac was brand new and smooth as butter which was good because the day before had been a draining and emotional day, and the easy riding meant I had time at least to begin processing everything we'd seen.

It was wet to begin with; the rain not heavy, nothing like the torrents we'd encountered between Axum and Adigrat when the streams burst and I'd seen people frantically trying to save their homes. This was gentle Ugandan rain and in the damp conditions, the hills and valleys reminded us even more of home.

We took it easy and crashed for the night at a hotel. For some reason Dai started going on about how we should be on the road much earlier tomorrow. We took it on board and it was agreed we'd be gone by seven the following morning. Seven came around and we were all gathered . . . all except the good doctor. Seven became ten past, then seven-fifteen and there was still no sign of Dai.

'He's probably busy with Barbara the sheep,' I muttered.

We went hunting, found his room and Russ rapped on the door. A couple of minutes later he appeared, great bear of a man that he is, all sideburns and chest hair, with a towel wrapped around him.

'Going to Cape Town, mate,' Russ said. 'Thought we'd let you know. Are you up for that or are you stopping here?'

Dai worked a hand over the stubble on his chin. 'Naw,' he said. 'Cape Town sounds good.'

22
Another Country

EWAN: Certain countries create certain impressions before you actually get to them: sometimes those impressions prove to be correct and sometimes they don't. Rwanda is a prime example of one that didn't. Thirteen years ago the country was in the grip of civil war. One million people were massacred in one hundred days while the West pretty much ignored what was happening. Bill Clinton said that not doing anything to help was one of his biggest regrets during his eight years as US president.

We were at the border in plenty of time to meet up with our fixer; our plan being to get to a lodge close to the Virunga Mountains before we stopped for the night. It took an hour of waiting before we realised we were at the wrong border.

The fixer was at another crossing eighty miles to the south.

Finding the place on the map, Charley and I set off into the mountains. As we hit the twisty stuff the good tarmac suddenly gave way to dirt. We were climbing, the road switching back on itself, and the riding was much tougher than either of us had expected. These eighty miles were going to take longer than we anticipated, but as we keep saying, it's the interruptions that make the journey. Heading into a narrow pass, we saw a line of trucks backed up, and a little further discovered that an articulated lorry had overturned and was blocking the road both ways. It had clearly been there a while because the spilled cargo was being loaded into other trucks.

There was no way Russ and David would get through so Charley got on the phone and told them they would have to find an alternative route. The overturned truck had left the slimmest of gaps however, and we nosed the bikes between the cab and the grassy bank.

We thought the trucks would be miles behind and as they had the carnets were sure we had no chance of crossing into Rwanda that night. But then Charley heard them talking over the radio and looking down we could see them on another stretch of road hundreds of metres below us. Their detour had been quicker than the original route. We got to the trucks, grabbed the carnets and sped off again. If we could get to the border before it closed we might persuade the Rwandans to wait for the others.

It was the strangest border crossing I've ever seen: a single dirt track edged by terraced hillsides with no vehicles save one bus and our bikes. People were walking, carrying great loads on their heads, there was the odd bicycle stacked with wood, but that was about it and I didn't really believe it was the right road until we actually got there. It was the crossing, though, no matter what it looked like, with a ragged looking bloke with no uniform operating the barricr.

The trucks made it and a couple of hours later we were again doing what we'd vowed we wouldn't – riding in Africa at night. It was fantastic, I loved it; every time I crossed to another country I got the same feeling: I could never quite believe I was riding my bike there. It was such a privilege. I could smell wood smoke and eucalyptus; it reminded me of Ethiopia. I felt quite emotional riding through a country with such a terrible history of unbelievable violence, but still so beautiful. Just a couple of miles in we stopped for a moment and were immediately surrounded by adults as well as children. As I looked at their faces all I could think of was what this nation had been through. I wondered how on earth it had managed to heal itself.

CHARLEY: We were going to Virunga to see the mountain gorillas made famous by Dian Fossey.

We would have just an hour with them – more than that and any coughs, colds or infections we might be carrying could be transmitted to the animals. We stayed the night in the lodge and the next morning drove an hour and a half to a village at the edge of the rain forest. We were introduced to armed rangers who would guide us, then started out on foot. We were at eighteen hundred metres and the gorillas lived at three thousand metres. From the village we could see the mountains shrouded in a blue mist. There were lots of villages round here – it was farming country, coffee growers mostly, and one of the most densely populated areas of the country. The land was very green, the soil looked good and we walked a mud road laced with heavy stones and bordered by green hedges.

It was tough going and the air was thin and damp, though fortunately it wasn't raining. It was quite cold, though, and we were wearing waterproofs; once into the forest proper we'd be waist-high in foliage.

Our guide told us that poaching was still a problem, and with ongoing fighting in neighbouring Democratic Republic of Congo the gorillas on this side of the border had to be monitored carefully. He spoke English with a French accent – many people speak French in Rwanda because it was once a Belgian colony.

'Ewan speaks French,' I said. 'Exquisite French, don't you, Ewan?'

'Yes,' he said. 'It's a particular kind of French that's actually called "exquisite". Not fluent, just exquisite. I don't know many words, or French grammar or anything, but what I do know I can say very, very well. Not much use but nice to listen to.'

The guide told us the mountains were too cold for snakes so we didn't have to watch our feet or the branches directly above our heads. He showed us elephant fruit, hard and yellow, tough skinned and very bitter. Elephants chewed them, and the people broke them open then mixed the innards with water and used the solution to wash their clothes: it was very effective apparently.

We climbed into the forest now, the villages far behind; the fields where we'd seen people tilling the soil with hand hoes. We were following a narrow path that drifted through a sea of green and every now and again we'd come to a clearing and get another view of the mountains. Then suddenly we saw movement in the trees, a smudge of black; a couple of young gorillas playing high in the branches. I couldn't believe it; they were about twenty metres away.

As we came out of the trees there in front of us was a female lying on her side with three youngsters, including one new baby. Very quietly we sat down to watch them. As we looked on the baby started suckling. It was amazing to be this close – the guide had explained that if we were lucky we might get within seven metres but they were no more than a metre away.

The guide showed us how to make grunting noises that indicated we meant no harm; he also said if we blew raspberries it would get their attention – both were noises that gorillas made themselves.

Then suddenly he told us to get up and move back.

A massive silverback was striding up the slope. He walked on his knuckles, belly hanging, massive shoulders; his head was absolutely huge. We moved up the hill to let him past and he ambled slowly by, looking sideways at us from about ten feet.

EWAN: They were all around us now. The mother got up and wandered off and behind us another silverback appeared. He was even bigger than the first one, sitting there chewing on a stalk; they eat the wild celery that grows here and that sticky grass you get in Britain that clings to your clothes. The food was everywhere in abundance; they didn't have to move very far, just reach out and grab whatever they wanted. Another smaller gorilla sauntered by, long arms and short legs. Charley blew a raspberry and it stopped and studied us.

'She is beautiful,' Charley said. 'Amazing eyes, really beautiful. I think I'm falling in love.' He paused for a moment then added. 'Normally I prefer blondes but this one . . .'

'I think it's a young male, Charley.'

It was the most incredible hour and as we came down we saw another silverback, sitting on a mound so most of his body was visible above the foliage. He watched us, great head, huge shoulders, an air of nonchalance about him, and then he stood up and, like a king surveying his domain, gazed across the forest.

The minister of tourism had arranged the trip and we met her in the Bourbon Coffee Shop in Kigali later that day. She explained that tourism was an important way for Rwanda to establish a stable economy. In the past year thirteen thousand tourists from ninety-five different countries had visited Virunga, and 5 per cent of the revenue generated by the gorillas was reinvested among the village communities of the area. She explained that since the war ended the people were only looking forward: the whole country was determined to move on. It was all about moving forward; the genocide of 1994 was part of Rwanda's history, it wasn't going to decide the future.

We chatted to the owner of the Bourbon Coffee Shop, a very cool guy who served great coffee. He said that since the genocide, people would say they were no longer Hutu or Tutsi, they were simply Rwandan. He'd quit the corporate life he'd been living to open his cafe and now he dealt directly with the coffee growers, most of whom had had no idea of the value of their product or indeed had ever tasted a cup. The place was vibrant, heaving with people; NGOs, doctors, nurses, aid workers and volunteers. We spoke to a couple of American girls who told us that at the end of every month there was a day of public works where the people would do something for their country. For such a historically divided nation there was an overwhelming feeling of unity.

Before we left, the minister of tourism invited us to her brother's wedding reception that evening. We didn't really have the right clothes, but turned up (rather underdressed), got past security and met the president (as you do), Paul Kagame, who had raised an army in Uganda and overthrown the Hutu militia. Half an hour later the minister found us again and told us that the president had asked us to his country house at eleven the following morning.

Over dinner there was a note of caution. Charley pointed out that we knew nothing about this man at all. We'd heard different rumours about his reputation – some good, some bad – but we decided in the end that we should go and at least try to make up our own minds

While we were discussing the matter I asked our fixer, Daddy, why the West hadn't got involved. He just shrugged and said that Rwanda was a small country and back in 1994 Nelson Mandela was being sworn in as president of South Africa. He reminded me that there had been war raging in the Balkans and a football world cup in the USA. He said that most people couldn't find Rwanda on a map and with so much else going on, no one was that bothered. Canada had led a small peacekeeping force, but when they requested more troops and permission to intervene in the slaughter, the UN had turned them down. The French sent soldiers – not to stop the militia but to protect them from Paul Kagame's invaders.

An audience with the president and we had nothing to wear. We'd already turned up at one function underdressed and didn't want to do so again. So we bought suits and shirts; the trousers too long and held up with gaffer tape. I found a pair of white pointed shoes that made me laugh. Suitably dressed we set off on the bikes for the Rwandan President's residence.

CHARLEY: We left tarmac for dirt road and finally a track that was fenced on either side with fields stretching away and cattle grazing beyond. The house was big but not too big, understated, maybe, compared to what you'd expect in Europe. It nestled among some trees like a big old ranch house only made of brick. Inside we were shown to a meeting room with an absolutely enormous round table. An array of spears decorated one wall.

We stepped onto the veranda, the back of the house overlooking pastures where black cattle with gigantic horns were grazing. The president kept them for milk and later we tried some. It tasted like natural yoghurt and was delicious. Beyond the pastures there was a lake surrounded by hills; beyond that was the Tanzanian border – our next destination. It was very beautiful, tranquil, and it was only then I thought about how clean Rwanda felt and noticed that livestock were fenced off from the road. Though we saw plenty of people walking, some carrying huge loads on their heads, there were no donkeys, sheep or cattle on the streets.

The president arrived and we shook hands again. We discussed the challenges he had faced, and asked him what motivated him.

He explained that war was part of Rwandan history, both before independence from Belgium and certainly since. He and his family had fled to Uganda when he was three and he grew up in a refugee camp. He'd spent twenty-five years there and needed no motivation other than that. He formed the Rwandan Patriotic Front, raised an army and invaded. After he became president he asked the people a question: 'Why did we lose a million people in less than a hundred days?' He made them think about it, the everyday Rwandan.

The answer was bad politics, bad leadership and extremism.

Kagame said that he was determined not to see that repeated and pointed out that investment follows if a country can show it is both secure and stable.

Paul Kagame has many critics as well as supporters, and neither Ewan nor I could claim to be experts on Rwandan politics. But we both sensed, riding through Rwanda, that this is a country full of hope and optimism. The progress in thirteen years seems incredible. The Rwandans have succeeded where others maybe have failed – perhaps in part because they never forget what happened, and are so determined to make sure it never happens again. Genocide is part of their history but it isn't going to decide their future.

When this unexpected visit was over, we visited the Eglise Natarama, a Catholic church where five thousand people hid from the Hutu Interahamwe militia in 1994. They'd fled from villages and taken refuge in the old brick church with its concrete pews and dirt yard, the huts of wattle and daub. The militia arrived and lobbed grenades through the windows. The ones who survived ran outside and were bludgeoned to death with hammers and machetes or decapitated with *pangas*, a native tool poachers use. Others were herded into the outbuildings and burned alive: five thousand people in one day.

Their bones lie on shelves in the old church; thousands of skulls, some still impaled with spear shafts, others smashed where hammers hit them. From floor to ceiling, thousands and thousands of skulls. The clothes of the victims hang in a macabre collage, torn, burned, blood-stained. It was one of the most disturbing sights I've ever seen. It brought home old newscasts and TV pictures, and felt so at odds with the Bourbon Coffee Shop, the bustling streets, the sense of progress in the country.

Time and again we had seen the effects of war and brutality on this trip, just as we had ridden along the Road of Bones in Russia. We had spoken to mine victims in Ethiopia, child soldiers in Uganda. Now here again we were in a country that had been ripped apart by war; the genocide of a million civilians that, as

Kagame said, had achieved absolutely nothing. But in each of these countries we also found hope for the future.

I'd recommend anyone to visit Rwanda and if the people can go on rebuilding, continue to heal, then who knows, perhaps one day the bones at Natarama can be laid to rest.

23
Destination: 'Transit'

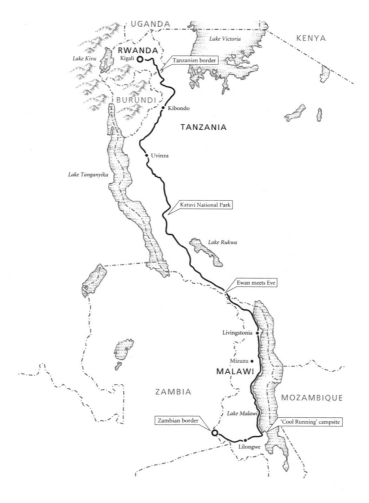

CHARLEY: We'd allowed ourselves five days in Tanzania, but Eve was on her way and would be meeting us at the border with Malawi, and I knew Ewan would be itching to get there. Still, it would take as long as it took and the roads looked pretty . . . interesting. Virtually all of Rwanda had been tarmac. Now we were in Tanzania it would be mostly dirt.

Once again, there was a huge change as we crossed the border. Rwanda was vibrant, very clean. Crossing into Tanzania we were back on the veldt, the great savannah; the world drier and dustier, yellow grass and grey dirt, a horizon marked only by the distant mountains.

We stopped for fuel at a petrol station that was no more than a collection of tented huts. There was one pump and it said: 'diesel' but the guy dishing it into jerricans assured me it was petrol.

'Really?' I said. 'It says diesel right there.' I tapped the pump with my glove that had been missing the thumb and index fingertips since before Ethiopia.

'No, no, petrol, petrol.'

I can't tell the difference between the smell of petrol and diesel, so I had no choice but to trust him. The bike didn't conk out, though, and once Ewan was fuelled up we were off again.

Just as with Long Way Round, it had taken a while to get into the groove of travelling. These bike trips are so different from the rest of our lives that it's bound to take a little time. Post-Addis though, everything had fallen into place, we were bouncing off each other, having a laugh and really enjoying the trip. Ewan was riding off-road really well and we were both less tired. It occurred to me that when we're not riding round the world our lives are so busy that we don't see as much of each other as we'd like. Two blokes together twenty-four seven for the best part of three months; it's bound to take some time.

We were having the time of our lives now, aware of just how lucky we were. We were determined not to take anything for granted.

We camped close to the road, and got our heads down early.

The following morning we were off at dawn. We stopped in a little town for lunch at a small cafe with circular tables built round poles that held up the thatched roof. The raw meat was in a locker that didn't look refrigerated but we'd learned to eat where the locals eat and most of the army seemed to be here. Not just the regular soldiers, but the captains, the officers; they were hunched over tables devouring chicken and pretty quickly we were following suit.

Ewan took a phone call; Eve in Malawi. He was like a dog with two tails. 'She's here, Charley, flew overnight from London to Jo'burg and she's in Malawi now.' His grin couldn't have got any wider.

He did stop, though, and pretty quickly. We left the cafe and were not quite out of town when he pulled up sharply, jumped off the bike and hauled his jacket off.

'What's up?' I asked.

'Fucking bee flew up my sleeve and stung me.'

I could see it, three angry looking bumps already rising on his forearm.

'I felt it fly up my sleeve,' he said. 'I tried to wriggle it out but the bastard stung me.'

'They seem to like you, the bees, don't they? The last time, remember?'

'Yeah, that was in my helmet. Rather up my sleeve than in my helmet, Charley.'

EWAN: As if bees weren't bad enough, that night our tents were surrounded by ants, really nasty looking ones with massive pincers. My arm was swelling nicely; three great lumps that were gradually coming together.

The following day the riding was much tougher – it seemed clear now that yesterday we had been on the good dirt. Now we were in sand – and I mean *really* deep sand. Then with no warning the sand would be gravel, then rock; really bumpy stuff, and you had no time to get used to it before it changed again. One minute we were up on the pegs, elbows out and easing our way through the technical stuff and the next the back end was squirrelling all over the place.

Claudio went down, I went down . . . even Charley went down. I was getting tired again. I'd enjoyed the dirt yesterday but this was purgatory; really deep troughs and there was no way you could stand on the pegs, you just had to squat in the saddle, try and steer whilst paddling away at the ground with your feet. The front wheel would be bucking, the rear wheel snatching and losing traction in equal measure and all the while my wife, whom I hadn't seen in weeks, was winging her way to the Malawi border. Mustn't think about that, mustn't think about Eve, concentrate, McGregor!

Crossing a bridge with a piece of scaffold pole as a rail, we paused to watch a group of hippos wallowing; they lay under the water with just their backs showing and every now and then one would lift his head, expose his tusks and grunt at us.

'What do they call a group of hippos, Charley?' I wondered. 'A herd, a flock, a gaggle maybe?'

He shrugged. 'Their backs look like rafts on the water, don't they?'

'A raft then,' I said. 'That's what this is. A raft of hippos, Charley.'

We rode on, the road no better. I suggested we stop for lunch. We ate cold boil-in-the-bag which actually tasted better than it does hot. We had a kip and rode on and after twelve hours of sand, rock and dirt we came to the camp. We were due a day off the bikes and in any case we were in a national park and it would be mad to rush through without checking out the wildlife. Before we got to the camp, however, we hit the gnarliest piece of road we'd come across yet: a final two kilometres that felt like eighteen, a real kick in the balls just when you needed it least. It was a rutted road and I mean rutted; troughs that were so deep they could've drawn water and there was nowhere for the bikes to go but through them. They were dry and grassy, slippery and bumpy, bordered by thirsty grass and acacia trees. If we thought we were paddling before, we were paddling now and by the time we finally got to the camp my legs felt as though someone had taken a piece of two-by-four and beaten them.

It was worth it, though, that ride. We pulled up as the sun was sinking and it really is that huge fireball you see in the movies. The savannah stretched out endless before us. A herd of elephants wandered towards the stream we could see cutting the plain like a sliver of silver. Peter told us that was the Katuma River; all there was until the rains came, at which time most of this grassland would become swamp. Taking our helmets off we sat side by side in total silence. The camp itself was fantastic; old school colonial with big tents, our own bathrooms where water-filled barrels created showers with strings to turn the water on and off. We had wooden beds with white linen and real pillows – oh, was I looking forward to hitting the hay tonight.

In the morning my forearm was one massive bruise, puffed up like Popeye's, the three stings finally coming together. It itched more than hurt, though, and I knew it would go down again in a couple of days.

We took off in search of wildlife, the pair of us sitting in the back of an open jeep. The Katavi National Park is part of the Serengeti and, unlike other parks, if we did see wildlife we were allowed to leave the jeep and walk. There were lions here and leopards, cheetahs, but we didn't see any. We did see elephants and zebras, gigantic herds of Cape buffalo, and we saw . . . the sausage tree.

We were trundling along close to some trees I'd not seen before and I noticed weird grey things hanging off the branches. Our guide told us it was a sausage tree; Charley said the sausages looked more like haggis. We bowed to our guide's superior knowledge, of course, when he told us the sausages were actually a form of fruit. Not juicy so much as dense and heavy, and when one fell you didn't want to be underneath. In the dry season elephants ate them, baboons too, and there were none lying around so hyenas (that eat anything) had been cleaning up the scraps.

We came across a great herd of zebras, masses of them gathered at the river. With the land parched into plates of mud all the animals congregated more tightly together. As we watched we realised that even in the herd we could pick out separate family units: one stallion to seven or eight females and their combined young. Apparently once the stallion has his harem sorted they remain together for life. There is no serious inbreeding because when his daughters get to about two they come into heat for the first time, stand in this really sexy zebra way and drive the other stallions wild with desire. It gets so bad that Dad has to rush around trying to beat them off. In the end, though, the number of young males outweigh the father's energy and the young females are driven off to join other families. The young studs, the sons, just drift away naturally when they are about eighteen months old. They join bachelor bands and run together until they are strong enough to pick up some wives of their own.

CHARLEY: Ewan spotted a foal through his binoculars. I know, a nightmare, isn't it, what with donkeys in Ethiopia and baby rhinos in Kenya . . . give him a chance and he'd be setting up his own game reserve in his back garden when we get home. I have to admit it was cute, though. We weren't close enough for a kidnap, thank God; and back in the truck we went in search of elephants.

The next day Ewan was up at some ungodly hour, packing his bike wearing a head torch. It wasn't light but it was less than forty-eight hours until he would see his beloved wife. Not so much the dog with two tails now as a cat on a hot tin roof.

We were away at dawn but before we'd properly left the camp I was down the road without my bike. We were riding the shitty track, the two clicks we mentioned before, staying to the side and trying to avoid the sand. I saw the tree stump. I watched the tree stump. Don't hit the stump, Charley, you can't hit the stump. I hit the stump, stove in my pannier and landed face down in the dirt.

There was nothing broken, though, just another dent in the bike and it would survive.

Thankfully we left the really bad road behind and by early afternoon we were on hard dirt and doing seventy miles an hour. Ewan was on a mission now; we knew that Eve was already at the border and he couldn't wait to get there. We crested a hill and up ahead saw two motorbikes and three girls by the side of the road. They were just standing there as if they were waiting for us and it seemed so out of place that we pulled over.

'Hi,' we said. 'Are you girls OK?'

They were fine: they lived here. They introduced themselves as Brooke, Casey and Shelby. They were American, and part of a missionary group. Brooke was a youth worker and the other two girls were sisters, and were about to go to bible school. They asked us home for a soda.

I could see Ewan umming and aahhing and I knew what he was thinking; got to get on, got to get on because Eve was already at the border. The reality was, of course, that no matter what we did today we'd not be there until tomorrow anyway, so we followed the girls a couple of miles to their home.

They lived in a white stone house close to a village and a primary school. Through the trees we could make out another series of buildings – a college for Tanzanian pastors. Casey and Shelby's mother came out to meet us. Their dad we'd passed earlier apparently, on his way back to the city with a man he'd brought out to castrate their dogs. One of them, a Doberman cross called Harrison, looked particularly sorry for himself. The girl's mother asked us how long we'd been on the road.

'You're making good time,' she said when we told her. 'We had a couple of cyclists here last October who'd been on the road eight years.'

'A Swiss couple?' I said.

'One was Swiss yes, the other German. Kurt and Dorothy. Do you know them?'

'We met in the Sudan,' Ewan told her. 'They were on their way home to look after her parents, though it was going to take them another six months or so.'

The girls' mother told us that the couple we'd met at that cafe had spent a week with them here in Tanzania while Kurt recovered from a bout of malaria. Kurt, Dorothy: if you're reading this, it's a small world, isn't it? Even on a bicycle.

The family was looking after a little lad called Stephen, an orphan from the city. Shelby's mother told us that in Tanzania if a child's mother dies kids are referred to as orphans regardless of whether the father is still around. In Stephen's case, his mother was dead and his father had remarried. The problem was he worked away a lot and when he did Stephen's stepmother wouldn't feed him. Apparently that wasn't uncommon. The little boy had spent some time with his grandmother but she ran the local distillery and liked to give him the odd nip now and again. This family had come across him badly malnourished in an orphanage.

'Food and love,' the girls' mother told us. 'That's all these kids need. Food and love.'

That night we camped in a little orchard and ate more boil-in-the-bag. I was a lot better since Kenya because Claire had given us a stash of her homemade chilli sauce. It was so good we considered selling it – you know, a picture of Ewan and me on the label like Newman's Own, but then of course we remembered the recipe was Claire's of course . . .

EWAN: I couldn't wait to get to bed, sleep and wake up in the morning. Now I knew Eve was so close I was just dying to get to her. I was up at the crack of dawn, we were on the road by seven and it was four hours to the border. We left the last of the dirt behind and hit tarmac and now I could really put the hammer down. We kept the speed down in towns, of course, rolling past people waving, rectangular brick houses with the ubiquitous tin roofs. We stopped for petrol at a proper station – all forecourt and lights and electronics. Charley said it was so nice to have a pump nozzle that fitted the tank and that the pump read 'petrol' and not 'diesel'. I didn't care. I just wanted to get going.

'What about an early lunch?' he said with a grin. 'I'm pretty hungry, Ewan. There's bound to be a cafe around here, a nice restaurant, maybe. Or a hotel even. We could get washed, peruse the menu for a while, have a siesta afterwards.'

Yeah, right. See you, Charley, it was nice riding with you.

We were off again and at last the hours were ticking into minutes. Finally, my heart hammering away in my chest, there was the border. Another dirt road cutting through a gully with green hills rising in the distance – somewhere over there was my wife and I was so impatient to see her I cannot tell you. Charley fetched the paperwork and I filled in my name, address, my nationality and occupation. Then I came to the box for destination.

I gazed beyond the barrier, the yellow hut, beyond, the people wandering around in football shirts. I was here to meet Eve, to see some country and ride on together – now the three of us.

Destination: 'transit', I wrote, and started the engine.

24
Lilongwe Down

CHARLIE: '*All by myself* . . .' That'll be me, then. Charley: remember me? I'm the one riding with Ewan down through Africa. Charley Boorman, Long Way Down, remember?

Just kidding.

I'd never seen Ewan quite so excited. As soon as the last of the paperwork was completed he raced across the border to where Eve was waiting. I could understand how it felt; if it had been Ollie waiting for me I'd have been jumping the fence. I made my way through and there was Eve. Ewan pulled up, leapt off the bike and she was in his arms. She looked terrific in her LWD hat and yellow singlet. He just held her and held her. In the end I had to look away. I mean, there was lots of kissing and hugging, lots of you know . . . Steady, Charley, best to leave it at that.

It was great to see her and a relief she'd made it safe and sound. Rick, the last of our fixers, had freighted her bike all the way from South Africa. He was driving a Nissan pickup that had been decked out with stickers like our trucks so it would be a unified front when we crossed the finish line in Cape Town.

Talking of stickers, Eve's bike was naked. Ewan quickly pasted a Long Way Down sticker onto the bike while I gave Eve a squeeze.

'How are you?' I asked her.

'I just can't believe it,' she said. 'I can't believe I'm here.'

She was, though, and I could see Ewan was delighted. A little while later she was kitted out in a rally suit and crash helmet and was ready to go. She climbed on her bike, very nervous but determined to ride. She told us afterwards that the difference between being on the bike and in the car was amazing; the atmosphere was so different. She loved how much closer she felt to everything: the people, the landscape, all the different sights and smells of the country.

Ewan rode up alongside. 'OK, Eve?' he called.

'I'm so nervous,' she said. 'I don't know if I can make it.'

'You'll be fine. Charley will go ahead and you follow him. I'll be right behind you.'

I swivelled round in the saddle. 'Now listen, Eve,' I said, 'no wheelies, all right?'

'Yeah,' Ewan echoed. 'Keep the front wheel on the ground.'

We set off at a gentle pace and I checked my mirrors to make sure Eve was all right. She was doing fine; she seemed relaxed and was riding smoothly. I watched her easing into the bends and getting a feel for the bike. I really admired her; it's gutsy what she was doing, not easy being dropped into Africa when you're inexperienced and getting on a bike with your husband and his mate who've been riding every day for months. Eve was looking good, though, and I was more worried about Ewan – he wasn't used to seeing his wife riding and I figured he'd probably be more nervous about it than she was.

EWAN: I probably was, once I'd got over the initial excitement, anyway. I still couldn't quite believe Eve was here. I cast my mind back to that Sunday when she first said she wanted to go – remembering the delight, and then the subsequent worry. I recalled the arguments we'd had, the discussions with Charley, and yet here she was in front of me riding a 650 through Malawi. I was singing I was so happy. Don't you just love it when a plan comes together?

It had taken an hour longer than we had hoped to reach the border, and then the crossing itself had taken quite a while, as usual. In winter (July is winter in this part of the world) it gets dark around five-thirty and the afternoon was already waning. Peeling off the highway we hit dirt road, heading for a remote lodge at the northern end of the lake. I was conscious of Eve: she'd been riding in London but only had half a day's off-road experience in her life, and that had been on bikes that were too big for her. The dirt wasn't too bad to begin with, though, and she was cutting along beautifully. Then she dropped her bike right in front of me. My heart was in my mouth, my wife on the deck in Africa. I'd never seen her fall off before. But she got to her feet immediately, picked the bike up and was back in the saddle again.

I yelled out to see if she was OK. She was fine, she said, determined to carry on. Knowing Eve her pride was probably more bruised than anything. Back in the saddle she walked the bike forward, paddling with her feet and trying to make it through the sand. Then she was down again and I had visions of myself back in that town in Sudan.

This was a tricky section of road, much trickier than it had first looked. The soft stuff just crept up on you – it would be firm under the wheels one moment then loose as shit the next. We suggested to Eve that she ride in the truck for this last section, and David jumped on the bike. He was wearing a T-shirt with no helmet or gloves: he dropped the bike, grazed his elbow and got back on. We got a little further and he dropped it again. I could see his elbow was bleeding and now he'd hurt his hand.

Finally we made it to the lodge. David was fine, if a little bloody, and the bike was christened at least.

'Are you all right, mate?' I asked him.

'Now I know about sand. Jesus Christ, how the hell have you guys managed to cope with so much of it?'

'A case of having to, Dave,' I told him. 'You get used to it.'

'Not if your name's Claudio.' Clouds walked past me, shaking his head. 'Fucking sand, it's shit. Slow down, power on: it doesn't make any difference.'

Eve was tired and a bit shaky from picking the bike up but she told me the pain was worth it. 'I only did half a day off-road before,' she said as I started unpacking my gear. 'At home, Ewan, in England, and it was nothing like the sand. Sorry if I wasn't very good.'

'You were great. In fact you were more than great.'

'The sand though, it's just much harder than it looks.' She glanced across to where Dai was taking a look at Dave's cuts and bruises. 'Is Dave OK? He didn't have any gear, not even a helmet.'

'Dave will be fine. Won't you, mate?' I called.

He lifted a hand. 'Oh yeah, no worries.'

The lodge was built above a small beach, with an open area of tables on a veranda, and the lake stretching blue and grey to the horizon. It was owned by a British couple who told us they'd lived in Africa for eighteen years – he'd been a tour guide and she a doctor. They had just built a cottage, but the place was so beautiful they thought they ought to share it. It was indeed spectacular: our bungalows overlooked the beach, a handful of trees, and water as far as the eye could see. Just about the perfect retreat for a man who hasn't seen his wife in a couple of months.

CHARLEY: Enough of that. Come on. There I was on my lonesome with Ollie back in London and Ewan had his wife with him. No wonder I was up before the sun. Last night I'd read the newspaper Eve had kindly brought me, I'd eaten the chocolate, had a swim, a shower, eaten dinner and generally twiddled my thumbs.

I slept pretty well though, not a hint of envy – honestly. Now I was on the balcony outside my bungalow, watching the sun coming up across the lake. I'd seen some pretty spectacular sunsets in Africa but this was wonderful, the sun rising in pale gold as if from the water itself. It was a quiet moment and I was having a few of those now. We were on the downward slope of the trip I suppose and as I looked back over the past few weeks, I realised just how much I was enjoying myself. In the early stages I'd been worrying too much, missing Ollie and the kids. I don't think I settled into the rhythm of the journey until much later than I expected. But since Ewan and I cleared the air in Ethiopia it had really kicked off in the way I'd hoped. Every morning I'd wake up with a sense of excitement and couldn't wait to get cracking on with the day.

This morning I would be 'all by myself' though (like it or not I'm going to enjoy singing that song, might as well aim for all the sympathy I can get). This was Eve's first full day on the bike, so to ease her in she and Ewan would stay on the tarmac and head south to tonight's camp site with Claudio. *The Three Amigos*, that's what Ewan was saying. I'd been one of the amigos and now it cut to the quick. (My dad would be proud of this, there's a future in acting, Charley!)

I was on my own then (wringing it dry), heading up a mountain track to where Dr Livingstone had lived. I said my goodbyes and hoiked a monster wheelie which Ewan told me later drew cheers and applause from a bunch of kids on bicycles.

Livingstone reached Lake Malawi in 1859. He was the first European to see it – this was long before Stanley met him in the bush. Seeing how beautiful the lake was, he asked a local what it was called.

Strange question, the local thought, it isn't called anything. It's just a lake; you know, a body of inland water. *Nyasa*, he said, *nyasa*. So Livingstone called it Lake Nyasa, only to find out later he'd actually named it Lake Lake. The country became known as Nyasa too and it was only in 1964, when it gained full independence, that the people got the name Malawi back.

Livingstone built a town in the mountains overlooking Lake Lake and it's still up there, looking a little shabby these days, but it has a college and there are still little reminders of its British origins, such as the 30 mph signs on the roads. Livingstone built the town so high up because of the mosquitoes – they were so prevalent and malaria was so rife that his only option was to live at an altitude where they couldn't survive.

While I was there I visited an old stone house that had been erected in 1903 as a meeting place for the elders of Livingstone's church. It was a museum now, right on the hill overlooking the water. I found lots of references to missionary work; records of people being ordained and churches being built, boxes of old glass slides with etchings of ships and shipyards engraved on them. There was an oxygen machine for surgical operations, a film projector, even an old rickshaw. I tried to imagine some poor soul hauling the rickshaw up that mountain road. It had been easy on a motorbike but a *rickshaw*?

In a way I was enjoying my day on my own without the 'three amigos'. I was able to do some Dakar-style riding – did I ever tell you I did the Dakar, by the way? I had taken it relatively easy on the way up, but on the other side of the hill I was catching air, popping the odd wheelie and backing it into the bends.

EWAN: *The Three Amigos.* Charley's an amigo: he'll always be *the* amigo. But Eve wasn't up for the mountain road, and it was fantastic to have the day with her as she got used to riding in Africa. We pootled along at about fifty; the road was tarmac but potholed and pretty twisty – nice bends, mind you, not really tight stuff – and Eve was picking her line, watching the vanishing points and really getting into the riding. I was so proud of her. It was weird not having Charley there – my wing man for so many miles – but we'd catch up tonight, and tomorrow the three of us would ride together.

We stopped for a break and Eve said she was beginning to

relax. At first she'd been tense and stiff, gripping the bars too hard. I told her she was doing really well; she'd picked a pace where she was comfortable enough to take in the scenery: the sweeping hills, the forests, the baobab tree – these massive trees that look as though they've been planted upside down. Eve loved them: she told me she'd heard a tale where God got so annoyed about something he pulled up the trees and replanted them so they had their roots in the air.

We were passing lots of people riding bicycles; what I call the standard third world machines, with no gears but sturdy and with a headlight and twin bells. Most had decorations on the frame and an old fashioned dynamo on the back wheel. I quite fancied the idea of one of those for London.

We took our time and stopped for lunch at a place called Mzuzu. It rained hard and Eve said it reminded her of riding in England, but by the time we came to camp for the night the light was that incredible African blue. There were lots of roadside vendors, mostly kids selling balls that looked as if they were made from thousands of rubber bands. The woman who owned the lodge where we camped told us that's exactly what they had been made from – the rubber having been stolen from various plantations in the area.

Charley arrived. We were waiting for him as he sped up, locked the back wheel and skidded to a halt. Helmet off; he was full of the day. He showed us a rubber-band ball he'd bought that was about the size of a tennis ball.

'I was ripped off,' he said. 'fifteen hundred *kwacha*, which I reckon is about ten quid. But he was just a kid with these big panda eyes and . . .'

We took a walk on the empty beach. The lake stretched to the horizon, and it felt as if we were by the sea. It was hard to imagine the water was fresh and not salt. As it was still quite warm, Charley and I went for a swim.

'Eve's really into the bike,' I told him. 'She really understands how it allows you to get closer to the people and the countryside in a way you never can in a car. By the way, did you see the chickens?

'You mean the suicide squad?'

We'd seen them all day, like the geep in Ethiopia, chickens that skittered out in front of us, just appearing from nowhere as if they had some kind of death wish.

'And that cheese or whatever it was?'

'Ah, yeah, the really smelly stuff.'

Along with the kids selling rubber balls, we'd seen lots of sheets laid down by the side of the road with squares of white patties spread on them. They stank to high heaven – made of some kind of goat's cheese, I think.

It was weird in a way: this was the first day when I hadn't ridden with Charley, yet we'd seen the same things, and apart from his sojourn into the mountains we'd still travelled the same stretch of road. All the way to Cape Town, the same sights and sounds and smells, in a way it was nice to know that, although we'd made our own way to the camp, we'd all shared some of the new experiences on the road.

CHARLEY: I was glad Ewan and Eve had had a day to themselves; if it had been Ollie coming out I'd have done it for sure.

And it was great having her around. I know that when the idea was first mooted I'd had some reservations, probably born of not knowing how the dynamic would work. I'd had plenty of experience being on the road with Ewan. We'd been through the pitfalls, both emotional and physical, and we knew how to handle them together. Adding a third person even for a short time, especially one of our wives, had raised the odd question. I needn't have worried of course, Eve was fantastic: I'd known her for years, what kind of a person she was and deep down I'd always known she could handle it. Now she was here and, far from being any kind of burden, her presence was very refreshing.

From then on the three of us rode together. The pace was easy but that didn't worry me, this wasn't a race and it's vital that no one in a group feels pressurised, otherwise people start taking risks and accidents happen.

Eve was riding well, she kept it smooth and I was pleased for her because I wasn't sure how much she'd be able to do once we got to Zambia. We kept hearing conflicting stories about how good or bad the roads were, but the latest news was that there was some pretty serious off-roading ahead of us.

I loved Malawi. I've heard it called a 'hand-out-state', and it's true that UNICEF is active here, as is Christian Aid. But hand outs or not, there's not much of an economy. The people were so friendly; they didn't hassle or crowd you and I hadn't once felt threatened. But then I'd felt that about every country we'd been through. All the horror stories we'd been told were just ridiculous.

There was one weird incident, mind you. We were headed for a place called 'Cool Running', a campsite at the southerly end of the lake. Rounding a bend, two blokes leapt into the road waving their arms at us and screaming away like banshees. They were wearing only loin cloths with canvas wrapped round their heads and were covered head to toe in soot. It was totally unexpected and pretty unnerving. We never did find out who they were or why it happened, but it was kind of spooky.

Every time we ventured down to the lake we had to leave the tarmac, and Eve found herself on dirt once again. She didn't fall through: feet out, she paddled the bike all the way down the slope until we got to the camp site.

'You're doing brilliantly, Eve,' I told her. 'I mean it. You're not scared to fall and that's the most important thing.'

'Charley,' she said, 'thank you for being so patient.'

'Patient, Christ. You're doing really well.'

She was. The last bit was really mad, though, stones and ruts and divots; massive holes where the front wheel would just stick. In the end Eve decided discretion was the better part of valour and jumped in the truck. Dave got on her bike and guided it down the hill.

Arriving at 'Cool Running' we went for a walk along the beach and came across a group of fishermen mending their nets which was fascinating to watch. The nets were a patchwork of squares, intricately formed and all manner of colours, white and lobster pink, bright red and blue. We also helped a couple of younger guys launch a canoe they'd shaped from a log.

At the site we met Steve and Dana. Steve was this crazy guy from Cape Town, and Dana was from Israel. They'd met at a trance party. Steve was a massive *Long Way Round* fan, and couldn't believe it when we showed up in the very spot where he was camping. He was living in a roof tent on top of a truck. It was all he owned these days, apparently. He told us that he'd been so inspired by *Long Way Round* that he decided to follow a dream he'd always had. He sold everything: house, business, the lot. He bought the truck and the tent, hooked up with Dana and drove all over Africa. They'd landed here in Malawi and planned to start a lodge somewhere close to the lake. I'd never met a more infectious soul or someone who laughed quite as much. He told us how much he admired what we'd done, but we were well known and didn't have to take on a challenge like Long Way Round; we could've stayed safe in our careers back in London.

'We're not that hardcore,' Ewan told him. 'I mean, there are plenty tougher than us. Remember Addis, Charley?'

I rolled my eyes: 'Oh God, yeah.'

Ewan explained. We were riding out of the city and had pulled up for a moment. This little kid walked over and in the strongest south London accent imaginable, he said: 'Where is you boys from, innit?'

'London,' I told him.

'London, is it. I'm from London. Whereabouts in London, innit?'

'Fulham,' Charley said.

'Fulham!' He looked aghast. 'You posh boy rough riders then, innit.'

EWAN: It was the middle of Ethiopia, for God's sake, and there was this little hoodie telling us how it was. In a way I suppose he was right. Then again, at least we were doing it.

Steve was a great guy and hats off to him for following his dream with nothing to his name but a few quid in the bank and a roof tent. His parting shot was: 'Give my regards to Cape Town.'

We set out again and Eve carefully negotiated the dirt from 'Cool Running' and as we hit tarmac she came alongside me.

'Did you see that, Ewan? Zambia will be like a tea party for me.'

We stopped early that day at another lodge near the capital Lilongwe; there were so many lodges, it was winter and we were happy to just chill out whenever we could. The rest of the team was there and Russ said he and David wanted to interview me for the website. We were sitting on a veranda overlooking a few head of cattle that grazed the land and I was thinking how mellow it was meandering along with my wife. Russ disappeared for a few moments and I was thinking, Where's he gone now? I thought we were doing an interview. He came back again and said he'd ordered a coke for me, which of course was very thoughtful. David started asking me about Tanzania and I was thinking, what the fuck are we talking about that for?

I looked quizzically at Russ. 'I thought you said you wanted an interview for the website.'

He had the biggest smile on his face. 'Yeah, that's right I did.' He glanced at David, aimed a mock kick. 'That's right, isn't it, Dave?'

'What the . . . ?' I looked from one to the other, both grinning like a pair of prize Cheshire cats.

'Here's your coke,' Dave said.

I looked round and the waitress handed me the coke. 'Thanks,' I said then jumped, and I mean physically. The waitress looked just like – the waitress was my mum. I did a double take. The last time I'd spoken to Mum she'd been at home in Crieff and now here she was in the flesh handing me a can of coke.

'Hello,' I said. 'What're you doing here?'

She gave me a big hug and told me she'd come out to make sure I was behaving myself.

It was fantastic, a real surprise, just about the last thing I would've expected. You're on a bike trip with your mate and then all at once there's your mother handing you a coke. She told me Russ had brought her out, arranged it as a surprise and suggested she could kill two birds with one stone by looking in on Sightsavers, a charity she's involved with here in Malawi.

'It was last year,' Mum said, sitting down. 'He suggested it to me at the premiere of *Miss Potter*.'

'*Miss Potter*!' I couldn't believe it. 'That was a year ago.'

'Planning ahead, mate,' Russ said with a smile. 'Dave and I thought it would be nice, you know, given Eve would probably be here too.'

I was gobsmacked. I really didn't know what to say: typical Russ and Dave, thinking about a gesture like this as far back as a year ago. Like when I broke my leg and missed out on the ski trip, they'd been concerned about me being on my own and had come round to make sure depression didn't set in.

It was wonderful to see my mum. We took a walk in the grounds and she told me that she'd been to see someone undergoing a cataract operation and visited some schools where visually impaired kids were being integrated into the mainstream.

All too quickly, our time in Malawi was coming to an end and I was so glad Eve was staying on through Zambia. She had wanted to come for the trip itself, of course, the landscape and the experience, but it was also for the UNICEF visits. I'd been to Malawi before when we put together a TV programme about AIDS called *The Missing Face*, but this was Eve's first time.

Hooking up with Sarah and Wendy from UNICEF, we set off for a community childcare centre in Chimteka to see how under-fives whose lives had been affected by HIV were being assisted. UNICEF supports thousands of these centres all through Africa – they're usually set up in or close to villages and the young kids go there in the morning. They get food and some basic education, they play with their mates and are able to just be kids for a while. This time out also gives whoever is caring for them (often no longer their parents) a chance to earn some money. One in every thirteen people in Malawi is HIV positive and over half a million children have lost either one or both parents to an AIDS-related illness. The communities struggle to cope with the enormous amount of orphans left behind, and centres like this give them a chance to keep going.

In the afternoon older children come to the centres; not to play but to receive psychological support. When there are so many children affected it's easy to collectivise them emotionally and forget that each one is an individual and that their loss is as acute as yours or mine would be. They're encouraged to create 'memory books', a brilliant idea; it helps them come to terms with the loss of their parents and allows them to grieve properly. It also seems to give them the confidence to face a future without a parent supporting them.

CHARLEY: The young kids were amazing, racing around like any other children, laughing, shouting, playing. We received a fantastic welcome; songs and dancing, lots of colour and hand clapping. We had lunch of maize, beans and cabbage. The children were so happy to be around us, full of mischief and laughter. It always staggers me how positive even the youngest of them are.

After lunch we sat down with some of the older kids. Fausita, a thirteen-year-old girl, lost her parents when she was six. Since then she has lived across the road from the centre with her aunt. Fausita told us she loved coming to the centre because she had a lot of support from the people there, both the helpers and the other kids. She wanted to be a doctor when she grew up. The only problem is that secondary education in Malawi costs money and she has no parents to fund her. Fausita is a good student, though, her favourite subject is maths and she works very hard. UNICEF told us that because of that she has a good chance at secondary education and there are bursaries available with only a small contribution necessary from the child.

Malawi is such a small country, and it's all too easy for it to be forgotten. There's only one doctor for every 100,000 people and UNICEF, along with other non-government agencies, is doing all it can. Because the spread of HIV is so rife, extended families take on thousands of orphaned children. Fausita's aunt, for example, has seven to care for in all.

Often it's the grandmother, and we met a lady called Haviloina who couldn't tell us how old she was, she only knew her husband had been born in 1938. She thought she was around seventy, maybe, and had seen three of her six children die from what she called coughs and swelling. We weren't sure whether she said that because she didn't know they had AIDS, or just because of the stigma. She had four grandchildren that she was now effectively mother to, and two of them were under five years old. It was such a lot for an older woman to take on, and yet she accepted her situation with grace and courage.

This was our final UNICEF visit and we said our goodbyes, thanking everyone for their hospitality, and thanking UNICEF for the care they continue to bring to these remote and potentially forgotten corners of the world. It's a privilege and a responsibility to make sure we keep their profile high because the people that read our books and watch the TV shows have been superb in supporting our charities financially. It's not just UNICEF, but CHAS of course and Riders for Health. While we were in Kenya, the Day of Champions auction was held at the British Moto GP at Donnington Park. Every year the proceeds go to Riders for Health and, as we were watching elephants at a waterhole, we took a phone call and were told that two guys had paid a combined total of £22,000 to fly out and ride with us into Cape Town. It was an amazing gesture and, given that we found out while we were watching some incredibe African wildlife, I think it really brought the trip home for both of us. We were approaching the southern tip of Africa and I realised that it wasn't just Ewan and I travelling; we had every fan, every reader, every biker who followed our trail, all on the back of the bikes with us.

25
Out in the Cuds with the Girls

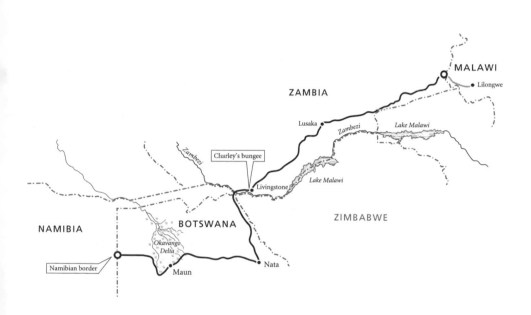

EWAN: Eve rode with us for seven days and her riding got better and better. The time passed far too quickly though, each morning I'd wake with her beside me and think about the day ahead of us and then in no time it seemed to be evening again.

In Zambia the roads were actually much easier than we'd thought and she was hammering along at seventy, avoiding the potholes like a veteran.

Stopping for a break, she got talking to a lovely woman in her fifties called Festina who lived in a collection of huts just off the road. There was a maize store and a vegetable patch where a couple of pigs were snuffling. It had been built in the shade of a mango tree that was in flower but wouldn't bear fruit until November.

Festina introduced Eve to her grandchildren and told her they came to her for Bible teaching in the evenings, along with their friends. They would sit outside and she would read to them and explain the importance of school, though she had only had primary education herself.

She was very aware of the risks of HIV and made sure the children understood the dangers. She told them that as far as she was concerned the only real protection was abstinence. One of her neighbours – a young woman – had chosen to go to the traditional doctors rather than attend a clinic and had tragically died just three weeks previously. It was a reminder to us of the kinds of dilemmas people out here faced; not just the medical ones but what to do when you are sick. Villagers live in much the same way they always have, and the traditions and beliefs go back hundreds of years.

We said goodbye and shook hands, Festina bowing slightly. I noticed that most of the people did that: everyone was so polite, full of smiles and handshakes. Again we'd heard the horror stories, how you couldn't camp because it wasn't safe, but as usual the rumours had proved unfounded.

I watched Eve ahead of me, her confidence had grown immeasurably and I was hoping this would be the first of many motorcycle trips together. Back when she started learning, Eve had been adamant that this would be her only trip, and she wouldn't go on riding once we were back in London. Maybe she'd change her mind. We'd wait and see.

A few miles later we were rattling along with Charley leading, Eve in the middle and me bringing up the rear. A dog ran out from nowhere, suddenly there on our left. I'd not seen any animal move so quickly in all the time I'd been in Africa. It came charging out of the trees and straight across the road. Eve must only have seen a flash of something dark, with no time to do anything about it, before it clattered into her foot.

It was one of those moments that happen so fast and all you see is disaster. Eve saved it, though I don't know how. The dog bounced off her foot and rolled away. I saw it get up a little groggily and lope off as if it had decided the road wasn't worth crossing after all.

We rode on a little further before we stopped. I came alongside and shouted across to Eve. 'Lucky it wasn't a couple of seconds earlier, the dog would've got caught up in your front wheel.'

Nice one, Ewan: that'll be good for her confidence.

She was a little shaken up but took it in her stride and we rode on. Stopping for lunch I took the opportunity to get the trousers of my rally suit mended. For the past few weeks I'd had a hole, and embarrassingly it was right in the groin. While we were grabbing a bite to eat, I noticed a guy sitting outside in a woollen hat with a pedal-powered sewing machine in front of him. Fetching a towel from my bike I wandered over and asked him if he could fix the trousers.

Certainly, he said, so I whipped them off and stood there in the towel while he got to work. Problem solved.

CHARLEY: What an image. It wasn't just the towel; it was the baggy socks – a lurid blend of multi-coloured hoops.

I was tired, I mean really knackered, and for the last couple of days I'd been feeling fluey. I'd missed the odd malaria tablet and was beginning to wonder. On the bike I was lethargic, only popping the odd wheelie, and my hands were aching much more than they had been. On the longer stretches I'd find myself taking my right hand off the throttle and working it with my left as I'd done before. I hoped I wasn't getting sick, not this late in the trip.

Looking for somewhere to camp, we caught a glimpse of a village not far from the road and thought we might rock up and ask the elders if we could stay with them. There were a few children wandering around, and lots of chickens and goats. Getting off the bikes, this smallish man in a black and white T-shirt greeted us.

We shook hands and he bowed. I bowed too and asked him if he was the chief. He said no, the chief was a man called Mpancha. This chap's name was Sanfajo and I asked him if it was possible to camp. He took a moment to think about it and then said it would be fine so long as we didn't steal their wives or eat their goats. No, I'm joking. Happily he showed us a clearing close to their huts. The huts were a little different from what we'd seen earlier: the roofs were thatched and the walls covered with animal dung as before, but the poles that formed the structure were interlocked horizontally, like a sheep hurdle only long and circular.

Sanfajo had a contagious smile and he seemed really pleased that we would be his guests for the night. As we unpacked the bikes he was joined by his wife, then a few of his friends came over and watched us put the tents up. We chatted about where we'd come from, and they told us that in the town where Ewan got his trousers fixed there was a guy called Nkanda who only wore a hat – nothing else. He'd strut around all day with his hat on and as far as he was concerned that meant he was dressed. He'd stop and talk to people, carry on with life as normal but as soon as he took his hat off he was naked and no one could look at him. Unfortunately we didn't get to meet him.

Ewan was trying to get a fire going; he'd gathered sticks and the dried outer leaves from cobs of maize and he had my lighter but all he could raise was smoke.

'I've got firelighters, Ewan,' I told him.

'Quick, get them. Get them, Charley. Eve'll be back in a minute and she'll get the thing lit in a heartbeat like she always does. What about petrol? Have you got any petrol?'

Eve was talking to Sanfajo's wife; we'd given them some bananas and oranges. She wandered over now, glanced at the flameless fire and knelt down to have a crack herself. This time, though, she didn't fare much better and meanwhile we could hear flames crackling merrily from most of the huts. In the end Ewan took a walk down to where Sanfajo was cooking his supper on a triangular grid over a perfectly smokeless fire.

'Can I borrow a log?' Ewan indicated the blaze.

'Of course.' Sanfajo was on his feet and picking up the biggest flaming log.

'No, no,' Ewan said, 'just a little one. Thank you, sir.' Armed with fire, ours was soon burning and we squatted down like the desperadoes we thought we were.

Still feeling groggy, I found my malaria testing kit and set about trying to work out what to do with it.

'You need to give yourself a little prick, Charley,' Ewan said. 'Eve, give Charley a prick would you?'

Getting to her feet Eve shook her head. 'Out in the cuds with the girls,' she muttered. 'Come here, Charley. Let me look.' Taking the needle contraption she pricked my thumb. I yelled, of course.

We worked out that we had to dip the needle thing in the solution then put it in the holder and wait to see which line registered: A, B, or C. C meant I didn't have malaria.

EWAN: We waited ten minutes and the tester registered C. No, Charley didn't have malaria.

Eve poked at the fire with a stick. 'That's fine,' she said, 'great. But the next worry is, what *do* you have, Charley?'

Charley grinned. 'Road fatigue,' he said.

We invited Sanfajo and his mates over for something to eat: a boil-in-the-bag between them. They looked less than delighted. They had already eaten, and had used fresh food, of course, so I'm not surprised the aroma of processed chilli wasn't so appetising. They chewed on it, however, sharing my cup and spoon; one guy in a pink baseball cap smoking a massive, flat roll-up while he ate. I don't know if they liked it but they were very polite.

As usual we were in bed by eight; it had become the norm when we were camping. The village was settling down, just a few fires burning and the gentle tones of muted conversation. In bed by eight and up with the sun, a burst of gold breaking through the leaves of acacia. Sunset and sunrise aren't things you notice much in London but out here you lived by them and personally I'd never get tired of it.

We were heading for Victoria Falls where Charley planned to throw himself off a bridge with a bit of elastic tied round his feet. Good luck, mate. I couldn't imagine doing it. Strangely, I'm not into anything where I think I might die.

The roads were empty, tarmac but potholed, banks of yellow grass and thick with trees. We bumped into another biker, a guy from South Africa who'd zigzagged his way through Namibia and was heading for Malawi before drifting south again through Mozambique. Like us he was loaded to the gunwales, still on road tyres with a set of knobblies strapped on the back. It was good to chat to him; we'd met plenty of cyclists en route but few bikers. He told us he worked in China and once his trip was over he was headed for Beijing and a language course in Mandarin.

There were only a few days left now before Eve took off and I didn't want to think about it. It was only a couple of weeks or so until I'd see her again of course but I'd really miss her. She'd been a breath of fresh air and it wasn't just me who thought so: we were all going to miss her. I pushed it to the back of my mind and concentrated on the journey, the time we still had together. As I rode along, I just kept looking ahead and seeing her riding there in front of me, smooth as silk and dancing around the potholes.

On our travels we had heard about an old guy from Scotland called Ian McGregor Bruce who ran a crocodile farm. He sounded like a cross between Robert Shaw's character in *Jaws* and

Crocodile Dundee. So we decided to drop in. They had two properties: a farm out in the sticks and another in the city. When we arrived at the farm, he was at their educational centre in Livingstone, so we were greeted by his son.

They'd started the place twenty years ago when Ian was sixty. At eighty, he still played beach volleyball every day. His son told us he'd been a big game hunter and used to wrestle crocs. Gaining something of a reputation, he was called in by villagers to deal with problem crocs, big bastards that ate cattle and people. He started to catch them and bred them to provide skins for the leather industry. One thing led to another, and realising the tourist potential, they opened the educational centre in Livingstone. Ian's son showed us one massive beast lying beside his pond, as fat as a horse. He must have been twelve feet long. They'd caught him after he ate a couple of cows followed by the men who owned them. When they brought him in there was one other male croc on the farm. This new guy was eighty years old already and he took on the other male, bit him in half and stole his nineteen wives.

Later we met Ian himself and he was exactly as I imagined. He had a broad Scots accent even after spending most of his life in Africa, he wore a green cap and wandered around with a long spiked pole. In one enclosure he messed about with a hissing, albino crocodile that moved so fast it was frightening.

'She's out of her element,' he told us, 'vulnerable on land.'

Vulnerable! She looked about as vulnerable as a tank.

'Steve Irwin used to get the crocs to chase him at his place in Australia,' Ian said. 'But then he could jump the fence. Me, I'd get stuck and have my arse bitten.'

CHARLEY: He reminded me of my dad, a slightly smaller version maybe, but just as sharp and funny. He introduced us to Maramba, another maneater who was even bigger than the cattle killer. He was lying in the mud with Peggy, so named because her right hind leg had been bitten off. Ian explained that even in the most filthy, rancid water a croc's wound never becomes infected. He told us that at two hundred million years old this reptile was about as evolved as it got. Its stomach could digest pretty much anything, although not a life jacket apparently. A few years ago they'd caught one dangerous croc with bait, tied its jaws and unfortunately it vomited into its lungs. In the morning it was dead and cutting it open they found a perfectly good life jacket – but not the person who'd been wearing it.

Ian introduced us to his right hand man Morgan, who went out with him in the boat when they were called out. The boat had no sides because they had to get the crocs on board and Ian said that he liked to do what he called the spearing: lassoing the beast around the jaws. Once he had it caught, he handed the dangerous part of getting it on board to Morgan. He told us how they were trolling along one time about two in the morning when Ian heard a splash. Morgan, having fallen asleep, had slipped overboard. Ian said he never saw a man move so fast: like Jesus walking on water he came skating over the side.

Morgan showed us a collection of snakes, hooded cobras and various others that spat venom into your eyes to blind you. Their aim was perfect and the only way to get rid of it was with water, immediately, and from the most easily available source, out in the bush with no waterhole nearby. Ewan said that he'd happily . . . no, we won't go there.

We also saw a black mamba, which has to be one of the scariest snakes there is. It can grow to twelve feet long and can swim. On land it moves at twenty kilometres an hour with one third of its body upright, weaving through the bush. Its skin is grey – it's the inside of its mouth that's black, and when it bites it injects enough venom to kill ten full-grown men. If you don't get anti-venom immediately you're toast.

We had just enough time to hear some grisly stories of Ian's hunting days, and see his collection of loaded rifles, before we had to head off. I had an appointment to keep with that length of elastic. Before we left he told us to remember when we were camping in the bush that the leopard is the most treacherous animal in Africa. If you wound one, he will play dead and wait for you. A lion will roar, but not the leopard, he'll lie in the brush and won't make a sound. When you get to him he'll pounce. A leopard did that to him once, ripped his cheek with a forepaw, nearly got his jugular and only narrowly missed ripping his stomach open with its hind legs.

Ewan was singing softly: 'Farewell and adieu to you fair Spanish ladies, Farewell and adieu to you ladies of Spain . . .'

Remember *Jaws*? Quint, Brody and Hooper sitting round the table swapping scars? You've got him, Ian McGregor Bruce.

The bridge was one hundred and twenty metres above the Zambezi, that's almost four hundred feet in old money.

Our first glimpse of the falls was through a V-shaped cleft in the landscape. We rode up to the bridge I was planning to leap from and initially all we could see was the spray lifting like smoke. Riding closer we saw them, the Victoria Falls, millions of gallons of water, the largest in the world. They were magnificent, incredible; the river was wide and flat as it approached a great fault in the land and the water just fell away. It cascaded in great curtains, the rock walls vertical in some places and not quite in others, before being forced through the cleft into narrow and raging rapids. That was where I would plummet, and it had seemed like such a good idea when I told everyone I'd do it back in London. The roar in itself was amazing. If you're old enough you might remember Tarzan on telly on Saturday mornings. Ron Ely, standing on the rocks above these very falls, looking just as cool as the legend he was portraying.

I wasn't the only one jumping; we'd hooked up with the support crew and Jimmy Simak was up for it as well. We stood together beside the little metal platform that only had three sides. Jimmy told me he'd never felt so nervous in his life.

I wasn't exactly a bundle of beans myself. I stepped on to the platform first and this smiling Zambian was chatting to me.

'How many times have you jumped before?'

'Never.'

'So this is your first time.' He laid a palm on my shoulder. 'Let's hope it's not your last then, eh?'

With that he strapped my legs together, attached a rather frayed-looking cable and stepped away. 'All yours,' he said. 'We'll count to five and you go.'

I glanced at the other side of the platform, the bridge side, the safe side where Ewan and Eve were looking on.

'I feel sick just watching,' Ewan called.

'Thanks, mate. That makes me feel a whole lot better.' I hopped to the edge of the platform.

'Big jump,' I said.

'We'll count you down,' the Zambian told me. 'Say goodbye to your wife. Five, four, three, two . . .'

'Aagghhhh!' I was gone, a huge leap, a swallow dive, well, falling very fast anyway. The first few seconds it was 'Holy Shit!' but then 'Wow! Fantastic'. There was a lot of pressure on my face but God, I'd do that again.

EWAN: Jimmy made his jump, plummeting to certain death before being hauled up by the cable and bouncing around like a yo-yo above the rapids of the Zambezi. Not for me, boys, not for me – but hats off to you guys, that's for sure.

In the morning we were heading for the river crossing that marked the border with Botswana and Eve was leaving for home. God, I was going to miss her – seven days was nowhere near long enough – but she'd ridden her bike, tasted the journey and I was very proud of her.

When the moment came there were a few tears. Actually there were more than a few – the whole crew would miss her. Bags packed, we stepped apart from the others for a few moments.

'Two weeks,' I told her. 'Two weeks and I'll see you again. I love you. Kiss the children for me.'

'I will. I love you too.' There were tears behind her sunglasses. She got in the car and lifted her hand in a wave. I watched as the driver turned the car around, and then she was gone.

Charley came over. 'Are you all right, Ewan?' he said.

'Fine, I'm fine.' I needed a few moments to myself. Eve's time with us all seemed so short and I was trying to work out why she couldn't have stayed on at least while we were in the Okavango. I don't know, another one of those remote-control decisions being made perhaps, by whom and when and where I'm never quite sure.

Walking back to my bike I could see the ferry approaching. We loaded up, paid the fare and I stood by myself on deck. I needed some space. I watched a crewman throw off the ropes. Zambia was behind us, Eve was flying out, the rattle of engines filled the air and we headed across the river and into the trees.

I woke to the sound of footsteps.

Lying there, I tried to work out who it was and how close the footsteps were to the tent. Out here your hearing is so hypersensitive it's difficult sometimes to work out the distances. I thought it might be Charley going for a pee, or one of the others maybe. We were just over the border in Botswana, and had decided to camp together for the first night.

Rolling over I closed my eyes to go back to sleep.

Then I heard it again, slow, heavy footsteps. My heart began to thump. I stared into the darkness. I heard something crunch in the undergrowth, the swish of branches and a deep rumbling sound.

Jesus Christ. Elephants.

We'd seen their droppings when we arrived, but they were old and there was no sign that any had passed through for days. They were back now, though, and my tent was right in the middle of their path.

I had to get out – they'd never see the tent, just trample it with me inside. Wearing only a T-shirt, I unzipped the flysheet and stuck my head out. Quickly I grabbed a pair of shoes.

'Ewan!' A sharp hiss. 'Ewan!' It was our fixer Rick. Grabbing some jeans I pulled them on, trying to call to him in a whisper that was loud enough for him to hear.

'Ewan!'

'I'm coming.'

'Ewan! Come over here. You need to get out of the way of the elephants.'

'I'm coming, Rick. I'm coming.' I was about to set off through the darkness when I realised my mosquito door was open. Better zip it up, I don't want to be bitten by mosquitoes after I've been trampled by elephants.

In the morning I found their tracks, massive footprints. They were oval shaped and three times the size of my hand. I found where they'd snapped off some leafy branches, then came across an indentation in the dust where one elephant had snuffled something with his trunk. He'd been twenty feet from my tent.

They worry about foot and mouth disease in Botswana and there's a line that runs right across the country – a chemical dip. We rode through it and, pulling out on the other side, Charley popped the front wheel. The road was pretty good and we were cutting through grasslands, this was real savannah again, a massive kind of openness, the land stretched for mile after mile, the horizon no more than a shimmering wave of heat. Eve would be home by now and I wished she could still be with me, especially as we were taking a couple of days off at a lodge in the Okavango.

We flew up in a small plane, all crammed together – a mass of fresh water and islands below us, delta country, swamp and grasslands, with pockets of solid ground. It was an amazing sight.

We were met by our guide, a man who called himself 'Doctor'. He wore a leather bush hat and drove a jeep with high-lift suspension and raised seats in the back. There was a spotter's chair fixed to the front wing so his mate could locate the wildlife. Doctor gave us some quick dos and don'ts as regards life in the

Okavango then we were off, bouncing along a marsh road right through the swamp itself. Clearly Doctor knew the trail because one minute we'd be on land and the next water was rushing by like waves across our gunwales.

Our destination was Mapula Lodge, a ranch style house with adjoining cabins built right on the edge of the lagoon with an amazing, uninterrupted view of the waterland that made up the Okavango Delta. We were introduced to the staff, had a quick cup of tea then we were back in the jeep and heading into the wilderness.

CHARLEY: We saw an elephant almost immediately, a solitary bull wading through the shallows. He was a massive animal with enormous ears and half-length tusks that showed the wear and tear of his years. He turned his rear end on us then wandered into the trees. Doctor told us that elephants are non-territorial and follow the food trails, seeking vegetation between the mass of watercourses.

We spotted giraffes and jackals, and a small herd of wildebeest that galloped over to take a look at us, the sturdy bull stepping away from his wives to make sure we didn't come too close. I'd never seen these animals in the flesh. They were big and athletic with massive heads. Black manes ran the length of their spines and with their heads down they bellowed at us like cattle.

Deeper into the swamp we saw another elephant, bigger and younger than the last, with huge curving tusks that sat high and pointed. We learned that the males hooked up with other males at different times of the year. The family groups were made up of the young elephants and females, with a dominant matriarch organising them. The males would fight when it came time to collect a mate and this guy looked like he could handle himself.

At six a.m. we were back in the jeep and heading out once more: dawn and dusk are the best times to see animals and we were going to find a pack of hunting dogs. The African wild dog is the most endangered species in southern Africa. That notwithstanding, Doctor told us they were by far the most successful hunters in the dog family, wolves included. They hunted as a unit to bring down impala. When they caught one, they devoured it very quickly so larger predators like hyenas and leopards didn't have time to steal it from them.

Doctor took us to the den where the pack was rearing pups. The adults were a tawny brown colour with massive ears and dappling across their hides. The pups were darker with white socks and they bumbled around hunting for scraps while the alpha female looked on. As long as the alpha pair was healthy and breeding, the pack would continue to grow, but if one or both of the alphas died, the pack would split and new packs would form.

While most of the pack would join together to hunt the impala, babysitters would stay behind and look after the young. The other dogs would bring food back and regurgitate it for them.

Sitting in the jeep we saw another elephant. He came closer and closer and only shied away when Doctor started the engine. The elephant hadn't seen us – to him the jeep was just another bit of landscape like a rock or a tree: it was only the noise and movement that told him we were there.

We saw baboons crossing the road carrying babies on their backs and we saw kudu: large antelopes with huge ears that walked with their heads jerking.

Back at Mapula we climbed into log curraghs; canoes that our guides poled across the lagoon. Now we were really out there, eye-level with the grass, the water, the wildlife. Doctor pointed out flowers that floated on the surface – day lilies he called them: they closed their petals at night. We saw fish eagles just above the trees, then moments later and very close we heard the grunt of hippos.

'Doctor,' I said, nervously, 'my eyesight's really good, we could go over there.' I pointed way across the lagoon.

'No, no,' Ewan cut in. 'Let's get a little closer.'

So we did, close enough to stand up in the canoe and see half a dozen of the massive beasts lolling below the surface. This was the most dangerous animal in Africa and we were on the water with them.

EWAN: I had another elephant moment back at the lodge. I took a walk and found a couple among the trees. I was filming myself with my back to them, doing my best impression of David Attenborough. This one big guy was getting closer and closer as I was muttering away. I suddenly realised just how close.

Turning round I looked up at him and him down at me. He must have been about ten feet at the shoulder with huge ears and massive tusks. I realised then I had no experience of wild animals, let alone one as big as this. Suddenly he came at me, so I dived for the cover of a tree. I was still some distance from the safety of my cabin with a mass of tangled undergrowth in between. It was undergrowth that the elephant could go through easily while I had to follow the path around. He flapped his ears and tossed his head, trumpeting at me. That was it; I took off at a run. I could hear him coming. Oh, shit. And I thought the other night I was in trouble.

Suddenly Doctor appeared on the path, lifted his arms to make himself big and shouted at the elephant. It stopped, considered him for a moment then half-charged. By now I was on the veranda looking back. Doctor stood his ground and shouted again. The elephant made another false charge and then finally wheeled away. Right, I thought, now I know what to do. If he makes a false charge, stand your ground and yell at him. You'll be fine, Ewan. Unless of course it's a real charge. Then you'll be dead.

That night we went out again and came across a large-spotted hyena with her pup. We'd heard them in Ethiopia but hadn't seen one before. She was very close and unafraid of the light, nursing her pup and watching us with relative disinterest with her long and large head, and massive bone-crushing jaws.

A porcupine scuttled across in front us. It got trapped in the headlights, thought 'oh shit', and hid behind a bush about a quarter of its size.

We can see you!

Can you? Really? All right. It scuttled off into the night.

We heard a weird call ring out from some distance away. Doctor swivelled round in the driver's seat. 'That's buffalo,' he said. 'A distress call.'

We were off, racing into the swamplands. He thought the buffalo might have been attacked by lions and this was our chance to see them. We drove for two hours trying to find where the call had come from and pretty quickly we were surrounded by hundreds of bawling, snorting buffalo. Again they didn't seem to be bothered by the jeep and we were literally within touching distance. Then Charley shifted his position only fractionally and the whole herd took off. We hunted for the kill but didn't find it. We did find a cat, however, hunched down in the grass, slanted eyes staring up. It was as big a cat as we saw; what looked like a domestic kitten. It just sat there and meowed at us.

Just a couple of days off and yet it felt like a week. I was refreshed enough to get back on the bike and ride 120 kilometres of shitty sand road. Since Kenya I'd got the hang of it and though I still came off now and again I enjoyed it much more.

'What do you reckon, Charley?' I said, as we prepared to ride out. 'We can make it, can't we?'

''Course we can. And if not, we'll flag down a truck and load the bikes on the back.'

We bumped into a couple of German cyclists, Rosvita and Roland. Their bikes had panniers front and rear and they were towing a trailer where they stored camera gear powered by a solar panel. It was ingenious and they were using it so they could create film for a website. They'd been everywhere: Israel, Palestine, the Yemen, and all over Africa, and they reckoned that despite what they'd been told, the most dangerous people they'd encountered were the kids throwing stones in Ethiopia.

I reckon we made eight or nine miles before I fell off and

buckled a pannier yet again. We'd left late, with only an hour or so of daylight remaining, and the hard packed dirt had quickly given way to sand.

A mile or two later, I was forced off the road altogether by a passing pickup. I figured it was time to stop. Finding a good camp site well off the road, we checked for elephant dung. I was taking no chances but there didn't seem to be much sign of any animals so we put the tents up.

I woke up feeling very positive and looking forward to the challenge but as we pulled back on to the sand a truck stopped with a couple of missionaries in it. They'd been bikers in a previous life and told us that the road was appalling, dangerous even, and we had to be very careful. They'd been in this part of the country for four and a half years and ours were the first motorcycles they'd ever seen on this road.

No pressure then.

CHARLEY. Actually it turned out to be nowhere near as bad as we thought. It took a while because we had seventy-odd miles to do, but we stayed on and rode well and the worst thing we encountered was someone else's puncture. A group of people from an AIDS awareness team had sprung a leak in their nearside front and were stuck beside the road.

Fortunately we had everything we needed to fix it and on hands and knees we set about the task. They were a great bunch and from mixed backgrounds: one lad from the ghettos, another from the capital, and they were visiting Bushmen villages in remote areas like Kai-Kai.

I chatted at length with a girl called Likopaini; she had gold teeth and was what she called an AIDS activist. HIV positive, she was on antiretroviral drugs and as full of life as anyone I've ever come across. She laughed all the time, showed us how to make the traditional clicking noises the locals make and told us she spent her time travelling the country, educating people about the dangers of HIV. She herself had tested positive when her husband died in 2004. Previously a health worker, she saw his deterioration and guessed what it was.

She said that the threat was everywhere, both in the cities and the country, and her job was to make sure people knew about it. She promoted safe sex and gave out free condoms, explaining that in remote regions some people weren't even aware that HIV existed. Some of the bushmen in particular chose not to go to school; they had no TV or radio and preferred the traditional life of hunter and gatherer. She spent a lot of time telling them what HIV was and that the disease knew no boundaries.

It was incredible to realise that after such a mammoth journey we only had ten days to go. My mood fluctuated between tremendous excitement about seeing Ollie, Doone and Kinvara, and pangs of sadness that I'd no longer be throwing my leg over the saddle every morning. The thing about travelling like this is you get so used to it, so excited about what each day might bring, that you can't quite contemplate stopping. I remember after Long Way Round I'd be home in London asleep with Ollie and wake up thinking, 'I'm late and Ewan's packed and on his bike waiting.' It was hard to contemplate going back to normality.

But I couldn't and shouldn't think about that now. I considered the cyclists we'd met, Kurt and Dorothy, on the road for nine years. I thought about Steve in Malawi, his entire life packed on the roof of a truck. I realised just how fortunate we were to be able to make this trip, see places like the Okavango and take on roads that hadn't seen a motorcycle in years. This particular road was easier now and standing on the pegs I settled into the rhythm. I was relaxed and happy, excited: thinking no further ahead than the upcoming Namibian border.

26
A Motorcycle Diary

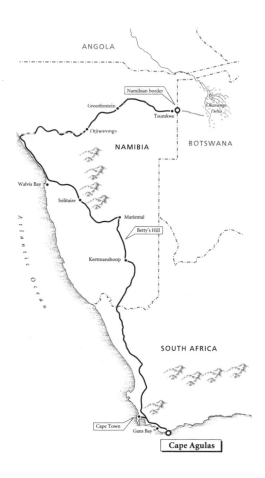

EWAN: Only a handful of days more to go and the trip would be over. I was feeling torn, dying to see my kids and yet not wanting the wheels to stop rolling. There was so much more to see in Africa.

We were in Namibia, and now had only one more border to cross. I glanced at Charley as he packed away his passport. Two women wearing huge colourful dresses were watching us and I was reminded of Egypt when we'd seen the smugglers packing their bloomers with boxes of cigarettes. These women were wearing headdresses I hadn't seen before – they were like headscarves only with a piece of cloth rolled horizontally at the front that looked like a pair of horns.

I spoke to a Namibian policeman who was really interested in the bikes. 'Do you get many motorcycles coming this way?' I asked him.

He shook his head. 'Almost never.' And with that he waved us over the border.

Charley pulled the obligatory wheelie and this time I popped one of my own. The police closed the iron gates behind us and we were into the desert, an 'elephant crossing' sign beside the road. I'd heard that the Namibian desert elephants were the tallest in Africa.

We pulled over at a craft centre run by a reverend and his wife. They told us how they visited the Kalahari bushmen villages and exchanged locally made goods, like bracelets and necklaces, for food. They sold the goods in their craft shop; the only problem was there were so few tourists in this part of the country. I bought a bracelet made from fragments of ostrich eggs and we also picked up a couple of woollen hats. It was chilly at night: we were in the desert, it was winter and the temperature could really plummet.

At the craft centre we met a bushman called Ali and asked him if it was possible to spend the night in one of the villages. He said he'd take us to his home.

CHARLEY: I was really excited about seeing it. The bushmen have lived in this part of Africa for more than twenty thousand years and it's only in the last fifty that their way of life has altered at all.

The village looked like many others we'd seen, small circular huts built from poles and plaster, campfires dotted here and there with people squatting on their heels around them. The bushmen reminded me of the people of Ethiopia; long-limbed with elegant features. Ali took us over to one fire where a group of men were gathered, and introduced us to the chief. It turned out he was also the local medicine man, or shaman. He was tiny, thin-faced with thin arms, small hands and feet. With Ali acting as interpreter we asked if we could camp and the chief said that would be fine. We had just enough time to put our tents up and grab something to eat before they started dancing.

It was dark now, and the firelight played over the faces of the people. We hadn't realised but it was during these ceremonies that the sick were brought to the chief and using the music and his shamanic powers he would try to heal them. The villagers brought a young man wrapped in a quilt and laid him on the ground. The chief sat over him while another guy in a headdress began the dance. The women were standing around the fire, clapping their hands with flat palms and splayed fingers: it created a hollow sound. They were singing in the traditional way, a sort of wail.

The chief took up the song, making clicking noises, half shrieks and high-pitched grunts while at the same time working his hands over the body of the sick man.

It was incredible to watch how the music grabbed him: as if it was part of him and he was part of it. The dancer got involved too; lying on his belly he put his head under the sick man's quilt, jerking his body like a snake.

Ali explained that this was elephant dancing and the bushmen had only been doing it for a hundred years. Before that they performed the giraffe dance, the difference being that here the women were standing round the fire, swaying and clapping, whereas historically they'd be sitting while the shaman performed the healing ceremony. We watched him working on the young man who later on, healed or not, was sitting up rather than lying down. I don't know how sick he'd been when they brought him in but he definitely seemed a lot perkier. The dancing had stopped and things were settling down now and we decided it was time to withdraw gracefully, so we thanked the chief, said our goodnights, and headed off to the tents.

We woke to the sound of a cock crowing and a radio playing. We had a long way to go today, so packing the tents we loaded the bikes and got moving.

We hit hard gravel and I had a rush of excitement as I realised I was only a week away from Ollie. I'd thought about her a lot while Eve was with us in Malawi; now it was just a matter of days until I'd see her.

The land was flat, the road a faint ribbon with nothing but sand and cactus drifting to hills that could have been a mirage on the horizon. Namibia was an enormous country, vast and empty, and we seemed to be the only people on the road.

It was good gravel, dusty and hard with no real sand to speak of, not that it mattered now because since Kenya Ewan had proved he could cope with anything. He was on the pegs, elbows out. One of the real pleasures of the trip had been watching him getting better and better. In Sudan and parts of Ethiopia he'd gritted his teeth and got on with it, but now he was really confident and I could see how much he was enjoying it. God, I'd loved these roads. I'd miss them when this was over: Ethiopia especially had been fantastic and I'd ride there again any time.

We left the dirt behind for a while, though. On good tarmac, we put the hammer down all the way to Grootfontein. The towns in Namibia were very clean, the streets wide and there was a distinctly colonial feel. From Grootfontein we rode to Otjiwarongo then back into the desert, heading west all the time. Eventually we'd come to the Skeleton Coast.

That night we camped in the desert, the landscape huge and

empty, baked sand and cactus, and weird looking quiver trees that were all trunk with just a canopy of short branches that stuck up like feathered arrows.

Ewan and I were both having the odd quiet moment now. I was savouring the mornings particularly, rolling up my sleeping bag, packing away the billy cans and stove. For the last three months everything I needed had been on this bike and I was going to enjoy every last moment of the experience.

Stopping for breakfast we met a couple of Dutch people on an organised bike tour. They were riding 650s with no panniers or gear to weigh them down. They told us that so far they'd only been on dirt roads, but their guide was taking them into the Namib so they could get their fill of the dunes. The previous night while camping they'd had a dodgy moment with an elephant. They'd pitched their tent under a tree and through the moonlight saw this big bull wander over to pluck a few juicy leaves from the upper branches. They were in the tent with the mosquito door open as he brushed the flysheet with his trunk.

We were into the desert now with the wind cutting across the plains, the country arid and dusty. The road was edged with dry yellow grass and thinly spaced quiver trees. We crossed bridges spanning waterless riverbeds and climbed into shallow black hills where the sand turned grey. Volcanic rock jutted on all sides, sharp as razors, the landscape almost lunar. Coming down again, we were gliding into basins where the roads were red dirt. We rode across the desert all the way to the sea.

EWAN: Parking the bikes we sat for a few minutes and I thought, my God, that's the Atlantic. We'd ridden north to south and east to west and now we were on the infamous Skeleton Coast. This was the region the bushmen called 'The Land God Made in Anger' and Portuguese sailors referred to as 'The Gates of Hell'.

I told Charley. 'From the Road of Bones to the Gates of Hell – do you think there's something in that?'

'Something about us you mean?' He laughed. 'I don't know, I'll look it up.'

'Look it up where?'

'I told you at the pyramids: the Charley book of everything. Remember?' He gave me a hug. 'It's been great riding with you, Ewan.'

'You too, Charley.'

We shook hands.

'What do you reckon,' I said. 'Shall we do it again?'

'I'm up for it. I think I might have another appointment with the Dakar first, though.'

I nodded. 'I've got a couple of things to do myself. But there's always the Long Way Up.'

'And the Long Way Across or the Long Way Over, or Under maybe, I don't know.'

'We could do South America, India, maybe, or China.'

Charley thought about that. 'Can you ride a motorbike along the Great Wall d'you reckon?'

'I don't know. I doubt it. Anyway, it's only a few thousand miles: we'd do that in a weekend, wouldn't we.'

'I expect it's got steps too. I'm not sure I could be bothered with steps.'

I looked out to sea once more where the wind was howling and rollers broke against the beach. 'They named this place for all the ships that have gone down,' I said. 'There are serious rocks out there; ships used to plough into them in the fog.' I gestured across the sand. 'The sailors that made it ashore starved, mostly.'

'Hence the skeletons,' he said. 'Shall we move on?'

We camped by a quiver tree under a full moon and got one of our better fires going. We were wrapped up against the cold in our bike trousers and fleeces, wearing the hats we'd bought near the border. We ate boil-in-the-bag for the umpteenth time and began to reminisce.

The following morning we were riding south, still on the dirt. Strangely now I didn't want to leave it. Once we left these roads in Namibia that was it, tarmac all the way to Cape Town. I'd savour it, throw in a couple of punctures maybe to make it last a bit longer.

We met a group of people on an overlander, a big red lorry with seats in the back and a blue canopy stretched over the top. It was full of various nationalities, a few Brits and one Australian who'd watched *Long Way Round* just before he left. If you jumped an overlander your travelling companions were random; you just showed up at the stop and got aboard. This group was going all the way to Nairobi.

Another desert road; we'd not seen this much desert since Sudan. Around lunchtime we pulled into Solitaire, a tiny spot that exists pretty much solely as a place for people to fill up on petrol before heading back out into the desert. It does have one cafe, though, and it was here that we bumped into Johannes again – a young guy we'd met when we crossed into Namibia. He was from South Africa and had been on the road for a few months.

I was surprised to see him so soon; he was on his own and had been meandering, taking his time as he rode through Uganda and Kenya. He didn't gauge his trip by distance or time: it would take as long as it took. I asked him when he'd be home and he said he didn't know. He still had two books to read yet, and a story to write.

He joined us for sandwiches and apple pie at the Café Van Der Lee run by Moose McGregor. Moose is the descendent of a Scotsman and an Irish woman who landed here in 1906. The apple pie was a family recipe that had been handed down for generations and had featured on a BBC food programme. Moose was a big guy (well he would be, wouldn't he), with a ponytail and goatee beard. White scars laced his forearms as if he'd been in a fight with a lion.

I asked him about it, thinking I'd get some Ian Bruce-type tale about a leopard playing dead in the bush. Instead Moose admitted the scars were burns from the sharp-sided pans he used for apple pie.

Oh well.

Leaving Solitaire, we continued on southwards. The dirt roads of Africa were almost finished with us. I was quite emotional; leaving the dirt would be the first little ending of the trip and I was quite choked when I thought about it. The enormity of it all was beginning to come home to me – how it had been put together, how because of Russ and Dave, Charley and I were able to ride through Africa without worrying about logistics, border crossings, paperwork. It enabled us to really be touched by the country, uncluttered, our hearts and minds were open. If people were then moved by what they read or saw on TV it was because we'd been touched, humbled by the experience.

I would miss the dirt road, can you believe that after Sudan and Ethiopia? As it turned out, however, they weren't quite finished with us yet: a couple of hundred miles before the border he spotted Betty's Hill. The dirt roads might be almost over but we could have one final excursion. We had been joined by Dai, our medic, and Julian Broad who had arrived to take photographs. And of course there was Claudio. Five desperadoes and four bikes. We opted to use the 650 Eve had been riding. It was the lightest; the least encumbered with panniers and it wasn't ours. It did have road tyres, though, which might be a problem.

The aim was to get as far up the hill as possible before we came off. Lots were drawn as to who would go first. Each name was scribbled on a slip of paper. We shuffled them and the names were read out in order: Ewan, Jules, Claudio, Charley and Dai.

Me first then; OK. I set off at a run, up on the pegs, the bike wobbling around on loose shale and stones. I was climbing though, higher and higher, then suddenly I was in a ravine that had been invisible from below. Shifting gear I stalled trying to climb out. Looking down the hill, however, I wasn't unimpressed with how far I'd got and using my jacket as a marker I rode the bike back and handed it over to Julian.

He beat me, the bastard. I put it down to knowledge accrued while watching me, of course, but patted him on the back anyway.

Claudio went next; his strategy was to follow Charley's advice about always going after the virgins . . . I mean virgin ground. Off he went, a bus ride from any recognisable line and stalled the bike close to the ravine. He rolled a good distance backwards thus missing both Julian's and my marker.

Then it was Charley. After pretending to be nervous he roared off, taking a totally different line from anyone else. He rattled up the hill beyond the twin green water towers we'd been using as a marker, then on and on until he was at the very top. For a moment I thought he was going for the next hill as well, but, fist in the air, he wheeled the bike around.

Dai was watching with a sour grin on his face. 'Right,' he said. 'Follow that then, shall I?'

CHARLEY: Seventy miles from the South African border Ewan got a puncture. We were riding along having a laugh about Betty's Hill when his bike started to fishtail. Looking down we saw the rear tyre was almost flat. There was a big hole right on the edge, big enough to require most of a tube of glue and two plugs. We weren't sure if it would hold but got it pumped up and made it to the border. Our last crossing on two wheels – I couldn't quite believe it.

The immigration office was next to a covered bridge that looked like something from *Sleepy Hollow*. We had our passports stamped for the final time, shook hands and got back on the bikes. 'You all set, Ewan?' I called.

He nodded. 'Are you?'

'I suppose.'

'The last leg, Charley.'

I was grinning now. 'Only until the next time.'

I pulled my last border wheelie, the biggest of the trip so far. The wheel came down sideways, wobbled a bit but I held it. Then we were in South Africa and the next stop was the lodge and Ollie, Doone and Kinvara. Yeehaw!

Apart from dying to see them I had no idea what I was feeling. We would have covered almost fifteen thousand miles by the time we finished, a convoy of riders following us into Cape Town. I'd miss my bike, my tent, my sleeping bag. I'd miss the African skies and talking to all my family on the phone while watching the most wonderful sunsets. I'd miss riding with Ewan. It had been three years since we'd rode the first time; would it be another three until we set off again? I'd get withdrawal symptoms, I knew I would, just like the last time. I'd wake up and expect to see Ewan, only it would be Ollie beside me.

That night we stayed at a small motel where we were the only guests apart from this one guy who'd been there a week. I think he got a bit of a shock when he came in and there we were lounging around in motorcycle gear. We got chatting and discovered he worked in adult education, training the teachers who taught the adults in the poorer areas of the Western Cape. He told us that much had changed in South Africa since the days of apartheid but even now there were still pockets of racism. The real divide between the people, however, was economic.

He couldn't quite believe that we'd ridden all the way through Africa. He said that many South Africans didn't travel the continent. They'd been told – taught even in some cases – that Africa really was a dark continent full of violence and murder. It was the same story we'd heard from the scaremongers back in Britain. Apparently when South Africans went on holiday it was usually to Europe or America, rarely their own continent. It's crazy the things people are told, and it was driven home a little later when we were stopped by the Western Cape traffic police and they said the same thing. The truth is, all that is bullshit. Africa's no Mecca for machete wielding mercenaries, it's a continent full of people who just want normal everyday things like a home and somewhere for their children to go to school. In all the time I'd been here I'd not felt threatened once. I realised then how lucky Ewan and I had been to stumble into Russ and Dave; they'd put this whole thing together and because of that we were allowed to ride across Africa and hopefully we'd learned something along the way.

We were up before it got light. It was winter now, and cold. Rain had been forecast and we had three hundred and forty miles to go. Ewan told me he didn't want the trip to end. He told me he'd miss his boots, the big off-roaders he'd worn the long way down. He'd miss hunting down a campsite and lighting a fire. He'd miss geep and elephants, and camels on the road.

He was concerned about his back tyre, though. The plugs had held so far but now we were in civilisation he thought he ought to get the tyre patched from the inside. We filled up with petrol and the guy serving told us there was a tyre place just up the road. Ewan went ahead while I filled mine and Claudio's bikes.

Paying the guy at the petrol station, I headed into town, not quite sure where Ewan had gone. I was messing about now, speeding up and hitting the back brake, sending the bike into a slide. The hard stuff was over, the adventure of it all, and I was relaxed and dossing around with stoppies and wheelies. Spotting the tyre garage off a slip road, I locked the back wheel and put the bike into a deliberate skid.

The next thing I knew Claudio hit me and slid past, the bike on its side and him whacking his head off the tarmac. His bike slithered down the road, glass shattering and sparks flying. I pulled up and jumped off.

Thankfully I saw him get up. He looked dazed and angry. Shit, I thought. Shit, shit.

'Claudio, are you all right?'

'Yes, I think so.'

'Man that was a big one.'

'Fucking hell, Charley, you just hit the brakes! I was going to hit you and I had to swerve and that was it.'

'I had no idea you were so close. The last time I saw you, you were miles back.'

'You left me at the petrol station, I had to catch up.'

'Oh, man, I'm sorry.' I hugged him. 'Are you all right? God, I'm so sorry. I was dossing around, having fun, locking the back end. I'm sorry, Claudio, it was all my fault.'

'It's all right,' he said. 'It's OK.' He looked at his bike, lying on its side with the beak broken and headlight shattered.

I noticed the oil radiator was buckled.

Ewan was alongside now. His bike in the workshop, he'd heard the back wheel lock up and the unmistakeably hideous sound of a bike sliding down the road. 'Fuck,' he said. 'What happened?'

'My fault,' I admitted. 'I was dossing about with the back brake and Clouds was closer to me than I realised. I saw you, hit the anchors and he crashed into me.'

EWAN: Claudio seemed to be more angry than anything else, but he'd come down hard on his right hand side and the lack of any pain was probably the adrenalin working. The bike didn't actually look too bad: the headlight was gone and the beak had broken, but we had gaffer tape and got it bandaged up. The oil radiator was bent back but it hadn't fractured and the bike was rideable. It was the old story: the last five minutes of any trip are the most dangerous – that's when complacency can set in and accidents happen. I knew it from bitter experience, when a car had crashed into me in Canada during Long Way Round.

Metaphorically we were five minutes from home now and this was by far the worst spill any of us had taken.

I got my tyre patched and we were back on the road. Not for long, though, Claudio's radiator burst, spraying oil everywhere. Claudio was really pissed off; all this way and now he couldn't ride his puppy into Cape Town.

Or maybe he could.

Between us we rearranged the gear on the back of the fixer's truck and loaded Claudio's bike. Getting on the phone, we arranged for the parts we needed to be brought to the lodge so we could get the bike fixed in time for Claudio to ride to Cape Town.

I checked my mirrors as we pulled away. I had no idea what I was feeling, it was so strange. When we finished Long Way Round I had a definite sense of achievement, I could recall specifically how I felt when we crossed the George Washington Bridge and there was Manhattan. This time I wasn't sure, I felt a bit numb.

Eve was in Kenya now with my daughters and I was going to fly up to join them as soon as all the press stuff was over. My mum and dad had flown out to South Africa and they would be at the lodge to meet us, along with Charley's family. I knew he was itching to see them all.

Forty minutes out we were wet, cold and it was pitch black. We had only one decent set of lights: Charley's. We weren't exactly sure where the rest of the team were so we tried calling various mobile phones, but nobody was answering except my mum. I told her we thought we were about forty miles away and we'd be there shortly.

It was all very strange, slightly surreal, but then I think that's how it is for anyone who's covered this amount of miles and been away from home for any length of time. I thought again about the cyclists and how they would adjust to life after having been on the road for more than nine years.

We'd left the desert behind, the dirt roads, the scrub and sand, the wildlife. For some reason I thought of Ethiopia and the market town of Bati where they sold goods on one side of the hill and livestock on the other. I could picture this young boy who'd showed me around. Older kids had tried to get rid of him, to take his place as my guide. But I wouldn't let them. There was something about him that seemed to sum up the trip for me. I hadn't known it then but in a way he personified the experience: yes, I'd been a guy on a motorbike and no doubt I would give him some money, which I did. But for the couple of hours we were there, there was a bond between us and for me these trips are really about the people. People make up the places, the roadside; without them the landscape is beautiful but empty.

We made it to the lodge and that was the second little ending of the trip. My mum and dad were there with the rest of the crew and it was great to see them. We met Paul and Keith, the two guys who'd paid so much to ride with us into Cape Town. The money was going to Riders for Health and thinking about it, I realised that those visits had been some of the most memorable and moving moments of the whole trip. Riders for Health had been hugely inspiring: the work of the clinic and the community health workers on dirt bikes. I thought about Scotland, CHAS and the people we'd been privileged to meet at Robin House. I thought about UNICEF and the mine-affected children in Zelambassa. I could see the village in Kenya where twenty-two children had been massacred. I could hear Daniel's voice, a child soldier in Uganda. All at once the memories began to flow. I could see Bulwer Street on the night we decided to do another trip; the Royal Geographical Society; the first time we saw the workshop at Avonmore Road. I recalled the moment when my bike arrived and I had her painted with zebra stripes. I thought about the Friday back in February when I hit that pedestrian and broke my leg.

We'd done it. It was coming to an end, but we'd done it. Only I didn't want it to end. Right then I would happily have turned my bike around and ridden back along the west coast.

CHARLEY: Finally we got to the lodge and there they were: my wife, my daughters. I hadn't got my helmet off and Ollie had her arms wrapped round my neck; Doone and Kinvara were hugging me. At last I did get the helmet off and kissed Ollie, kissed the girls.

'Hello, my darlings,' I said. 'How are you?'

We hugged and kissed. I held Ollie for all I was worth and in that moment I realised just how much I'd missed her and just how lost a soul I'd be without her. I picked up Doone and Kinvara, kissed them, hugged them, kissed them again. I couldn't stop holding them.

I parked the bike and there was Ewan's mum. 'Hello, Charley,' she said.

'Hello, Carol.' I gave her a hug. 'Told you I'd bring him back safe.'

Ewan was hugging Ollie and my daughters, Russ's mum and dad were there, as well as Emily his daughter. It really was a welcome party. Before we went inside I took a look at my bike. I couldn't quite believe that tomorrow would be the last time I threw my leg over the saddle.

The following morning we left the lodge for Cape Agulhas and the final stage of our journey; a great convoy of bikes, the support vehicles and our families. On perfect black tarmac, Ewan and I rode side by side, taking in the coast where the sea was green and the sand flat and white. And then finally, beautifully, wonderfully, we came to a last bit of dirt road that would take us to the point.

We'd made it. Cape Agulhas, the most southerly tip of Africa and we'd started at the most northerly tip of Scotland. Almost journey's end, I couldn't get my head around it. We were standing at the foot of the world with the Indian Ocean on one side and the Atlantic on the other. We needed a moment just to take it in.

'We did it, Ewan,' I said.

'We did. You and me, mate. To the bottom of Africa, fifteen thousand miles.'

'Hell of a trip,' I said.

'But good, I mean really, really good. Maybe we should do it again sometime. What do you think?'

'I'm up for riding back right now.'

'You know what, mate? So am I.'

EWAN: Hundreds of people had turned out to ride with us. Lachlan from BMW South Africa had done a tremendous job organising bikes for our friends and the people who'd helped us put this thing together. It was brilliant, the perfect finale. The trip had been Charley and I for sure, but it was more than that – it was our families, friends, it was the fans of *Long Way Round*, it was Dai Jones and Jim Foster, it was Jimmy Simak and Claudio. And not just them: it was everyone back in the office, everyone who'd seen us off that first morning that felt so long ago. It was wonderful to honour all that effort now with so many motorcycles.

People crowded round us, asking all sorts of questions. And in a way it gave us a moment to reflect, to begin to step back and think about what we'd done, what we'd seen and how the whole experience had affected us. I turned to Charley.

'What do you reckon,' I said, 'shall we go to Cape Town?'

'I suppose we could. I mean, from here it seems like as good a place as any.'

'That's what I was thinking.'

Outside everyone was waiting: a sea of faces, and lines and lines of motorcycles. I took a moment to consider my bike: she looked about as battered and beat up as the old bike had done by the time we rolled into New York three years ago. This was different, I felt different; I still couldn't quite take it in. Africa had been unbelievable, complicated, difficult. In some ways the place was so unjust: the poverty; AIDS; conflict; hardship. I had such an awful lot to think about, I had no real sense of a high just then, I mean personally, and I think it was perhaps because the trip needed so much reflection.

I glanced at Charley, at Russ and David as they prepared to get back on the bikes they'd ridden from the lodge this morning. My dad was there and I caught his eye. He smiled at me.

Russ was already on his bike, engine running, he was itching to get going. David had ridden Eve's bike in Zambia and he was riding again now. This whole thing was about motorcycles and it was fitting that the team that put Long Way Down on the map would ride the last leg together.

I called across to David. 'What do you reckon, mate? Shall we rock up to Cape Town?' I turned to Russ. 'Cape Town, Russ; are you up for it?'

We fired up the engines and pulled away from Cape Agulhas. We were on the blacktop: Charley alongside me, I reached across and grabbed his hand. The noise of the engines was drowned suddenly by another, larger, meatier engine altogether: a helicopter. It dipped above us like a bird of prey, a cameraman hanging out the door. I thought of Colin, my bother and former Tornado pilot; he'd arranged a fly-by to launch the trip at Castle Mey. Perfect, I thought, a tornado to begin and a chopper to finish. Kicking down a gear, I tucked in and cracked the throttle.

And finally there was Cape Town cradled in a valley – the sprawl of skyscrapers, suburbs and shanties dwarfed by the might of Table Mountain. I realised this was a dream, a childhood dream: motorbikes and meeting people in the most extraordinary places, people who basically have nothing and yet share what little they have.

I felt like I wanted to turn round and ride back up. We'd met so many fantastic people and seen so many fantastic places, and yet I felt that we had only scratched the surface. There's so much more to learn about Africa. I know I'll be back, and I can hardly wait. It feels more like the beginning of a journey than the end of one.

CHARLEY: On the outskirts we pulled over and draped the Scottish flag Ewan's nephew had given us across the back of Ewan's bike. I could hear him singing 'O Flower of Scotland' and then we were on the last leg, cruising through the streets to the Arabella Sheraton. I thought about a final wheelie but strangely perhaps I was more reflective. The enormity of what we'd been able to achieve began to sweep over me, brought home I think by the little bit of gravel we'd ridden to get to the very tip of the continent at Cape Agulhas. I was suddenly humbled, a little bit of dirt where we stood on the pegs and stuck our elbows out. I thought of the Sudan, Ethiopia, Kenya, I thought of Zambia, Tanzania: all those gnarly, muddy, sandy, potholed roads. It occurred to me that ten years from now, five even, those roads would be gone, buried for all time under tarmac. The Africa Ewan and I had ridden through would be changed forever.

Finally we pulled up outside the hotel and   were the support vehicles and the bikes that had ridden on ahead. I slowed down, winding back the gas and stepping down through the gears for the very last time. I considered the height of the hotel as I heard the roar of motorbikes on the expressway.

Ewan took his helmet off and worked a hand through his hair. 'Charley,' he said. 'Thanks, mate; it was a pleasure riding with you.'

We shook hands, southern Africa style, then embraced Ewan-and-Charley style. 'You too, mate,' I said, 'you too.'

Appendix A

ROUTE

Countries	Locations	Date	Km	Miles	Cumulative
UK	John OGroats – Crieff	12th May	472.0	295.0	295.0
	Creiff – Scotland/England border – Holy Island	13th	310.0	193.8	488.8
	Holy Island – Silverstone	14th	535.0	334.4	823.1
	Silverstone – London	15th	117.0	73.1	896.3
France	London – England/France border – Rimes	16th	478.0	298.8	1,195.0
Italy	Rimes – Dijon – France/Italy border Just East of Mont Blanc tunnel near Courmayeur	17th	697.0	435.6	1,630.6
	East of Mont Blanc tunnel – Lake Como – Camp site north Fidenza/Parma	18th	446.0	278.8	1,909.4
	Camp site – Siena – Rome	19th	517.0	323.1	2,232.5
	Rome – Amalfi Coast – Pompei.	20th	372.3	232.7	2,465.2
Sicily	Pompei – ferry to Sicily – Palermo	21st	710.0	443.8	2,908.9
	Palermo – Trapani	22nd	109.0	68.1	2,977.1
Tunisia	Trapani – Sicily/Tunisia border by ferry – Tunis	23rd	0.0		2,977.1
	Tunis – Sfax	24th	284.0	177.5	3,154.6
	Sfax – Matmata – Medenine – 40 km west of Ben Gardane	25th	271.0	169.4	3,323.9
Libya	Camp – Ben Gardane – Tunisia/ Libya border – Tripoli	26th	246.0	153.8	3,477.7
	Tripoli – Leptis Magna – Surt	27th	465.0	290.6	3,768.3
	Surt – Tobruk	28th	810.0	506.3	4,274.6
Egypt	Tobruk – Libya/Egypt border crossing – Marsa Matrouh	29th	377.0	235.6	4,510.2
	Marsa Matrouh – Alexandria – Cairo/Giza	30th	503.0	314.4	4,824.6
	Cairo – Suez – Luxor	31st	778.0	486.3	5,310.8
	Luxor – Aswan	1st June	222.0	138.8	5,449.6
	Flight from Aswan – Nairobi for Riders for Health visit.	2nd	0.0		5,449.6
	Flight from Nairobi – Aswan	3rd	0.0		5,449.6
Sudan	Aswan – Egypt/Sudan border – Wadi Halfa (ferry)	4th	0.0		5,449.6
	Wadi Halfa	5th	0.0		5,449.6
	Wadi Halfa – Camp in Desert near Kosha	6th	142.0	88.8	5,538.3
	Kosha – Argo	7th	198.0	123.8	5,662.1
	Argo – Dongola – Mulwad	8th	108.0	67.5	5,729.6

Countries	Locations	Date	Km	Miles	Cumulative
	Mulwad – Khartoum	9th	501.0	313.1	6,042.7
	Khartoum – Qallabat	10th	561.0	350.6	6,393.3
Ethiopia	Sudan/Ethiopia border – Shehedi	11th	30.0	18.8	6,412.1
	Shehedi – Gondar – near Simien National Park	12th	238.0	148.8	6,560.8
	Simien NP – Adi Arkay	13th	74.0	46.3	6,607.1
	Adi Arkay – Aksum – Adrigat	14th	215.0	134.4	6,741.4
	Adigrat – Day trip to Zalembessa with UNICEF – Adigrat	15th	0.0		6,741.4
	Adigrat – Mekele – Adisho	16th	172.0	107.5	6,848.9
	Adisho – Kombolcha	17th	252.0	157.5	7,006.4
	Kombolcha – Addis	18th	336.0	210.0	7,216.4
	Addis Ababa	19th	0.0		7,216.4
	Addis Ababa	20th	0.0		7,216.4
	Addis Ababa	21st	0.0		7,216.4
	Addis Ababa – Langano	22nd	215.0	134.4	7,350.8
	Langano – Yirga Alem	23rd	149.0	93.1	7,443.9
Kenya	Yirga Alem – Kenya/Ethiopia border – Moyale	24th	448.0	280.0	7,723.9
	Moyale – Walda	25th	149.0	93.1	7,817.1
	Walda – Marsabit	26th	74.3	46.4	7,863.5
	Marsabit – Lewa	27th	276.0	172.5	8,036.0
	Lewa – Nakuru	28th	215.2	134.5	8,170.5
	Nakuru – Lake Naivasha	29th	89.3	55.8	8,226.3
Uganda	Naivasha – Kenya/Uganda border – Mbale	30th	445.0	278.1	8,504.4
	Mbale – Jinja – Kampala	1st July	232.3	145.2	8,649.6
	Kampala fly to Gulu for UNICEF project	2nd	0.0	0.0	8,649.6
	Gulu, fly back to Kampala	3rd	0.0	0.0	8,649.6
	Kampala – Fort Portal – Near Kasese	4th	389.0	243.1	8,892.8
Rwanda	Near Kasese – Uganda/Rwanda border – Volcano National Park.	5th	408.3	255.2	9,147.9
	Gorilla tracking	6th	0.0		9,147.9
	Volcano NP – Musanze – Kigali	7th	119.0	74.4	9,222.3
	driving in hills around Kigali	8th	217.4	135.9	9,358.2
Tanzania	Kigali – Rusumu – Rwanda/Tanzania border – Ntumaga	9th	299.0	186.9	9,545.1
	Ntumaga – Kibondo – Kasulu – Uvinza – Bush camp near Kaloma	10th	323.2	202.0	9,747.1
	Kaloma – Katavi National Park	11th	227.8	142.4	9,889.4
	Katavi Rest Day	12th	3.5	2.2	9,891.6
	Camp – Sumbawanga – Camp 100 km before Tunduma	13th	282.0	176.3	10,067.9
Malawi	Tunduma – Mbeya – Tanzania/Malawi border – Chilumba	14th	483.6	302.3	10,370.1
	Chilumba – Livingstonia – Rumphi – Nkhata bay- Chinteche	15th	269.7	168.6	10,538.7
	Chinteche – Salima – Senga Bay	16th	311.2	194.5	10,733.2
	Senga Bay – Lilongwe	17th	127.1	79.4	10,812.6

Countries	Locations	Date	Km	Miles	Cumulative
Zambia	Lilongwe – Mchingi – Malawi/Zambia border – Chipata	18th	220.5	137.8	10,950.4
	Chipata – Petuake – Kachalola – Camp by Luangwa river 60km from Kachalola	19th	399.1	249.4	11,199.9
	Camp by river – Lusaka – Choma	20th	493.4	308.4	11,508.3
	Choma – Livingstone	21st	211.0	131.9	11,640.1
Botswana	Livingstone – Zambia/Botswana border – Camped just north of Nata.	22nd	320.0	200.0	11,840.2
	Camp – Maun – camped in the delta in Mapula	23rd	377.0	235.6	12,075.8
	Day in Swamps	24th	0.0		12,075.8
	Maun – Nokaneng – camp in bush on way to border.	25th	235.0	146.9	12,222.7
Namibia	Camp – Botswana/Namibia border – Tsumkwe	26th	218.8	136.8	12,359.4
	Tsumkwe – Grootfontein – Otjiwarongo – Omaruru	27th	690.0	431.3	12,790.7
	omaruru – Uis – Mile 108 – Henties bay	28th	401.3	250.8	13,041.5
	Henties Bay – Swakopmund – Bloedkoppie area, Namib Naukluft Park	29th	189.9	118.7	13,160.2
	Bloedkoppie area, Namib Naukluft Park – Sossusvlei	30th	245.3	153.3	13,313.5
	Sossusvlei – Keetmanshoop	31st	493.0	308.1	13,621.6
South Africa	Keetmanshoop – Namibia/South Africa border – Bitterfontein	1st August	628.9	393.1	14,014.7
	Bitterfonteln – Gansbaai	2nd	541.1	338.2	14,352.8
	Gansbaai	3rd	0.0		14,352.8
	Gansbaai – Cape Agulhas – Cape town	4th	394.2	246.4	14,599.2
Total			23,358.7 km		14,599.2
Total mileage including ferries and flights					19197.95

Appendix B

EQUIPMENT

List of Tools – all supplied by MacTools

12″ Adjustable wrench, 3/8″–1/4″ adapter, Brass drift punch, 16oz ball peen hammer, 3/8″ Super steel centre punch, 5/16″ Combination wrench 12pt, 11/32″ Combination wrench 12pt, KS2 Combo wrench standard (3/8″, 7/16″, 1/2″, 9/16″, 5/8″, 11/16″, 3/4″, 13/16″, 7/8″, 15/16″ and 1″), 3/4″ Super steel chisel, 6/12/24v Circuit tester, 3/8″ × 7/16″ Flare nut wrench, 1/2″ × 9/16″ Flare nut wrench, 5/8″ × 11/16″ Flare nut wrench, 25bld Univ Mstr feeler gage st, Bend-a-light Pro-new, 3/8″ × 7/16″ Halfmoon wrench, 1/2″ × 9/16″ Halfmoon wrench, Punch & chisel holder, 5/8″ × 16″ Lady foot pry bar, 8″ Mill bastard file/CG, 1pt, 1″–1/4″ Telescoping mirror, 1/4″ Ratchet 5″, Macinists pocket rule 6″, Telescopic pocket power magnet, KS2 Combo wrench metric 10mm, 5/16″ Standard socket 12pt, KS2 Combo wrench metric 11mm, 11/32″ Standard socket 12pt, KS2 Combo wrench metric 12mm, 3/8″ Standard socket 12pt, KS2 Combo wrench metric 13mm, KS2 Combo wrench metric 14mm, KS2 Combo wrench metric, KS2 Combo wrench metric 16mm, 16″ Speed HDL 1/4″ DR, KS2 Combo wrench metric 17mm, KS2 Combo wrench metric 18mm, KS2 Combo wrench metric 19mm, 1/4″ DR, 2″ Knurled extension, Metric Long Combo Wrench 21mm/12pt, Metric Long Combo Wrench 22mm/12pt, 1/4″ DR Universal joint, 10″ Big champ pliers, 7 3/4″ Curved diagonal pliers, 6″ Slip joint pliers, 1/4″ DR, 6″ Knurled extension, 1/4″ DR Spin handle/comfort grip, 3/16″, Standard socket 12pt, 7mm Comb wrench 12 pt, 7/32″ Standard socket 12pt, 8mm Comb wrench 12 pt, 1/4″ Standard socket 12pt, 9mm Comb wrench 12 pt, 9/32″ Standard socket 12pt, #1″ × 3″ Phillips Bolster/CG/Red, #3″ × 6″ Phillips Bolster/CG/Red, 5/16″ × 6″ Std tip Bolster/CG/Red, 5/16″ × 8″ Std tip/CG/RED, 1–1/2″ Flexible putty knife, 1/4″ × 1.5″ Std stubby, 3/16″ Long S/S pin punch, Foam profile, 8″ Needle nose pliers w/cutter, #2 × 1.5″ Phillips stubby, 8″ Round bastard file/CG, 5/16″ S/S roll pin punch, 1/8″ S/S roll pin punch, 1/4″ S/S roll pin punch, Ratcheting screwdriver (2), 8″ Square bastard file/CG, 9pc Metric hex key set with case, 13pc Speed hex key w/cset, 1/8″ S/S starter punch, Black frame clear safety spec, 3/4″–2″ ADJ hook spanner wrench, Pitch gauge bolt & thread, 3/8″ × 7/16″ Wrench, Open-ended wrench 9/16″ × 1/2″, Open-ended wrench 5/8″ × 3/4″, Digital mulitmeter, 10″ C-JAW Vise-Grip+R w/cutter, 7″ Straight jaw Vise-Grip+R, 10″ Ratchet 1/2″ drive, 10″ Extension, 1/2″ Socket 12pt, 18″ Flex handle w/comfort grip, 9/16″ Socket 12pt, 2″ Extension, 5/8″ Socket 12pt, 11/16″ Socket 12pt, 3/4″ Socket 12pt, 13/16″ Socket 12pt, 7/8″ Socket 12pt, 1/2″ Universal joint, 15/16″ Socket 12pt, 1″ Socket 12pt, 5″ Extension, 12mm Socket 6pt, 13mm Socket 6pt, 14mm Socket 6pt, 15mm

Socket 6pt, 16mm Socket 6pt, 17mm Socket 6pt, 18mm Socket 6pt, 19mm Socket 6pt, 21mm Socket 6pt, 22mm Socket 6pt, 24mm Socket 6pt, 3/8" Ratchet, 8" Flex handle, 3/8" Socket 12pt, 7/16" Socket 12pt, 10mm Socket 12pt, 11mm Socket 12pt, 3" Knurled extension, Universal joint, 6" Knurled extension, slotted bit (2), #1 Phillips ACR bit, #2 Phillips ACR bit, Metric pitch gauge, MacTools battery charger – 12v up to 100AH.

BMW spares

Emergency cylinder head kit (3), Rocker cover (2), Gasket (8), Bolt (4), O ring (1), Plugs (4), Coils (4), Clutch Field (1), Lever (2), F Pads (6), R Pads (3), Brake fluid (1), Headlight bulb (1), Tail bulb (1), Bracket hand (9), Bracket (9), Extra tank bags (3), Front and Rear discs (spare discs for bike) (2), Tyres (16), Extra keys (4), BMW front shock absorbers (2), Rear BMW shock absorbers (2).

Nissan spares

Air filter (2), Pollen filter (2), Sets of wiper blades (2), Dampers with bushes (4), Fuel filters (4), Alternator (1), Set of engine bells (1), Engine injectors (2), Car set light bulbs (2), Tin plastic Metal (2), Tin rad weld (2), Engine oil (1), Engine coolant (1), hi-lift jack (1).

Camping Equipment supplied by Touratech

Touratech – Ortlieb roll closing q packsack (8), Touratech – Ortlieb TRACK day pack (8), Touratech – Ortlieb premium travel mat (8), Powerstretch Gloves (8), Haglofs Barrier Jacket (L) (6), Haglofs Barrier Jacket (XL) (2), Anadir Sweater (XL) (2), Anadir Sweater (L) (6), Fram Pants L (6), Fram Pants (XL) (2), Roll Closing Q Packsack (XL) (8), Haglofs Bum Bag (8), Eagle Creek Undercover Security Wallet (8), Pack-It Sport (black) (2), Pack-It Sport (cherry red) (2), Pack-It Sport (neptune) (2), Cascade Pack Shower (3), Ortlieb T Pack (5), PackTowl (XL) blue (8), Pocket Soap (8), Hammock (2), Clothesline (2), Mutha Hubba Tent (8), Touratech Tent Bag (8), Marmot Sawtooth sleeping bag (2), Yeti Energizer 750 (6), eVent compressing packsack (L) (8), Travel pillow (8), Ortlieb Premium mat (8), Walkstool (8), Outdoor Mosquito net (8), MSR Dragonfly cooking stove (2), MSR fuel bottle (4), Ortlieb Collapsible dishes (2), Titanium Multi Compact (2), Snow peak titanium thermal tumbler (10), Stainless steel plate large (10), Stainless steel plate (10), Salt-n-pepper shaker (4), Curry-n-herbs shaker (4), Titanium cutlery (10), Nalgene loop top bottles (8), Nalgene wide mouth bottles (8), Drink powder 'Rouge' (20), Letherman charge Ti (8), Active thermos flask (8), Micropur water purifier (8), Ortlieb waterbags (8), MasterLED torch (8), Princeton Tec Aurora (8), Strap It Motorbike Adjustable (10), ROK All purpose Adjustable (10), ROK All purpose Flat 30cm (4), ROK All purpose Flat 60cm (4), ROK All purpose Flat 90cm (4), ROK All purpose Flat 150cm (4), Strap It Motorbike Flat 300mm (4), Strap It Motorbike Flat 450mm (4), Strap It Motorbike Flat 600mm (4), Strap It Motorbike Flat 750mm (4), Neck Brace (3), Mountain equipment pneumo stuffsack 5 ltr (1), Mountain equipment pneumo stuffsack 15 ltr (1), Mountain equipment pneumo stuffsack 25 ltr (1), Mountain equipment pneumo stuffsack 50 ltr (1), Haglofs Bum Bag Watatait (1), Pack-It Quick Trip toiletries bag (1), Packet Soap (8), Pack-It Quick Trip toiletries bag (1), Packet Soap (1), Yeti Sunrizer 800 (1), Touratech Aluminium Camping seat (3), Snow Peak GIGA Power WG (1), Trangia Spirit Stove Ultralight HA (1), Nova Multi Fuel Burner for Trangia cooker (1), Snow Peak Titanium Multi Compact cooking set (1), Snow Peak titanium thermal tumbler (1), Lexan Plate flat 25cm (1), Nalgene loop-top bottles, Lexan (1), Katadyn COMBI water filter (4), Airchamp tubeless tyre puncture repair kit (4), Tyre pressure gauge (2), eVent compression bag Medium (1), ProLite 3 Regular Therm-a-rest (1), Touratech Mess Kit (1), Zega Case (black) (1), Auxiliary Bag (1), Snow Peak GIGA Power WG (1), Twin burner stove – petrol (1), Honda generator-EU10i (1),Wayfarer Boil in the bag foods: spicy vegetable rigatoni, meatballs pasta in tomato sauce, chocolate pudding, chicken pasta and mushroom, sausage casserole, beef stew, beans & bacon in tomato sauce (various), Space Cases: various sizes (4), Mosquito repellent (30), Deet (30), Howling Moon 2-man roof tent (3).

Clothing

Powerstretch Gloves (8), Haglofs Barrier Jacket Large (6), Haglofs Barrier Jacket (XL) (2), Anadir Sweater (XL) (2), Anadir Sweater (L) (6), Fram Pants (L) (6), Fram Pants (XL) (2), Touratech Haglofs Fleece jackets (8), Belstaff customized jackets (2), Belstaff customized trousers (2), LWD beanies (8), Rain jackets (8), LWD Personalised T-shirts (60), Underwear, Socks, Shorts, Hiking boots, KSB Sport Sandals, Jeans, Cotton shirts, UNICEF LWD Buffs, LWD logo hats (8), BMW Rallye2 Suit (1), Zip-off cargo pants.

Video/ Photography equipment

Sony Z1 Camcorder (1), Sony HVR-V1e HDV video camera (3), Sony HRV-A1e HDV Video camera (3), Sony HDR-HC7E handycam (2), Sony HC96 Dv Cameras (6), Sony V1e hard drive (1), Sony MDRV150 headphones (1), V1e camera batteries (7), A1e battery charger – AC5Q950 (4), A1e battery charger (6), A1e batteries (12), Sennheisser boom mic and cable (1), V1e battery charger (4), Sennheisser EK100 radio mic(transmitter & reciever)set (2), Sony top mic (1), Swit S-2000 light (4), Audio splitter cable (1), Rode NTG-1 external mics with softie (3), Travel adaptor plug (8), Century Optics Wide Angle lens (1), Leica Dlux 3 digital camera (6), Velbon tripod (1), Sennheisser headphones (1), Sennheisser boom mic + cable (1), Hyperlight and charger (1), Sony top mic (1), Audio splitter cable (1), RSA1U-A1 raincovers (1), DV-970L lithium battery (3), Uniross AA/AAA battery charger + mains lead (1), Uniross AA rechargable batteries (16), Uniross AAA rechargable batteries (8), Canon DSR 450 zoom lens (1), RSPD170 raincovers (1), Sony toplight (3), Travel plug (10), Century Optics Wide Angle lens (1), Canon 30D SLR camera (1), Canon speedlight 430EX (1), RSA1U-A1 raincovers (1), Century Optics Wide Angle lens (1), Nikon SLR D200 (1), Plaubell Makina 670 stills camera (1), RSA1U-A1 raincovers (1), 1500GB raid 5 storage device with foam protection (2), Additional set of raid 5 drives and caddies (4),

Pelicase for 10 drives case-1520 (2), PC PCI-X SATA card for AVID (1), PCMCIA SATA adaptor for PC Laptop (3), Panasonic Toughbook 51 Core Duo 1.66Ghz 4Gb Ram 100Gb HD- laptops (3), Additional batteries for Panasonic Toughbook (3), Additional power supply to Toughbook (2), Pelicase for toughbook and HDV deck (3), AVID express pro software (1), Sony HVR-M15 deck (3), Sony VCL-HG0862K (0.8x Wide Conversion Lens for V1) (1), Sony HVR-DR60 Hard Disk Recorder (60GB) (1), Tripod GITZO Traveller (G0041587) MANFROTTO (701 RC2) (2), Sony Charger AC-SQ950 with car charger (for two 7.2V Lithium M batteries) (1), Hawk-Woods DV-MC2 Charger (for two 7.2 Lithim L batteries) (1), Hawk Woods DV970L DV link battery (15), Hawk Woods DV-RH1 (Sennheiser radio-mic holder) (3), Hawk Woods DV-CA12 Step-Up Adaptor (5), Sony Diversity URX-P1 receiver , +UTX-B1 transmitter (3), Sennheiser SK100Tx transmitter + EK100Rx receiver (2), Sankon tie mic (for Sennheiser radio mics) (6), Sankon tie mic (for radio mics) (4), Audio Technica tie mic (for radio mics) (4), Sony Gun Zoom Microphone ECM-HGZ1 (1), Rode directional mic NTG-1 + Rycote Softy (2), Headphone Sennheiser HD25SP (1), Sony AA+AAA charger (1), Uniross Sprint AA+AAA charger (1), Rechargable AA batteries (20), Rechargable AAA batteries (12), Surge Protection Multiple power socket (2), Leica HL-005 Batteries for Leica camera (12), Sonic helmet cameras and mics (6).

Page reference	Picture credit
3 (top), 6 (bottom), 7 (both pictures), 8 (bottom), 16 (both pictures), 18 (both pictures), 19 (top), 21 (both pictures), 22 (bottom), 23 (top), 25 (top right), 26 (bottom), 27 (top left), 32, 33 (both pictures), 34 (both pictures), 36 (both pictures), 37 (both pictures), 40 (both pictures), 41 (bottom), 42 (top and middle), 43 (bottom).	David Alexanian
29 (bottom), 30 (bottom), 43 (top) 45 (both pictures), 48.	Julian Broad
1, 2 (both pictures), 46 (all three pictures).	Oliver Blackwell
23 (bottom).	UNICEF UK/Ethiopia 2007/Sarah Epstein
38 (bottom), 39 (both pictures).	UNICEF UK/Malawi 2007/Sarah Epstein
31 (both pictures).	Chulho Hyun/UNICEF
4 (both pictures), 5 (all three pictures).	Rob Mcdougall
6 (top), 15 (top), 17 (top), 20 (bottom), 22 (top), 30 (top), 35 (top).	James Simak
3 (bottom)	Chris Mundle
8 (top), 9 (top), 11 (both pictures), 12 (both pictures), 13 (top), 14 (bottom), 17 (bottom), 19 (bottom), 20 (top), 24 (both pictures), 25 (top right), 26 (top), 27 (top right and bottom), 28 (both pictures), 35 (bottom).	Russ Malkin
10 (both pictures), 13 (bottom), 14 (top), 15 (bottom), 25 (bottom), 29 (top), 38 (top).	Claudio von Planta
9 (bottom).	Dai Jones

So what next?

When we got off our bikes in Cape Town at the end of Long Way Down, people started to ask 'So what next?', 'Will there be a Long Way Up?', 'Any more journeys planned?'. Well, we can now give an answer. There's definitely one more journey taking place and we're fully committed to make it happen. What is it? It's our journey to try and raise as much money as we can for UNICEF and children affected by HIV, poverty and conflict all over Africa. We're calling this journey 'The Long Way to Go' because whilst UNICEF is reaching millions of children across the continent already, we want to go all the way to help them in their mission to reach every single child, and that's no mean feat.

Having travelled across Africa on Long Way Down, it's been a privilege for us to work with UNICEF, meet children and hear first-hand about their lives. A lot of people ask us, 'Doesn't it get depressing hearing about these terrible things and seeing children living in difficult situations?' But the truth is, strangely, it doesn't. Because the children we have met on our travels are incredibly brave. They have hope. They have UNICEF and its partners, taking action to make their lives better. We've seen how it works with our own eyes: the education and opportunities that UNICEF gives children who have grown up knowing nothing but war, the simple miracle of preventing babies being born with HIV, the incredible care and love that UNICEF gives to children orphaned by AIDS. They have made a long lasting, incredible impression on us.

Crossing Africa we realised the enormity of what UNICEF has set out to do. Without any funding from the UN, they need money urgently to reach every child. So please join us on this new journey. You don't even need a bike. Just dig deep in your pockets and give something to UNICEF – however much it is – to help make the world a better place for every child. We've seen what a difference it can make.

www.unicef.org.uk

UNICEF is the leading children's organisation, reaching children in more than 190 countries around the world. We work with families, local communities, partner organisations and governments to help every child realise their full potential. We support children by providing health care, nutrition and education. We protect children affected by crisis including war, natural disasters and HIV.

UNICEF is not funded by the UN. Instead we rely on voluntary donations to fund our work for children worldwide. We need help from people like you in order to continue supporting and protecting children from the effects of poverty, conflict and disasters. Even the smallest donations can make a huge difference to a child who has nothing.

If you live in the UK, you can help UNICEF by donating or by taking part in a fundraising event or by lending your voice to our campaigns. Please go online and do something to help the world's children at www.unicef.org.uk/longwaydown.

Alternatively, you can donate by calling 0800 037 9797 and quoting 'Long Way Down' or you can send a cheque to:

UNICEF
Long Way Down
Freepost CL885
Billericay
CM12 0BR
United Kingdom

If you are outside the UK there are still many ways to support UNICEF, please visit www.supportunicef.org to find out more.

Children's Hospice Association Scotland

Sharing the Caring

Children's Hospice Association Scotland, CHAS is a Scottish charity committed to providing hospice services for children with life limiting conditions and their families. Sadly, hundreds of Scottish families are facing the fact that their child will not live to be an adult.

CHAS runs the only children's hospices in Scotland, Rachel House in Kinross and Robin House in Balloch, as well as an at home service called Rachel House at Home for families in the Highlands. CHAS provides respite care, practical help and emotional support to the whole family, from the day they are referred until the death of their child and beyond.

These services are free of charge to families but it costs CHAS £5 million each year to run Rachel House, Robin House and the Rachel House at Home service.

If you would like any more information about CHAS, please visit our website at www.chas.org.uk or contact us at the address and telephone number shown below.

CHAS
Canal Court
42 Craiglockhart Avenue
Edinburgh
EH14 1LT

Tel: 0131 444 1900

Scottish charity number SC019724

Motorcycles saving lives

10.8 million people are now receiving regular healthcare, sometimes for the first time in their lives.

Billions of dollars are spent each year to produce drugs and vaccines to prevent men, women and children dying needlessly from easily preventable and curable diseases. But they fail to reach the people who so desperately need them. This isolation from health care resources is due to the fact that the population of Africa live far from towns and major centres, the distances are vast and the best roads are little better than dirt-tracks. Even when vehicles are available, they quickly break down if no one has the expertise or resources to maintain them.

So Riders for Health addresses that vital missing link. We make sure, with our highly trained local teams, that motorcycles and other vehicles used in the delivery of health care withstand the harsh conditions and keep running day in, day out. We work in Zimbabwe, the Gambia, Nigeria, Kenya and Lesotho, training health care workers in safe riding and preventative vehicle maintenance.

Charley and Ewan's experiences on the ride gave them a first hand understanding of the distances and difficulties involved in riding in Africa. These are the same difficulties that the health care workers face every day.

To find out more about the work of Riders for Health or to find out about how to make a donation, please visit www.riders.org.

Acknowledgements

Olivia, Doone, Kinvara and the whole Boorman clan
Eve, Clara, Esther, Jamyan and our family

David Alexanian and Russ Malkin.

Lisa Benton, Sarah Blackett, Ollie Blackwell, Julian Broad, Kelly Bushell, Mike Clark-Hall, Dave Depares, Joanna Ford, Jim Foster, Jeff Gulvin, Daryl Higgins, Corin Holmes, Dai Jones, Asia Mackay-Trotter, Liz Mercer, Claudio von Planta, Andy Ryder, Robin Shek, Jimmy Simak and Lucy Trujillo.

Antonia Hodgson, Caroline Hogg, Marie Hrynczak, David Kent, Tamsin Kitson, Alison Lindsay, Duncan Spilling and everyone at Little, Brown Book Group.

Special thanks to:
Arai: Wendy Hearn
AST: Chris Wood and Tracey Harris
Belstaff: Manuele Malenotti and Michele Malenotti
BMW: Steve Bellars, Pieter De Waal, Lachlan Harris, Tony Jakeman, Juergen Korzer
Buff: Julian Peppit, Ignasi Rojas
Cafédirect: Sylvie Barr
Castle of Mey:
Eurotunnel: John Keefe
Explore: Paul Bondsfield, Peter Eshelby, Ashley Toft
MacTools: Adrian O'Nion
Media Insurance: Boyd Harvey
Michelin: Paul Cordle
Nissan: John Parslow, Bob Neville at RJN, Russell Joyce at Motormode
Nokia: Amooti Binaisa, Jenny Williams
Sonic: David Bryan, Wayne Schreier, Liam Thornton
Standford maps
Starwood: Amalie Craig, Rob Kucera, Robert Scott
Total: Iain Cracknell

Touratech: Herbert Schwarz
Virgin Atlantic: Richard Branson, Paul Charles, Bill Gosbee
Visit Scotland: Karin Finlay, Liz Ware

CHAS: everyone at Rachel House and Robin House, and Barbara Osbourne
Riders for Health: Andrea Coleman, Barry Coleman, Jennie Goodman
UNICEF: Sarah Epstein, Alison Tilbe, Wendy Zych

All stills photos by Julian Broad taken on Canon digital cameras.